# Public Television

# Public Television

## Politics and the Battle over Documentary Film

B. J. BULLERT

RUTGERS UNIVERSITY PRESS
*New Brunswick, New Jersey, and London*

6/99

# 37030640

Portions of chapter 3 have appeared in slightly different form in *Wide Angle* 16 (August 1994), pp. 6–39.

Excerpt from "The Vatican Rag," by Tom Lehrer, reprinted by permission of the author.

### Library of Congress Cataloging-in-Publication Data

Bullert, B. J., 1955–
    Public television : politics and the battle over documentary film
/ B. J. Bullert.
        p.    cm. — (Communications, media, and culture)
    Includes bibliographical references and index.
    ISBN 0–8135–2469–5 (alk. paper). — ISBN 0–8135–2470–9 (pbk. :
alk. paper)
    1. Public Broadcasting Service (U.S.)    2. Public television—
United States.    3. Documentary films—United States.
4. Documentary television programs—United States.    I. Title.
II. Series.
HE8700.79.U6B85    1997
384.55'4'0973—dc21                                                                97–17633
                                                                                          CIP

British Cataloging-in-Publication data for this book is available from the British Library

Manufactured in the United States of America

*The pen may be mightier than
the sword, but an eraser
is mightier still.*

# Contents

# Preface

On November 7, 1985, I met with a PBS programmer in Washington, D.C., to discuss an airdate for my first documentary, "God and Money," a one-hour program about the U.S. Catholic bishops' pastoral letter that strongly criticized the U.S. economic system. I expected she would have good news for me—that PBS would air the program in prime time around Easter and put some special effort into promoting the broadcast.

The programmer sat upright in her office chair. She didn't smile as she ran through a list of her concerns about the documentary. She didn't like the "loaded" tone of the narration, and she felt some of the interviews with those critical of the bishops weren't strong enough to make the program seem "balanced and fair." She didn't believe the bishops were unanimous in their support of the pastoral letter, and she questioned why we had not interviewed any "dissenting" bishops. She requested documentation to back up narration about a correlation between Reagan administration policies, growing economic inequality, and homelessness. As a web of tension tightened around us, she asked me to justify why the program deserved airtime on PBS. Our conversation ended when she said she would not let the program on the air unless certain changes were made either in specific sequences or in narration.

A knot formed in my stomach. I thought we had done everything right and that the access to the PBS airwaves would be almost automatic. My partner on the project, John de Graaf, had a long, successful track record. Not only had he won several American Film Festival awards, he had produced a feature story on the bishops' pastoral letter for *The MacNeil/Lehrer NewsHour*. We had done extensive research and worked on the project for two years. The Corporation for Public Broadcasting had funded the entire project with a $100,000 grant back in 1984. We had even hired a crew from KCTS, Seattle's public television station, to ensure the program would meet PBS technical broadcast standards.

What had gone wrong?

Years later, I realized we had not done anything wrong. I was simply inexperienced in the ways and concerns of PBS. After several conversations with the programmer, my work partner and I rephrased some of the narration, and "God and Money" aired at 10 p.m. on PBS on November 9, 1986, the same day the Catholic bishops released their economic pastoral letter. This was just over a year after I first met with the programmer.

The timing and nature of the program as well as the way we handled the situation influenced the ultimate outcome. My interaction highlighted how decisions about programs are made by real people with specific concerns at specific times who operate within conscious and unconscious constraints. PBS programmers don't exist in a vacuum. Further, each step in my encounter with the programmer was contingent on the preceding one, and each of us could have reacted differently.

This experience at PBS planted the first seed of this book. I wondered: How do PBS programmers decide which programs to put in the national schedule and which to reject? What compromises have independent producers made to get their programs accepted? What factors enter into the PBS programmers' decisions, especially regarding productions by independent producers of stand-alone documentaries? These initial questions eventually led to broader ones about how specific programs by independent documentary producers became controversial.

Because I am an independent producer, portraying the worlds of independents and the world of PBS programmers has been a personally and professionally challenging experience. While researching this book in San Francisco,[1] a mecca for independent documentary film makers, I visited with other independents and felt an easy kinship, an unspoken understanding born of common experience and challenges as well as common fears and perceived enemies. We spoke the same language; more often than not we were motivated by the same passion to draw public attention to social issues and share the gems we created in film or video with a larger public. Our goal was to be listened to, if not to influence the way viewers see the world. This solidarity proved a handicap when I sought to enter the world of PBS programmers. Viewed from the trenches of the independent producers' community, PBS programmers were the official gatekeepers who kept our programs off the air. Independent producers held them responsible for PBS's failure to live up to its promise as a genuine forum for a wider diversity of perspectives on public television.

A few months after interviewing independent producers in San Francisco, I traveled to Washington, D.C., to meet face-to-face with several PBS national programmers. On the same trip, I finished the archival research on my own documentary "Earl Robinson: Ballad of an American," a one-hour profile of the Seattle-born composer of the labor anthem "Joe Hill," and other songs made famous by singers, such as Joan Baez, Paul Robeson, Frank Sinatra, Josh White, and the groups Three Dog Night, and Peter, Paul, and Mary. Daily I moved back and forth between my professional world as an independent film maker and the PBS programmers' world, a journey that underscored the differences of each.

As I interviewed the PBS programmers, I gradually immersed myself in their perspectives, and I stifled a quiet voice of allegiance to my independent colleagues who wanted me to champion their particular causes and be a messenger of their complaints. The aim of my interviews was information, not confrontation. I also wrestled with an awkward dilemma from the convergence of my film-making life and my scholarly vocation: a rough edit of my documentary on Earl Robinson sat on one of my interviewee's shelves. (My program would eventually be screened by a new PBS programmer in the cultural programming department with whom I had had no previous contact.)

When conducting my interviews with PBS programmers, I made a short speech at the beginning of my interviews acknowledging my two roles—independent film maker and scholar—and stating that for the purposes of the interview I was a scholar, not a film maker.

As I listened to and empathized with the programmers' institutional constraints, I felt accepted. Now I had the heady feeling of being an insider, while the independent producers seemed distant and flawed. When I identified with the programmers and I felt their power to say yes or no to the projects before them, I also recognized that they saw themselves as more accountable to stations than to independent producers or viewers; they weren't free agents who could put whatever they wanted on the air. Like the scholar Carol Cohn, who shared the sympathies of peace activists and interviewed the nuclear scientists who created and designed nuclear weapons, I was impressed by the programmers' humanity but often puzzled by the reasons that justified their decisions.[2] I felt a bit like a traitor to my independent friends for seeing the programmers as gatekeepers who were "just trying to do their jobs."

I was so put off by feeling like a traitor that I sought out an anthropologist, who reassured me that this was all part of the process of doing good fieldwork. "If you go into a project with the conclusions fixed in your mind, the good guys and the bad guys clearly differentiated, you're not doing a proper ethnography," he said. This prepared me for the mind-twisting experience of being spun around when I interviewed different sources with contrary views and conflicting evidence asserted as fact.

I began to feel less like a traitor and more as if I had been drawn into a dysfunctional family with distorted power relationships, implicit and unstated rules, roles for "power parents" and children distinguished as "rebels," "heroes," "scapegoats," and "helpers." The power relationships between programmers and independent film makers mirrored the power relationships in family systems models, where everyone is part of the dynamic but no one accepts the blame. The appeal to the sacred beliefs of the system—mythologies—included an adherence to the conventional norms of "balance," the maintenance of a clear distinction between journalism and propaganda or advocacy. The maintenance of these distinctions disguised what was actually going on: the public television system was keeping most of its public affairs programming in the realm of elite cultural authorities who could be "trusted" to provide the programming the system is known for. Open secrets about what could and could not be said, as well as aesthetic formats for how stories should be told, kept elite authorities in their anchor or interviewer chairs, while independent film makers with strong opinions vied on the outside for the occasional slot in the PBS schedule. Everyone inside public television knows about the vital lie that keeps the system working financially: that what is fundable determines what is produced, and how.

For example, "everybody knows" a documentary series on the history of the labor movement would have difficulty attracting corporate underwriting, especially if it presented corporations as representing class interests at odds with those of working people and documented patterns of greed, deception, and the assassination of union organizers.[3] "Everyone knows" PBS would not air an exposé on how its marketing department had tried, with success, to make public television more attractive to corporate underwriters given the prospects of cuts in government funding.

When I voiced the general apprehension some station producers had expressed to me privately about their concerns that the reliance on corporate underwriting was pushing public television farther away from challenging programming to safer, educational programs, PBS president Ervin Duggan became very aggressive in defending this direction and dismissing his critics. "Public television has done a wonderful job of amassing corporate funding without ever compromising its independence or courage," he told me. "To imply that we are somehow prostituting ourselves is a hypothetical charge that has no basis in fact."[4]

Duggan seemed like an angry parent in a dysfunctional family who wanted to silence those who questioned him. With my tape recorder running, I felt positioned as an independent producer, for suggesting that the emperor had no clothes, and for questioning the "public-ness" of public television. A few minutes later, a public relations man tugged him away.

Ervin Duggan, the former FCC commissioner who became PBS's fourth president in 1993, oversees PBS from his perch in the president's office, but those under him are in charge of the day-to-day operations. PBS's National Programming Service, which is responsible for selecting programs for broadcast, has more than forty programmers on staff, but not all those programmers make overt editorial judgments.[5] Some are schedulers; others are administrators. To understand how editorial decisions were made, I interviewed the programmers who were paid to make those judgments and dealt directly with the program producers. These were the gatekeepers who bore primary responsibility for accepting or rejecting programs.

With one exception, none of these editorial programmers had worked in documentary production. Most came to their positions from the National Endowment for the Humanities, the National Endowment for the Arts, another branch of PBS, or else from a job as a gatekeeper at a local public television station or a public television series.

I interviewed six PBS national programmers. These face-to-face conversations lasted about an hour and were audiotaped. Later, I followed up with telephone calls. I also spoke off the record with these and other sources in public television.

Not all programs that became controversial between 1985 and 1993 were included in this book. Redundancy in the stories, lack of access to key participants, poor timing in terms of my schedule and others' availability led me to omit some controversial films, such as a cluster of documentaries on Central America, including the films of Barbara Trent.[6]

Two of the independent producers who declined to participate in the study were Michael Pack ("Campus Culture Wars" and "Inside the Republican Revolution") and Pam Yates ("When the Mountains Tremble"). I interviewed Steve Emerson ("Jihad in America"), but he, like others with something to gain by working with PBS, was unwilling to disclose the particulars of his interactions with PBS for fear of spoiling a deal in the making. I also spoke briefly with producer Ken Burns during a publicity tour, but given his demanding schedule, and mine, we were unable to do a proper interview. His GM publicist, Owen Comora, declined an interview on his behalf. Comora said he would not grant me an interview unless I made a formal request in writing, described how the interview would be used, the subjects I intended to cover, and a description of the book.[7]

The interviews with the film makers began as relatively straightforward transactions where I was trying to understand how each of my interviewees saw their role and those of others in the handling of their documentaries. Most were charming and seemed sincerely to want "their" stories told, and several remarked, "Finally somebody's going to put it all together." The controversies that swirled around their work left scars and pain years later, marked by long sighs in our conversation, as if by telling their stories they were revisiting and releasing a bad memory, or savoring a victory. The same seemed true for the other players.

These players included PBS programmers, gatekeepers at public television stations, journalists, and special interest groups. I found their names in newspaper articles, which also provided the initial framing of the disputes in the public arena.

To reconstruct how the disputes were created, I not only interviewed the available key players but also accumulated relevant correspondence and other documentation to have a paper trail against which to verify events and substantiate memories. I also cross-checked stories with relevant participants to articulate different points of view and clarify discrepancies.

When I found discrepancies in versions of events, I did what any journalist would do—I went back to the material, checked my information, and asked for reactions from different parties as I tried to get to the bottom of the story. "The truth," however, was not a fixed object or a certain destination. Rival versions coexisted depending on whom I chose to believe based on the available evidence. Usually these discrepancies were relatively unimportant, but others cast a different light on the players. For example, *P.O.V.* executive Marc Weiss told me he rejected "Roger & Me" based on a "very rough, rough edit" that did not include the film maker's narration, but Michael Moore said he sent Weiss the same rough edit he sent the Telluride Film Festival. This version was basically the same work that launched its theatrical success. Whose account was I to believe?

I learned "truth" is a verb, a process of discovering, fitting pieces of information together and arranging them in a kaleidoscopic collage, whose composition could shift depending on a twist of the wrist, a new piece of information, or a recalled memory that challenged that of another player. Several times a new piece of information sent me scurrying back to the library or my interview notes to check conflicting versions of events or alleged facts. It was a frustrating experience, especially when each party *insisted* his or her perspective was the most accurate, and independent evidence was not available to verify one version or the other. The narrative of these controversies therefore strives to accommodate more than one truth or the most accurate truth available given the information at hand.

My motivation was different from that of my interviewees. My objective was to make sense of my experience, shed light on the relationship between documentary film makers, public broadcasters, and the times, write a readable account, and complete my Ph.D. The other players were speaking with me in part because they wanted to help me. Others believed they had something to gain or they wanted to spin the story to their advantage. And some tended to withhold information that might hurt their cause or to offer information that would discredit another player.

For example, when I interviewed Marlon Riggs, he wanted to blast a group of African-Americans who were uncomfortable with his documentary "Ethnic Notions," but he didn't want to talk about his experience at KQED because he was in the process of negotiating a deal with the station.[8] Other film makers didn't want to go on record about their experiences with PBS because they feared it would jeopardize future relationships there, and some were actively producing programs funded in part by PBS. Others were coproducing with public television stations, so they were selective in the information they gave; fearful of leaking information about the station, they would only talk "off the record."

Some public television sources also hid behind namelessness. One PBS programmer requested anonymity after agreeing to speak with me on the record, and did so months *after* our interview. Another balked at my writing about my firsthand experience at PBS, fearing she would appear foolish. Other sources sought to distance themselves from their own statements, fearing that their words would be misunderstood and their authority or reputations undermined. In addition to being aware that my sources had vested interests in making themselves appear in a positive light, I learned that this type of research requires the ability to step back and keep the alternative perspectives in mind while remaining aware of my own evolving views and the perspectives of my sources. When I did, I saw a consistent pattern where independent producers and programmers collided head-on through misunderstanding and genuine conflicts of interest, especially when the programs contained voices from outside the mainstream unrepresented or underrepresented on American public television. I also saw a few opportunities for building common ground where provocative independent producers' and PBS programmers' mutual interests and agendas could, and did, converge as they struggled together to widen the range of voices on the national PBS prime-time schedule.

Most independent producers have to run a gauntlet of gatekeepers, and once they're inside the system, they are subject to additional pressures from station producers. Like feuding clans fighting over scarce resources, independents and station producers compete for foundation funding and underwriting of various sorts. Where there are more worthy proposals than funds to go around, or fewer time-slots in the schedule than programs a programmer would like to schedule, someone has to carry the hatchet.

The situation of independent documentary producers in relation to PBS is a microcosm of the national situation in the arts, where only the tenacious, fashionable, and funded survive. In this picture, the survival of the fittest is not necessarily the survival of the most original, talented, or innovative. (The same seems to be true in the publishing world.) Those who succeed have survived a process of selection that takes place out of the public forum in meeting rooms where grant givers evaluate proposals for funding, film makers negotiate in-kind or reduced fee services, station programmers and gatekeepers decide where to put their limited resources of services, funds, and broadcast time. The works of independents, like myself, sometimes find a forum and support if they can make it through this weeding-out process and are willing to make the compromises necessary along the way.

My documentary "Earl Robinson: Ballad of an American" was an independent coproduction with KCTS/Seattle, and it premiered on the station in April 1994. The station contributed the postproduction services that enabled me to complete it. The station didn't commit to the project until I received a grant from the National Endowment for the Arts, and I had a rough edit of the documentary to show for it.

The premiere took place as a community event. On a huge screen in Seattle's IBEW union hall, about a hundred friends and fans of Earl Robinson watched the five-year, labor-of-love, fifty-seven-minute profile. As Paul Robeson sang "Joe Hill" over the credits, the audience rose to their feet for a standing ovation that lasted about five minutes. Someone handed me a dozen red roses, and I remember staring with pleasant amazement from the stage at the crowd applauding the film and me. This is the currency of reward that most independent film makers cherish.

KCTS received more calls to rebroadcast the film than any other that week, so it had a special "Viewers Encore" repeat broadcast the following Saturday night. Working with KCTS publicity staff, we made the cover of the weekly TV section of the *Seattle Times* and Earl's photo smiled from the pages of *TV Guide*. I was on local radio.

Getting the show out nationally was another matter.

The work blended history with music so it fell between two categories in the PBS programming world. PBS national programmers rejected the program with hundreds of other submissions in 1994. With PBS national programming no longer an option, I sought out other ways to get my work out to the audience: nontheatrical educational distribution. Some of my music rights agreements stipulated that I distribute my program through a nonprofit distribution entity, so I sought out a distributor that would fit these parameters. I settled on PBS Video, which agreed to distribute the program to the nontheatrical market.

The film appeared in film festivals in New York, Santa Barbara, and Seattle, and it acquired a Silver Apple from the National Education Media Network. Other showings, including one at the Pacific Film Archive in Berkeley, California, drew enthusiastic crowds who knew Earl's songs and sang along on several tunes.

After finishing the film, I returned to writing this book. My effort to get the film out became less of a priority, though I continued to seek a national audience. My efforts bore fruit when the program was accepted by the Pacific Mountain Network (PMN), which showcased the documentary and offered it, for free, to public television stations in April 1996.

I don't know how many people watched it or had the opportunity to see it on their local stations. I do know that on September 3, 1996, 25,000 Chicagoans tuned in to the 11 p.m. broadcast on WTTW. The following Friday, with a repeat on Sunday, WNET/New York broadcast the program and an estimated 76,000 viewers watched. Public television stations in Philadelphia and Pittsburgh also aired the program. I found out that other stations broadcast it without notifying me so there was no way to publicize it in these markets. These are paltry numbers compared with those for a program with a national slot on PBS, which reaches millions of viewers.

Like other film makers fatigued by fund-raising, I turned to a more reliable way to make a living: I found a job with a salary.

# Acknowledgments

I wish to thank my teachers, past and present, who unwittingly inspired me to follow my heart in taking on this project. Howard S. Becker and Roger Simpson were remarkable guides through the research that culminated in this book. In addition, the influence of two teachers with whom I studied more than a decade ago, Howard Zinn and Alasdair MacIntyre, continue to shape the questions I ask and my scholarly motivations.

Thanks also goes to my sources, named and unnamed, in public television, the independent film-making community, and the press. Steve Behrens and Karen Everhard Bedford at *Current*, and Nancy Neubauer at the Association of America's Public Television Stations (APTS), were very generous with their time and information. So were Marc Weiss at *P.O.V.* and David Fanning at *Frontline*. All of them returned my calls. Friends and scholars who provided insightful comments on the manuscript include William Hoynes, Ralph Engelman, Diedre Boyle, Bob McChesney, Susan Ivers, Anthony Chan, Richard Kielbowicz, Michael McCann, John Campbell, Ernie Harburg, Leonard Rifas, Peter Knutson, David Tafler, and Sue Curry Jansen. Paul Loeb's remarks were especially useful in the early stage of the manuscript. Vicki Haire and Peggy Brooks helped edit the manuscript with care and charm. Friends whose companionship accompanied me through the lonely writing process deserve special thanks: Donna Petras, Hemda Arad, Hylah Jacques, Jill Gonet, Lisa Schillinger, Connie Veldink, Tom Ballard, John de Graaf, Carmine Winters, Hing Ng, and many others.

Public Television

# Introduction:
# The Anatomy
# of Controversy

Public television holds a special place in the American broadcasting landscape. It was initially envisioned as a noncommercial system, an alternative to commercial broadcasting that would "enrich our homes, educate our families and provide assistance in our classrooms."[1] This use of television would "appeal to the minds and hearts" of the viewing public, providing cultural, informational programming as well as in-depth public affairs programs "which will lead to a better informed and enlightened public."[2]

Public television's original mandate required the system to address issues of controversy and facilitate the inclusion of voices and perspectives that lie outside the "established consensus."[3] But attempts to include these voices have proven to be divisive, laying bare the fragile social, economic, and political foundations of public television, its organizational limitations, and revealing a communication system riddled with conflicting obligations.[4] The divisions within public television brought to the surface in these controversies mirror divisions within American society, the vulnerability of the public television system to political and financial pressures, the tenacity of independent film makers, and the resiliency of public broadcasters to internal and external attacks.

Several public television documentaries acquired the controversial label between 1985 and 1993. These works located the cutting edge of social change where nonmainstream or minority voices sought to enter the public media arena through PBS. All the works examined here were made by independent producers. This book is not so much about the producers themselves, but rather about the resistance to the views of reality they put forth. These film makers presented communities and viewpoints marginalized or missing from public television, such as the experience of being a black male homosexual, citizens who believe they have been harmed by the legacy of nuclear weapons and the Cold War, Americans concerned about the Palestinians of the Intifada, the unemployed and working people who saw themselves bearing the brunt of a major corporation's shift of jobs overseas and its quest for profits.

These programs sought to close the gap between the realities of these American citizens and the representation of these realities—or lack thereof—on American public television. The independent producers created documentaries that offered the viewing public a glimpse of another perspective of the world around them. Some of the producers were directly linked to social or political movements at odds with official U.S. government policies. In their films they sought to challenge prevailing myths and the country's direction.

The controversies unfolded within an increasingly polarized political climate, summarized in chapter 1: the Reagan administration's early escalation of nuclear weapons production, the war against Nicaragua, and the championing of traditional, heterosexual family values and mobilized grassroots movements to promote or counter these policies. On issues where the conservative, organized citizens groups stood on one side (in support of increased military funding for nuclear weapons, the Contras, the heterosexual family), and organized, progressive citizens groups lined up on the other (in favor of a nuclear freeze, cuts in aid to El Salvador, gay rights), charges of propaganda and censorship were hurled in the battle for public influence and media coverage. These battles raised questions about which views of reality would be allowed to contend on the public television airwaves, and which would predominate. Independent producers created programs from the front lines of these wars for public opinion, drawing the battle lines in the ether.

In this political tug-of-war, PBS programmers, like news editors across the country, stood at a crucial juncture. Programmers with their own biases and institutional and political constraints served as arbiters of the different perspectives because they determined which programs would have the imprimatur of PBS and therefore priority access to the national, public television airwaves through the affiliate stations. They stood at the gateway as traffic cops of perspectives. Chapter 1 examines the relationship between PBS programmers and independent producers in light of the constraints present in each of their worlds, and chapter 2 looks at the two primary venues for independently produced current affairs documentaries on PBS: *Frontline* and *P.O.V.*

Subsequent chapters focus on each of the controversies in turn. "Dark Circle," the subject of chapter 3, was a provocative documentary on nuclear weapons whose producers were Judy Irving, Chris Beaver, and Ruth Landy. PBS first accepted the program for national broadcast and then rejected it, raising the questions of whether the film was "propaganda" or "journalism," whether the film makers could be believed, and what is the relationship between independent producers and movements for social change.

"Days of Rage: The Young Palestinians" was a film by Jo Franklin-Trout about the Intifada that presented the Palestinians' perspective.[5] In chapter 4, we see how organized interest groups, PBS national programmers, and public television station executives diluted the views presented in this film when efforts to withdraw it from the national schedule failed.

Marlon Riggs made the documentary "Tongues Untied" to chronicle his experiences as a black, gay man. Chapter 5 looks at the challenges facing programmers, series executives, and independent producers when station gatekeepers—and a vocal part of the viewing public—do not want to hear what a member of a marginalized group has to say. "Tongues Untied" had a chilling effect on a subsequent program dealing with gay themes: "Stop the Church" by Robert Hilferty. This film, examined in chapter 6, was about an AIDS protest in St. Patrick's Cathedral in New York.

Two films critical of General Motors—Michael Moore's "Roger & Me" and Steve Talbot's "The Heartbeat of America"—were also controversial for public television. Chapter 7 not only chronicles these controversies but also contrasts the films with Ken Burns's PBS series, which have GM as their sole corporate sponsor and which serve to enhance the auto corporation's public image.

Finally, the conclusion ties all the controversies together through a discussion of their similarities and their general significance for society at large.

All of the documentaries examined here eventually made their way onto public television, and most of them became part of the national PBS schedule. The stories of their journeys, and the way the programs were ultimately framed by the broadcasters, and then by the press, show how the collective effort of programmers, producers, interest groups, and journalists tell the public what to think about a particular topic or issue, and how to think about the programs in question. The particular goals and activities of each group are essential to understanding the anatomy of controversy. They are also essential to understanding how different perspectives compete in the so-called marketplace of ideas, where citizens have opportunities to receive information necessary to make informed decisions about their individual and civic lives.

Before the discussion gets under way in chapter 1, it is useful to take a brief look at previous scholarship in this area as well as key terms and concepts that we will be using throughout the book.

## Previous Scholarship

Media critics and communications scholars have analyzed why public television tends toward safe, high-quality, noncontroversial programming as its standard fare.[6] The fear of alienating corporate underwriters, station subscribers,
and government officials reinforces what William Hoynes calls a "logic of
safety" and a culture of timidity inside public television.[7] Ambivalence about
public television's mission—whether it is primarily an educational tool for
high-quality programs or a venue for noncommercial, alternative viewpoints—
has never been resolved. This "goal ambiguity," in Hoynes's words, is played
out in the controversies I examine.[8] So is the trend toward commercializa-
tion so thoroughly documented by Ralph Engelman.[9]

Communications scholars have analyzed for decades the efforts of powerful special interest groups, government officials, and journalists to set the
public or media agenda on specific issues or topics.[10] The power of these groups
is measured by their effectiveness in shaping the discourse on these topics.
Agenda-setting studies have focused attention on the gatekeeping function
and decision-making process of wire-service editors, magazine and television
news editors, and newspaper editors.[11] Political and social movement theo-
rists have also examined the efforts of marginal, less powerful social or political groups to get their perspectives across in the mainstream media.[12] These
works analyze the strategies used as various players seek to influence what becomes "news" and how that news is presented to the viewing public through
the mass media. Other scholars have taken agenda setting a step farther by
examining how media coverage shapes the actual decisions of policy makers.[13]
Still others have analyzed the role of advocacy groups in influencing television programming decisions.[14] And certain scholars have explored the agenda-
setting function of the press to reinforce and maintain political myths vital
to the acceptance of the political and economic system.[15] Controversies
are often the by-products of these agenda-setting or agenda-reinforcing interactions.

## Key Terms and Concepts

### GATEKEEPING

Gatekeepers—whether they are newspaper wire-service editors or local television news executives or PBS programmers—are crucial in deciding which
stories the reading or viewing public will have an opportunity to see. Through
their routine decisions, gatekeepers help or hinder the flow of information and

perspectives to a viewing audience. For example, when PBS programmers justify their decisions to air or not to air particular programs, they make explicit
the usually unspoken rationales and criteria that underlie their routine decisions. These moments reveal much about the people and the institutions to
whom they're accountable and the sometimes conflicting interests they strive
to serve. Gatekeeping also enters into the communication process at other
levels: judgments made by journalists about whose voices to include in the
depictions of the controversies, and decisions within organizations about who
will represent their points of view to the press and the public. Once a controversy about a documentary enters the public sphere of newspapers, the dispute takes on predictable form: attacks on the film maker's credibility, charges
of "unfairness" or "lack of balance," and efforts of interested parties to shape
the perception of the work in question and to use it to their own advantage.

### FRAMING AND REFRAMING

Frames embody implicit theories about the nature of reality.[16] They presup-
pose the tacit use of principles of selection, presentation, and emphasis that
seem "natural" to us. Frames enable us to make sense of our world by serving
as the organizing filter through which we interpret and construct our realities
and our perception of others. Framing is an epistemological activity.

Media professionals use "media frames" to organize realities for viewers.
These frames are the persistent patterns used to select (or exclude), present,
emphasize, and interpret various views of reality.[17] Conflicts and controversies arise when representations of reality are reframed in such a way that they
challenge the dominant media framing, and someone is powerful enough to
protest it.

The case studies in this book show how the framing of disputes can be a
remarkably effective strategy for limiting public debate and keeping the discussion of divisive issues within the bounds of journalistic acceptability. The
persistent pattern of framing of the films deflects the discussion away from
the perspective intended by the film maker and provides a forum for interested parties to have their say. Public relations staff, as in the case of General
Motors, play a vital role in directing public discussion, showing how they are
powerful yet often invisible players in the news business.

### TELEVISION AS A SOCIAL UNIFIER

Television programs routinely frame reality and fantasy for viewers, and reinforce particular perspectives and prejudices. While viewers can disagree with
or distance themselves from the fantasies or realities depicted on television,

media images and stories suggest how we should see each other and ourselves, as well as how the media framers treat public issues and perspectives.

Independent producers, public television gatekeepers, journalists, reviewers, and members of interest groups are soldiers battling on a field of myths and beliefs—battling to maintain or resist prevailing ideologies that serve established, powerful interests that underpin our social, economic, and political order. This order is threatened by works that have a different view of reality, a critical or alternative perspective, or one that serves other interests. It's a kind of shadow play of mythology taking place beneath a spectacle of debate.

Television programs imagine, visualize, contest, and renegotiate views of reality.[18] In this role, they act as a forum through which cultural negotiation takes place. As we listen to and observe the ongoing stories of the day told to us by those who select, create, and present them, we watch reconstructed realities about other individuals, communities, and groups. We can agree or disagree with the content of what we see, but television programs are fundamentally about the framing of the world and about representation. Programs that speak to deeply divisive issues and present views of reality that are shocking to some, are usually contained, if not symbolically reconciled, in the programs themselves by familiar aesthetic styles and the conventional structures of storytelling. These conventions include the standard dramatic structure of stories with a beginning, a middle, and an end, and the cathartic ritualizing of fearful images through symbolic representation whereby what is feared seems safe and manageable.

The programs that became controversial did not use television to unify viewers or to reinforce dominant societal beliefs so much as to challenge viewers to rethink their realities and the world around them. They sought to push the boundaries of the acceptable and widen viewers' exposure to unfamiliar realities. Television's social role as a medium for unifying viewers, like a national hearth, militates against works of controversy. Because controversial programs pinpoint a departure from television's role as a social unifier, independent producers who create such programs stand out like wayward children in the public television family.

## CULTURAL AUTHORITIES

All societies have cultural authorities who define what is worthy of public attention and make decisions about whose realities are represented and how. All societies have particular procedures or routines that determine, generally, how the stories are told. In television, this communicative process involves broadcast producers, reporters, and technical staff (camera operators, audio technicians, video editors, etc.) who choose which images are projected, which words are used, and programmers who select what will be scheduled. In news and public affairs, cultural authorities sanction who speaks on the selected issues. They determine how those images of the issues are conveyed and, de facto, how groups of people and their lives are portrayed. They are key figures in the reimagining of our world. Only a few people in society have the status of cultural authorities.

The independent producers are cultural authorities, too. Yet because they are largely self-appointed, they are not treated with the same respect and regard as those elite cultural authorities who have prestige media institutions behind them. They are citizens with cameras who capture stories and voices that often lie outside the mainstream and reflect the realities of a wide diversity of the American public—a mix of economic and social classes, ages, and ethnic, racial, geographic, and gender identities. By producing works from communities that lie outside the dominant media frames, independent producers have sought to bring the perspectives of these communities to the public forum. The broadcasting of their works over public television can enhance our democratic culture by nurturing the role of public television as a genuine public forum for diversity.

### THE PUBLIC SPHERE

Much has been written about the limitations and potential role of mass media in creating a "public sphere" or a "public forum" whereby the diverse views of the people can be expressed, debated, and analyzed.[19] Jürgen Habermas, who first coined the term "public sphere," defined it as "a domain of our social life in which such a thing as public opinion can be formed."[20] A public sphere refers to the social spaces, such as town meetings, electronic bulletin boards, community groups and clubs, and media venues, where people come together to grapple with matters concerning the common good and with other issues.

The underlying premise of this work is that democracy requires a media system that allows for the relatively free expression of the people's views—venues where everyone's authentic perspective can have a place in the public dialogue. The media can serve as part of the "connective tissue" linking the people to their representatives and also to each other.[21] People in media can help facilitate democracy or participate in its betrayal.

CONTROVERSY

My working definition of "controversy" extends the commonsense meaning of the word as a matter of opinion in which opposite views are advanced and maintained by opponents.[22] This definition emphasizes the conflict between opinions, rather than the truth or falsity of the opinions themselves. I define "media controversies" as *collective activities that arise at particular times and places when someone decides to question the legitimacy or value of a perspective, and someone in the media considers the accusations valid enough to write about them in the press.* Controversies are distinct from mere private disagreements between two parties because they occur before an audience of readers or viewers. Full-blown controversies, like those I profile here, are complex interactions that involve a chorus of voices all seeking to influence the public perception of the documentaries in question and the topics they address. Controversies locate points of social conflict and reflect a lack of social consensus. They mark the efforts of various parties to set the agenda on matters of concern to them.[23]

Controversies are patterned communication events with initiators and specific turning points. Someone—whether that person is a programmer, a producer, a journalist, or a member of an interest group—initiates the controversy. Once a dispute reaches the pages of the newspaper, the controversy is set in motion as a public event. Seemingly little decisions and steps taken by actors sometimes independently of each other and sometimes in response to actual or imagined actions can turn a private dispute into a controversy as long as it successfully passes through the gatekeeping process of newspaper reporters and editors: the tests of timing and newsworthiness.[24]

Controversies are flashpoints for other conflicts and a tactic for mobilizing groups. They are wielded strategically by different players to publicize their concerns and to attack their opponents in the public arena, and are opportunities for various parties to flex their muscle on a particular issue. They can be a remarkably effective way for interested parties to limit or direct political debate, which often results in turning the issues the *film makers* are trying to raise into secondary issues.

Understanding how controversies occur involves reconstructing these decisions and actions, step by step. The truth about controversy lies in these details.

The following controversies about independently produced works took place in a political context where government funding for public broadcasting was under attack. In 1990, PBS responded to this situation by increasing the system's educational visibility through "brand" identification, grassroots organizing, and a publicity campaign to present itself to the American people as a cultural institution just as vital as the public library. The slogan "If PBS doesn't do it, who will?" was played repeatedly over the airwaves to muster support for the system, but many of the works on the cutting edge for the service, such as *Eyes on the Prize*, *The Civil War*, "Hoop Dreams," and "Roger & Me," were produced by independents who struggled for years to give the gifts of their labor to a broader public. They took risks, and given their legacy, it would be even more appropriate to ask, "If the independents don't do it, who will?"

# Chapter 1
# Independent Producers and PBS Programmers

$M$ost of the controversies presented in this study were sparked initially by clashes between independent producers and PBS programmers. Each group operated within its own institutional, organizational, and social constraints.

The political climate between 1985 and 1993 added another context to these controversies. As a battle in the culture war was fought over public funding of the National Endowment for the Arts (specifically around the work of photographer Robert Mapplethorpe, sculptor Andres Serrano, and performance artist Karen Finley), key Republican politicians and media critics targeted public broadcasting as unworthy of public funding. They charged public broadcasters with promoting a homosexual lifestyle and produced studies to illustrate PBS's "liberal bias" in programming. Several films examined here were cited as examples of such work. Provocative, independently produced documentaries became fodder in the ongoing debate over government support for public broadcasting.

## The World of Independent Documentary Producers

The community of independent documentary film producers is diverse. Such producers are the video equivalent of independent writers and artists who retain artistic, budgetary, and editorial control over their work, and usually the copyright.[1] Some lean more toward experimental video art, others produce documentaries shown in media centers and video festivals, and still others strive to make independent feature documentaries that are presented in movie theaters.

Independent documentary producers are scattered across the country, but most are concentrated in New York, Los Angeles, and San Francisco, where organizations exist to support their work. Numbers are hard to come by, but the Independent Television Service (ITVS) has a mailing list of 15,000 and the Association of Independent Video and Filmmakers has 5,000 members.[2] Only a few of these producers have regular contact with public television stations.

Those who work with public television are linked to the system through a complex relationship of politics, trade, and power. They compete with station producers for scarce resources and airtime, and the station producers usually have the edge because their programs generally take priority at the station level.

Independent producers are "outsiders" and "workers for hire" in the public television world, yet because they are removed from the day-to-day socialization of station producers, they are also freer to address topics they choose and do it in their own way. Sometimes they develop unconventional approaches to topics, taking risks outside the aesthetic and journalistic norms embraced by public television station producers.

Independent documentary producers tend to be individualists with a strong sense of personal vision as well as a tenacity and stubbornness that enable them to survive the gauntlet of fund-raising, rejection, production, negotiation, editing, and promotion. In addition, a wide variety of skills must be acquired and employed during each stage that productions pass through. It is obvious that film-making and managerial skills are essential, but producers must also excel at research and fund-raising.

### HOW DOCUMENTARIES GET MADE

Producers begin with an idea or a story they want to turn into a documentary. Story ideas arise from a variety of sources: newspaper articles, magazines, movies, conversations, suggestions, and so forth. The story idea must be personally compelling. Since very little funding is available for research and development on documentary projects, independent producers have to be sufficiently motivated to handle these tasks themselves. Research and development turn the story idea into a proposal for funding.

The next challenge is to figure out how much money and resources it will take to get the program off the ground and through the different phases to completion. The cost of producing the sort of documentary likely to be broadcast on national public television or released theatrically may range from an estimated $2,000 to $5,000 a minute or more, depending on the project. Independent producers must be able to handle budgets, raise funds, negotiate deals, hire and manage crew and technicians, and have faith in what they do to carry them through the rough seas of rejection. They must understand not only what makes a strong story but also what kind of story is likely to attract funding and an audience.

Given the expense of producing a documentary, independent producers often live on the edge economically, unless they are independently wealthy. Production and postproduction costs can quickly devour savings and soon put producers in debt unless they have their own equipment, a talent for bringing in grants and investors, or for negotiating in-kind services.

Since foundation funding for documentaries depends on the current priorities of the foundations, which tend to follow the social issues written about in the mainstream or alternative press, producers must know what these issues are. In the 1980s, nuclear disarmament, homelessness, and, toward the end of the decade, AIDS became major social issues tackled by the funders. This resulted in a spate of documentaries on these topics, and producers anxious to produce them.

Some independent producers have sufficient experience at fund-raising and production, and a timely project, so they can marshal all the money and resources necessary before beginning the production. Many others must instead follow a cycle of fund-raising and videotaping and fund-raising again as their needs arise and time allows.

Success in the independent producing community means being able to make documentaries the producers care about while maintaining a relatively comfortable standard of living (that is, having enough income to pay rent or meet mortgage payments and cover other basic living expenses). Many independent producers thrive in their twenties and thirties but can no longer sustain their passion financially when they have families or other significant financial responsibilities. Those who continue to produce independently may create their own production companies, freelance in commercial or public television, or work for video or film production companies as directors, producers, videographers, cinematographers, audio technicians, editors, production managers, fund-raisers, or assistants. Some take jobs unrelated to production. Others, like me, go into teaching and continue to produce on the side.

FOUR BASIC TYPES OF INDEPENDENT PRODUCERS

Independent producers fall into four general categories: mavericks, activists, pragmatists, and innocents. Although these categories overlap, in some cases the differences among independent producers are greater than those between independent producers and station producers. The mavericks are film makers who feel constrained by the usual conventions and seek innovations that set them apart from that world.[3] Outside public television's culture and institutions, they may develop their own styles and unconventional approaches to topics. Some, like Frederick Wiseman, may violate conventional norms of public television documentaries by producing works "too long" or "too short" to fit conveniently into the time-slots on the PBS schedule. Others, like "Dark Circle" producers Judy Irving, Chris Beaver, and Ruth Landy, create highly partisan documentaries that challenge conventional beliefs, years before those issues are given voice in the mainstream media. They are political or social activists who produce programs with strong points of view and an agenda for change. Still others—the pragmatists—moderate their presentations, adapting to the journalistic conventions of "balance" and "right to reply" in order to get their work accepted for broadcast on public television. And finally, there are the innocents, independent producers who are unaware of the rules. They do not know how to package their programs or tailor their proposals within the boundaries of what is acceptable in public television. They are naive and figure that if they make a program, it will be put on, and are surprised when they learn the process is not so simple.

Independent producers may adopt different approaches at various times in their careers and from one project to the next. Some producers start out as activists who seek to use the documentary medium as a tool for change, but over time they become more pragmatic. Others freelance at public television stations and sometimes are hired on later as staff. Yet most producers remain outside public television stations as mavericks, activists, or innocents; whereas the mavericks and activists understand their exclusion from the system, the innocents are unclear about the reasons why. Some of these producers would rather seek their fortune in theatrical film, cable, or commercial productions than in public television or cable.

Activists present the greatest challenge to viewers and to those who work at public television stations because they have strong partisan views, and their documentaries advance their perspective and speak for groups marginalized in the mass media. They may break with the conventions of journalistic balance as understood by public television journalists. Public television executives describe activists as producers who don't always feel it is necessary "to give the opposition its say" since they don't share its viewpoint. Some activists resent this charge and argue that they don't need to "give the opposition its say" because the mainstream media have already given it sufficient exposure. They argue that "fairness and balance" are inherently problematic because what is deemed "fair" by public television journalists is unfair in their eyes for it is skewed toward the powerful. Activists perceive conventional journalists as dupes. Activists may be sympathetic or active participants in organizations for social change. Because of this partisan involvement, public television executives view them with suspicion. "They're not journalists," a station staffer told me. Activists are often thought to be untrustworthy with public affairs topics, even if they can substantiate all the facts in their programs.

Unless an independent documentary producer acquires the rare label of "investigative journalist" with the credentials to back it up, public television gatekeepers and staff usually seek to determine if an independent producer is an "activist" or a proper "journalist." Gatekeepers distinguish activist film makers from journalists by a level of trust and credibility. They perceive the activist as not playing "fair," a key value in the journalism of public television. For example, they suspect that if the activist has information contradicting the main arguments in his or her film, the activist will not report it. So even if activists are accomplished film makers, they are not "journalists" in the public television sense of the term. Until someone inside the system determines that what they do is "journalism," public television insiders often label the work of advocacy film makers as "propaganda."

Pragmatists may also be activists, but they have found a way to work within the institutions of public television. They may do the same work as station producers, but without the benefits that go along with being on staff, such as medical insurance, a regular salary, and so forth. Sometimes they are later hired on as staff. They work within the stations' norms and conventions, and usually forfeit editorial control and ownership of their programs. Legally, they are "workers for hire."

Although pragmatists may have started out as advocacy film makers, they have adapted to the aesthetic and journalistic requirements operative at their public television station. All films have points of view, but pragmatists internalize the conventions of balance and fairness so their work is indistinguishable from that ideal aspired to by station producers. They strive to "educate and inform," just as their counterparts at the stations do.

Pragmatists tone down their work to fit public television's norms of journalism and aesthetic style, making compromises in both form and content that hard-core activists would refuse to make. They may still have strong personal opinions, but they tailor their proposals and programs to fit within the boundaries of acceptability in the world of public television.

## The World of PBS Programmers

The Public Broadcasting Service is a program distribution service founded in 1969 to provide for the national programming needs of the 346–member affiliate stations that make up the public television system in the United States, Puerto Rico, the Virgin Islands, Guam, and America Samoa.[4] It is a private, nonprofit corporation funded mostly by member stations with other income from the Corporation for Public Broadcasting (CPB), educational institutions, and other sources.[5]

PBS programming activities include educational programming to colleges, universities, plus telecourses and instructional programs for students in kindergarten through twelfth grade. PBS's National Programming Service (NPS) is the sole provider of the programs PBS is known for: *Sesame Street, Masterpiece Theater, Nova, The MacNeil/Lehrer NewsHour, Frontline*, and so forth. The programmers who work in this department, along with series and local affiliate gatekeepers, determine what viewers will see with the PBS logo.

PBS is not the only supplier of national programming to the stations. The American Program Service (APS) is a smaller national distribution network providing programs to stations. Regional networks, such as the Central Educational Network (CEN), the Pacific Mountain Network (PMN), and the Southern Educational Communications Association (SECA), also distribute non-PBS programs by satellite to affiliates throughout the system.[6]

The public television system is a decentralized network of semiautonomous stations that pays PBS for selecting and scheduling national programs from which the stations can then make their choices. Of the 1,815 hours of original-broadcast programs distributed in the 1993 fiscal year, public affairs programs (including news) comprised the largest share (46.1 percent), followed by children's programs (17.3 percent), cultural programs (16.7 percent), how-to shows (7.4 percent). Science and nature, and educational programs—mostly college telecourses—made up 6.1 percent each.[7] Only 0.2 percent of the NPS schedule were sports programs.

PBS programming is divided into three main departments: cultural programming, which includes drama, performance, and music programs; children's programming; and news and information programming with its subareas of news, public affairs, and science and history programs. All departments have a director and usually one associate director who handles program submissions and queries in his or her particular area. Directors supervise associate directors, and the vice president of programming oversees all the directors.

In the 1993 fiscal year, the individual stations paid PBS the largest percentage of the service's budget (29 percent). Corporations came in second (at 22.9 percent). The federal government through the Corporation for Public Broadcasting contributed 13.9 percent of this budget.[8]

With stations making up the largest single percentage of the NPS income, programmers of the national prime-time schedule are accountable to them and try to anticipate their needs and address their conflicting concerns. Programmers have a strong mandate to provide stations with shows that can be aired in places as diverse as rural Louisiana and New York City. Yet they also have a mandate to grapple with issues that lie outside the established consensus.[9]

"We're professionals employed to make judgments about television programs," explained Mary Jane McKinven, director of public affairs programming. "It's part of our journalistic guidelines that we will not shy away from controversy, that we will take on the tough issues of the day. That's part of our charge."[10]

PBS programmers live in a world where trust, a producer's track record, particular production and journalistic standards, and room in the PBS schedule influence their ultimate decisions to accept or reject programs. They are also mindful of PBS's mission to encourage "the highest quality" national programming, provide reasonable access to the schedule for programs that "reflect the great diversity of human thought, expression and experience," and to adhere to "accepted journalistic standards," but they are limited by the demands of scheduling and the number of slots available for programs.[11]

The bulk of PBS's schedule, especially in prime time (8 p.m. to 11 p.m.), is already filled by what programmers call "strand" series, such as *Nova, Masterpiece Theater, The American Experience,* and *Frontline.* Much of the rest is taken up by limited series. So not much time remains for specials and other single programs. The actual time window varies from month to month and sometimes from week to week. (In 1995, very few single documentaries were accepted for broadcast, even fewer than in the mid-1980s.)

"I only have a few hours of programming to fill each week, and I get around fifty submissions a month," McKinven told me. "I don't like telling 95 percent of the people that there's no room at the inn. And some of the shows are wonderful, too."[12]

Programmers say they try to separate their personal opinions from what they see as their professional responsibilities to provide stations with programs that meet "the high standards of excellence PBS is known for."[13] They want to select programs that the stations will carry and that will fit PBS standards of "quality" and "fairness."

Most programs are rejected because they fail to meet these "high standards of excellence." The shows are too local in focus, of poor technical quality, have an inappropriate narrator or an inadequate script. Sometimes the topic has already been covered. If the show has PBS money in it, or if it comes from a reliable, prominent station, most programmers interviewed said they will give it much more consideration than an unsolicited program from a first-time film maker or an unknown independent producer.

The background and day-to-day activities of PBS programmers illuminate how different their world is from that of independent producers.

PBS programmers live in a bureaucratic, administrative universe. They attend several regularly scheduled meetings a week where departments discuss programs they might want to acquire and discuss those they have acquired. At other, less formal meetings, associate director programmers lobby each other and the director on behalf of particular programs they would like to see on PBS. (The vice president of programming makes the ultimate decisions but usually doesn't interfere with the departmental directors' judgments.) Sometimes meetings are called to view programs that the department is unsure about accepting or rejecting or to discuss problematic or potentially controversial programs. In between meetings, programmers screen and answer queries about prospective projects from independent producers, distributors, station programmers, station producers, and series representatives. Their time is divided between dealing with future programs and current ones. They spend a lot of time on the phone.

## A Very Brief Political History of Public Television

PBS programmers are affected by the shifting political winds in the country as much as independent producers are. During the 1980s and early 1990s, both programmers and producers were especially on guard because political conservatives sought to cut federal funding for public broadcasting.

The Reagan administration called for the total defunding of public television in 1981.[14] This effort was not entirely successful, but significant cuts in government support of public broadcasting and the prospects of more cuts in the future led stations to embrace programming that would appeal to middle-class viewers to bring in more donations and subscriptions. Stations were also forced to seek out more private funders and corporate underwriters for their programs and operations to lessen their dependence on government funding.

The attempt by Reagan to shut down public broadcasting wasn't the first time a president used financial pressure to control the system. Since its inception in 1967, public broadcasting has been plagued with financial uncertainty and efforts to influence the content of its programming.

When President Lyndon Johnson signed into law the Public Broadcasting Act of 1967 two months before leaving office, the legislation didn't specify a long-term solution for how the new system would be funded.[15] Although funding was never intended to come exclusively from the federal government, it was not specified what the proportion of government funding to private contributions would be.[16] Those details were to be worked out later. The Carnegie Commission Report (which was the blueprint for the Public Broadcasting Act of 1967) proposed a tax on television sets or fees levied on the

commercial uses of the broadcast spectrum to provide a regular source of funding that would also insulate public broadcasting from political interference.[17]

In 1969, proposals for the long-term financing of public broadcasting did
not materialize. Historian Erik Barnouw implies this may have been partly by
design.[18] Nineteen sixty-nine was an especially turbulent year. While the Corporation for Public Broadcasting was still being set up, New York City's
National Educational Television (NET)—which later became WNET—
announced that it would broadcast a series of documentaries critical of the
U.S. role in Vietnam beginning with "Inside North Vietnam." This announcement set the station management—and public television—on a collision
course with the Nixon administration.

The story indicates how plucky yet vulnerable to political retaliation public broadcasters have been. After NET announced that it would air "Inside
North Vietnam," station executives received a letter signed by thirty-three
congressmen demanding that the station cancel the broadcast.[19] The station
went ahead with the broadcast, but NET's management didn't survive much
longer.[20] When President Richard Nixon ordered the secret invasions of Laos
and Cambodia in 1970, NET responded by broadcasting several more documentaries about the war and U.S. foreign policy. (Those programs included
"Who Invited Us?" about U.S. intervention; "Behind the Lines," a documentary about the FBI's use of agents provocateurs to infiltrate antiwar groups;
and The Great American Dream Machine, a satirical series produced by Al
Perlmutter, who later produced several Bill Moyers specials, including "The
Secret Government," and also the financial program Adam Smith's Money
World.)[21]

In 1972, President Nixon vetoed a three-year appropriation to public
broadcasting, and the word went out through his associates that he wanted
public television to get out of the public affairs business and to stick with less
controversial programming.[22] Although a scaled-down bill eventually passed,
Nixon pointed his finger at the Corporation for Public Broadcasting (CPB)
as the source of many problems, asserting that it had become "a focal point of
control and a center for power."[23] Embracing the concept of "localism," Nixon
sought to control the system he couldn't eliminate by vetoing government
funding of CPB and by decentralizing the broadcasting system so that the local stations, which tended to be more conservative in outlook, could exert a
conservative influence on national programming.[24] This strategy took the concentrated power and money away from the main national production centers
in New York and Washington, D.C., and spread it among the stations.[25] The
bill also tied federal funding to matching grants from the private sector. As
Patricia Aufderheide observed, "The era of balkanized public TV had begun."[26]

The 1972 veto was followed by a series of key resignations by Democrats at CPB, and Nixon selected several conservative Republicans to fill their positions. A former Republican congressman and Nixon supporter, Thomas B. Curtis, became the new CPB chairman of the board, and Henry Loomis, a former deputy director of the U.S. Information Agency, became the new president of CPB. Together, they set about "correcting" the "left leaning" tilt of public affairs programs on public television.

With the vision of a weaker and more accountable CPB, the Nixon appointees got to work. In 1973, the new CPB board of directors decided not to support programs perceived as "too controversial" and quickly dropped CPB funding for *Bill Moyers' Journal*, *Washington Week in Review*, and even William F. Buckley's *Firing Line*.[27] In March 1973, White House assistant Patrick Buchanan appeared on ABC's *Dick Cavett Show* and explained to the late-night talk show host why the Nixon administration didn't like these programs. Buchanan reportedly told Cavett and his listeners that *Bill Moyers' Journal* and *Washington Week in Review* were "unbalanced against us." He also considered Robert MacNeil of *The MacNeil/Lehrer NewsHour* as a person "who is definitely anti-Administration."[28]

PBS was also revamped. It still remained in charge of coordinating national broadcasts to the affiliates, but now members of the boards of local public television stations sat on its board, giving the stations representative control over PBS.[29]

While government funding for public broadcasting was under attack in Congress in the 1980s, Barry Chase, then the vice president of news and public affairs programming at PBS, described the political climate in public television during his tenure as "repressive." "There was a widespread fear that if the system were too troublesome, it could be shut down completely," he told me.[30]

Chase saw himself walking a fine line. In 1981 or 1982, he received a visit from "two large men" who introduced themselves as "friends" of the recently elected president, Ronald Reagan. His visitors urged him to accept for national broadcast a film narrated by Charlton Heston about communism in Poland. Chase felt uncomfortable and a little intimidated by his guests. The Republicans were not the only ones to lobby PBS for programs with partisan views. He said the Democrats under Jimmy Carter did the same thing.[31]

Although the vast majority of programs broadcast on PBS between 1985 and 1993 aired without controversy, a handful of public affairs documentaries shone a spotlight on what Chase called "the predicament of public television": how the system is expected to be both "a paragon of traditional journalistic integrity and a playground of free expression."[32]

Wrestling with this predicament was the challenge Chase faced when most of the controversies examined here took place. Chase and his PBS program-mers tried different ways to broadcast programs with strong points of view on passionately contested issues and yet not jeopardize PBS's credibility and its standards of "balance and fairness." For example, PBS would broadcast a pro-gram on a divisive topic and add a follow-up panel discussion so critics of the program could have their say. Chase also experimented with the notion of "op-ed television."

In 1985, PBS's Program Advisory Committee contributed $380,000 to KQED/San Francisco for three "theme nights," with about one-third of this money budgeted for acquisitions.[33] Each theme night was to provide a three-hour forum for opposing perspectives on contested public issues. Produced by KQED's director of current affairs, Beverly Ornstein, and hosted by reporter Steve Talbot, the theme-night specials presented partisan films (some by in-dependent producers) with an introduction by Talbot and a follow-up panel discussion with experts and advocates representing each side.

The first theme night addressed abortion and the second the Israeli-Palestinian conflict. WNET and WETA, two major East Coast stations, re-fused to carry the shows. Skittish about alienating significant numbers of view-ers with programs critical of Israel or as explosive as abortion, station managers and programmers didn't want to risk alienating a broad base of support. After Chase received dozens of complaints from affiliates, he canceled the third theme night, which was to deal with Central America, nuclear disarmament, or the death penalty.[34] He rethought his strategy on packaging programs with strong points of view about vital social issues. "There's a certain ethical re-sponsibility one has to have to those paying the bills," he said.[35]

Accused of bias by right-wing groups, such as Accuracy in Media, PBS programmers occasionally sought out documentaries with an overtly conser-vative political perspective. "Nicaragua Was Our Home" focused on the Miskito Indians of Nicaragua who were highly critical of the Sandinistas.[36] The program was produced by CAUSA, a group founded by the Reverend Sun Myung Moon, which reportedly funded the contras after the Congress's ban on government funding. PBS broadcast the program on June 17, 1986. Decisions like these were made because Chase understood federal funding could be cut if PBS were perceived to be "too left-wing" by the conservative watchdog groups and institutes, such as Accuracy in Media and the Center for the Study of Popular Culture. These organizations had the ear of Senators Robert Dole and Jesse Helms. Programs about homosexuality attracted New Right critics and liberal defenders, and either could launch subscriber boy-cotts. Threats to withhold government funding loomed ominously over pub-lic broadcasting during this period.

Chase knew what most programmers locally and nationally learned from experience: that one programmer's journalistic responsibility is another programmer's timidity. It was risky to schedule programs that major stations would not air, and Chase felt it was also embarrassing. He knew he was in for a bumpy ride with the stations so long as he allowed programs with strong points of view on the national schedule in the op-ed television format, yet he still wanted to find a format for programs with divergent points of view on the issues of the day. Chase didn't want to give up the fight entirely.

Gail Christian, the programmer under Chase who handled the specials, was also a programmer who actively sought to "push the envelope"—in the direction of social action, the questioning of authority—so it would be more difficult to be complacent in the 1980s. Director of news and public affairs programming, Christian figured prominently in many of the controversies examined here. She and Chase seemed to have a symbiotic relationship that allowed Christian to widen the range of views expressed on contested topics, while also allowing Chase to distance himself when he felt it was necessary.

Meanwhile in the late 1980s, independent producers organized their own campaigns to pressure PBS into broadcasting their programs and to increase funding available for their productions. As public television stations absorbed an increasing percentage of a smaller pot of programming funds, independent producers felt shut out of the system, a system that they felt was supposed to be a forum for diversity and to provide a venue for their work.[37] They succeeded in passing a law to create the Independent Television Service, a funding outlet for independently produced programs.[38]

## How Programs Get on the Air

Submissions to PBS programmers cover a wide range of queries and proposals for programs. Some are short letters from station or independent producers who have an idea for a program and wonder if it has a realistic chance of getting on PBS. Some are packets from producers with a sample videotape and supporting material. Sometimes producers seek a letter of support from PBS expressing interest in the project, for such an endorsement might help their fund-raising; other times they want feedback on how they could turn their proposed idea or rough edit into something PBS would air. Some submissions are completed programs from stations, independent producers, and foreign broadcasters all vying for a PBS broadcast in or near prime time.

Given the very limited time-slot to be filled and the stiff competition, most of these queries and proposals never become PBS programs. Like Mary Jane McKinven, the other programmers I interviewed estimated they reject

95 percent of all submissions that cross their desks. They figured they receive about fifty queries a month and said they try to respond to each query individually. Programmers felt overwhelmed by the stacks of queries and phone messages from producers wanting feedback on their submissions, an explanation for their programs' rejection, or a scheduling decision.

The methods of rejection vary depending on the nature of the submission, the topic, and the approach. For example, if an independent producer submits a query letter or a program on a topic that the programmer believes has already been covered, the producer will be told "the story has already been done." However, if the producer uses a very different approach or brings new information to the "old" story, it may have a chance for acceptance.

Programmers don't have time to watch all preview cassettes, rough edits, and programs in their entirety, so they devise shortcuts to get through the material.

For example, one programmer—the one who requested anonymity and did so months *after* our audiotaped, on-the-record interview—usually will not even read the supporting material that comes with a video sample but will simply pop the tape in the cassette player. "I'll look at the title, and I think that's fair because that's the way people look at television. They look in *TV Guide* and they channel surf. . . . We don't have time to look at every show that comes in its entirety."

If this programmer decides the program is not up to PBS standards, the tape is ejected after five or ten minutes. This allows at least a few minutes after the title to see how the producer sets up the story. If this programmer finds the program interesting or believes it has potential for PBS, the whole show will be watched.

"I'm basically looking at content. Sometimes something jumps out at me and says, 'Listen, our stations are not going to play this.' From my own experience, I know they're not going to use this, so why send it to them?—especially when I've got two or three other ones here that are roughly equivalent, and my sense is that they are more likely to be used by our stations. We have a limited amount of air time so it's a sort of a juggling act. . . . You can't send them everything."

If the work has high production values (decent lighting, shots in focus, clean audio, appropriate narration and voice quality, a well-written, clear, and credible story), and the story is deemed compelling for a national audience and not just of local interest, the typical programmer will watch the entire program, read or skim the material, and inform the department director of the program's merits, and then contact the scheduling department for approval. This department checks to see if there is room in the schedule for the program. Otherwise the tape will be sent back with a polite "no thanks" and sometimes some words of encouragement or a suggestion.

With the exception of series, PBS programmers accept only completed or nearly completed programs for broadcast. In recent years, PBS has helped fund several specials and limited series, and PBS programmers have occasionally taken a more active role in shaping programs at the editing stage to ensure that they will meet PBS standards, including those standards for "balance" and "fairness." This "ongoing conversation" with the program's producer is especially crucial if it is a program PBS wants to air but is not part of an already existing series such as *P.O.V.*, *Frontline*, *Nova*, *The American Experience*, or *American Masters*.

Some submissions would be acceptable given the technical standards and content but aren't compelling enough to the programmer to warrant a broadcast, especially given the competition. Programmers also distinguish between programs that are of topical interest and therefore must be aired during a limited time, and "evergreens," which are programs that can be put on the shelf and aired practically any time and still have interest.

Sometimes a well-produced program comes to a programmer on a topic that the programmer realizes is likely to offend a particular group or put the stations in a position to get calls from irate viewers. (Programs on abortion, the Middle East, and homosexuality fell into this category during the period examined in this book.) If the programmer feels strongly that this show ought to be on the PBS prime-time feed, a meeting of other programming staff will be called to solicit other opinions about it. Then more meetings are planned to decide how to handle the matter.

Potentially controversial programs are scrutinized carefully by staff and the vice president of programming. Occasionally these meetings evoke heated discussions about the program's suitability for PBS, but if the show is considered important enough, a discussion about damage control begins.

"Everybody will look around the room and say, 'Okay, who's going to write the response press releases? Who's going to answer the mail? Who's going to do the station relations on this one?'" Glenn Marcus, associate director of history and science programming, told me. The fear of reprisal isn't taken into consideration, at least not at the associate directors' level. "It's not something I get exposed to."[39]

Some programmers favor programs by independent producers that have been coproduced with or submitted through a PBS affiliate station because these programs have already passed through a screening process that covers both technical considerations and editorial content. "The stations will not approach us with a work coming from an independent in particular unless they have a fairly good sense that it will work for us and they're usually right," Marcus said. He said the percentage of shows that come from independents through stations and get scheduled on PBS is much higher than those that come directly from independent producers.[40] Other programmers disagreed and said station affiliation makes no difference in their decisions because they are looking for simply the best programs regardless of their point of origin or packaging.

All programmers I interviewed confirmed that single documentaries have a better chance of being broadcast on PBS if they are part of an established series. In the next chapter, we will examine the organization and operation of two well-known series: *Frontline* and *P.O.V.*

# Chapter 2

# Frontline
# and P.O.V.

Programs submitted for consideration to PBS documentary series pass through a gauntlet of screeners, each of whom uses specific criteria to determine which shows should be accepted for broadcast. Although independent producers typically lose editorial control and often copyright when working with series— the notable exception is *P.O.V.*—they know their programs are more likely to get on the air and to reach a wide audience if they conform to the imprint of an established series. PBS programmers rely on the series editors to prescreen the programs and hardly ever pull a program from a series.

Two PBS series specialize in independent productions and current affairs: *Frontline* and *P.O.V.* (*The American Experience* features historical work, which lies outside the scope of this book.) By taking a look at how these series operate—including how they select programs—we can better understand their relationships with PBS, independent producers, and special interest groups.

## *Inside* Frontline

Since its inception in 1983, *Frontline* has answered PBS's mandate to address the controversial issues of the day. It is the only long-format, public affairs documentary series on PBS that is sanctioned to deal with such material. During its seven-month season, *Frontline* provides about twenty-five hours of provocative programming in the PBS prime-time schedule.[1] Independent producers whose programs appear on *Frontline* must conform to the standards and styles of the series and have a topic that suits the series's mission.

*Frontline* has a special status in the public television universe because it has a guaranteed place on the national prime-time schedule, relatively secure funding from CPB, PBS, and the stations (so it is not beholden to corporate underwriters), and widespread respect within the public television system (based on years of award-winning programs). *Frontline* programs are routinely reviewed in the nation's newspapers, and they often become part of public debate. These programs set the standard against which other PBS public affairs documentaries—including independently produced documentaries—are often measured.

While *Frontline* offers independent producers a venue for their story ideas, few independent producers have been successful in turning their stories into series's programs. Those who do produce for *Frontline* receive funding for their projects (so they don't have to fund-raise) and a place in the PBS prime-time schedule. In return, they work with the series producers and turn over editorial and creative control on the final cut.

*Frontline* stands alone as the only long-format, current affairs documentary series on national American television, excluding series on cable. When the commercial networks gradually abandoned their one-hour documentary series, such as *CBS Reports*, NBC's *White Paper*, and ABC News's *Close-up*, *Frontline* filled the gap. The series is currently the highest-rated public affairs program on public television with an average weekly audience of over six million viewers. It is most popular with adult men, who comprise 54 percent of its audience.[2]

## A PROFILE OF *FRONTLINE*'S DAVID FANNING

David Fanning is the cofounder and executive producer of *Frontline*. He and his team of senior staff decide which stories to tell and which current issues to address. Like his associate Bill Moyers, Fanning has the power not only to select and sanction stories but also to put them on the public agenda, baptizing them into the mainstream media through a series that reaches millions of viewers. Fanning is an elite cultural authority. He is also a South African by birth. His father was a teacher-boatbuilder, and his mother gave him travel books and biographies to read while growing up.[3] He began his film-making career in 1970 in South Africa but later moved to California, where he directed and produced documentaries at a small public station, KOCE/Huntington Beach Channel 50. Fanning's major break into the national public television scene came with his appointment at flagship station WGBH/Boston, where he developed *World*, an international documentary series that ran for five years and presented over fifty foreign and domestic documentary films.[4] (*World* was a series similar to *Frontline* in that it presented programs produced specially for the series, in addition to some coproductions and acquisitions.) In 1980, one of those films, the docudrama "Death of a Princess," produced and written with the director Anthony Thomas, caused an international up-roar and put the thirty-four-year-old Fanning on the map as a provocative film maker with a distinctive style and sensibility.

Fanning went on to create *Frontline* with Louis Wiley, Jr., a lawyer turned television producer. *Frontline* programs generally emulate the investigative, hard-news documentary style of *CBS Reports*. They tend to use a male, third-person narrator (often Will Lyman) or to tell the story from the first-person perspective of an on-camera male reporter. Virtually all *Frontline* documenta-ries address important and topical social, political, or economic issues.

THE SELECTION PROCESS

*Frontline* receives hundreds of queries, proposals, and program ideas a year, but only a small fraction become *Frontline* documentaries. Independent produc-ers, public television station producers, producers who have worked previously with *Frontline*, and journalists all pitch story ideas to the series gatekeepers. The most promising are discussed by *Frontline*'s screening committee, which is composed of Fanning, executive editor Louis Wiley, Jr., series producer Marrie Campbell, and other senior staff members.

The screening committee typically meets around a table and goes through story ideas submitted to the series that haven't been already disqualified by the staff as redundant or poorly developed. Most proposals are rejected be-cause the group does not consider them "interesting," they have been "done before," or the story or topic isn't deemed "newsworthy."

Decision making at *Frontline* is not topic driven so much as *story driven*, and to some extent, *author driven*. For example, Fanning is not interested in "doing something on child care," but if a known producer pitched a story about a miscarriage of justice in a day-care center where three-year-olds accused adult day-care workers of sexual misconduct and the testimony divided the com-munity, raised questions about repressed memory and apparent loopholes in the justice system, *and* the adults were sent to prison for life, *that* would be a strong *Frontline* story.

The screening meetings sometimes generate new story ideas that spin off a proposed story but are distinct from it. A promising story idea may emerge because of the questions raised and the journalist or film maker raising them. For example, Fanning was intrigued when investigative reporter Seymour Hersh came across a legal case where a man was arrested for trying to export a nuclear trigger but got off with a slap on the wrist. This fragment of infor-mation became a story about nuclear proliferation, a detective story, with Hersh guiding the camera.

Occasionally, "a great story" will come along that most people in the group will recognize as worth doing or exploring. Or someone will come up with a story angle the group feels is fresh and exciting. According to Fanning, much of the process is simply "trusting your gut." "You get that instant reaction from other people [in the group] which is 'hey, this is a great story. I'm interested in that.' And that's the heart of this endeavor," he said.

Once a program idea is accepted, the next step is likely to be further research and development, followed by the actual production. Fanning and his senior staff divide up the projects. The person responsible for a given project—generally a senior producer—is charged with following up on details and finding out more about the individual proposing the story, specifically about whether that person has a vested interest in the project. This senior producer becomes the contact for the film maker and the "editorial guide" for the story.

Fanning objects to film makers who do "crusading investigative journalism" masquerading as "objective work" and who use "voice of God" narration to give a "semblance of balance." "I think journalism is always to be tested on your honesty, and there's something dishonest about pretending you're an objective journalist when in fact you're carrying a flame, a torch," Fanning said, but he doesn't dismiss point-of-view journalism in itself. "I think you've got to just say, 'I'm carrying a torch with this,' and that's okay if you tell me. . . . I believe very much in authorship."

Fanning insists on editorial control, as do the executive producers of all other major series except *P.O.V.*, because the medium of television, in his view, is so open to abuse. "It's such a manipulative medium. I mean all journalism is, but television, with its power to persuade, is particularly dangerous," he said. "There's a lot of fairly dishonest practitioners out there."

Fanning looks for film makers who combine journalistic curiosity and discipline with the authorial literary skills that make for good television documentaries. Often the person proposing the story doesn't have either the experience or the track record that would make Fanning confident that he or she would be able to produce a program with the standards expected of the series. Fanning will then try to match a regular *Frontline* producer to work with or to supervise the project, or the series will hire the less experienced film maker as an associate producer. If the outside producer has a solid track record recognized by Fanning, he or she would work directly with Fanning or one of the senior producers.

### *FRONTLINE*'S RELATIONSHIP WITH PBS AND THE STATIONS

*Frontline*'s relationship with public television means, for all practical purposes, Fanning's relationship with PBS and CPB. Fanning is the one who assumes editorial control of all programs the series funds and produces, taking responsibility for whatever is produced with the series logo. PBS programmers trust him with their logo, too. With some exceptions, station executives accept what he produces as "high-quality journalism," even if they disagree with particular programs and receive complaints from their listeners, annoyed underwriters, or interest groups who feel that their issues have been misrepresented or that they have been otherwise treated unfairly.

Years of trust and an established track record hold Fanning's relationship with PBS together. He also lobbies. When he believes one of his programs may be shocking or controversial and could cause ripples in the system for PBS programmers, he will make a special effort, like a good diplomat, to arm his PBS colleagues with ammunition against potentially irate station managers or interest groups so PBS or station staff can defend *Frontline* against attack. For example, Fanning knew the program "Innocence Lost," produced by Ofra Bikel, would be controversial.[5] The film asserts a miscarriage of justice took place in a North Carolina town. It investigates a day-care center where small children alleged sexual abuse by day-care workers and contains several descriptions of sexual acts. When the program was nearly finished, Fanning invited two PBS programmers up to New York to sit in the editing room and watch it.

"I wanted them to see this exhausted team of people that had spent three years, and [had] documents to the ceiling and hundreds of hours of tape shot, just so that they [the programmers] understood what a commitment we had made to this so they would go back to PBS and have a defense," Fanning explained. "I'm arming them because people will be upset, because . . . there will be small southern stations and other places who will be very scared of this program because they will take a lot of heat from right-wing conservatives and fundamentalist groups on even airing the subject, let alone the fact that we are essentially challenging two court verdicts."

Fanning enjoys an economic freedom that few others in public television have. Since *Frontline* receives all of its funding from PBS and the Corporation for Public Broadcasting, these organizations serve as a heat shield between *Frontline* producers and irate interest groups. Moreover, Fanning doesn't have to worry about alienating particular corporate underwriters or individual financial donors (factors that do come into play more at the station level). As far as editorial matters are concerned, neither PBS nor CPB know in detail what programs he has in production. He doesn't notify PBS of programming in the works until the programs are almost finished.

Fanning may release a rough edit of a program to select reviewers for an early press preview. Occasionally, the copies find their way into other hands.

This happened with "Losing the War with Japan," a documentary about U.S.-Japanese trade policy told through a case study of Honda.[6]

Honda got hold of a press copy of the film before the broadcast and produced an eighteen-page refutation of the film, which cast aspersions on the series's journalistic credibility. Honda sent this document to every station manager in the system the day before the scheduled broadcast. Although no copy was sent to *Frontline*, the station managers passed along the criticisms to Fanning. He did not have time to respond, but PBS broadcast the program anyway. Then *Frontline* spent a few weeks refuting all the accusations.

Another program that created a ripple in the ranks of station managers was "L.A. Is Burning: Five Reports from a Divided City." KCET/Los Angeles was, in Fanning's words, "extremely unhappy" about the ninety-minute *Frontline* special that analyzed the reasons for the three days and nights of beatings, looting, and burning that began on April 29, 1992.[7] The station manager felt the program gave too negative a view of the situation and expressed concern about its airing in Los Angeles the week before the second Rodney King verdict. KCET canceled the local broadcast, an act which then made other public television stations reconsider their decisions to broadcast it.

To ease the friction with the station, Mary Jane McKinven at PBS programming took several phone calls to reassure nervous programmers and station managers that the program was, in her words, "really very good."[8] A public relations professional, McKinven smoothed the ruffled feathers of her station constituents and defended *Frontline* against their attacks.

Preliminary research suggests that disputes over *Frontline* and Moyers's programs are handled privately and relatively quietly at PBS. Upset station managers or special interests typically call PBS programmers and David Fanning to complain about a particular program. PBS programmers defend the documentaries, standing firm with Fanning. Rarely are retractions given. Critics express their views, PBS and Fanning and/or Moyers respond, and the matter is basically over. Although Moyers and Fanning have a special status by virtue of being elite cultural authorities, they have also been the targets of organized interest groups who have sought to make controversy around specific programs and to pull the plug on government funding for public broadcasting as a way to rein in Moyers and *Frontline*.

The attacks on *Frontline* from politicians and political conservative groups have proven harder to smooth. Since its major funding comes from the Corporation for Public Broadcasting, *Frontline* has been drawn into the debate over government funding for public broadcasting as an example of the system's "liberal bias." It is also a favorite target of the Israeli media watchdog group CAMERA and, along with Bill Moyers, of the Committee on Media Integrity (COMINT), a conservative media group run by former leftists David Horowitz and Peter Collier.

## *Inside* P.O.V.

The idea for *P.O.V.*—a film maker's term for "point of view"—grew out of a conversation in 1986 at the Sundance Film Festival between David Fanning and Marc Weiss, a prominent figure in the independent producing community as a producer, promoter, and programmer of independent films.[9]

During a forum with independent producers, Fanning suggested PBS ought to have a series devoted to independent nonfiction films that had strong or unusual points of view. (At *Frontline*, Fanning often rejected these programs because they did not fit the aesthetic or journalistic standards of the series.) Weiss later asked Fanning how that series idea could be realized, and Fanning introduced him to the people who could help make it happen: Barry Chase, then PBS's vice president of news and information programming, and Henry Becton, the president and general manager of WGBH/Boston. Eventually, at the suggestion of these prominent PBS insiders, Weiss met with David Davis, executive director of *American Playhouse*, who agreed to back a new series just as he had done with other series.[10]

The idea for *P.O.V.* dovetailed with Barry Chase's concerns and those who shared his interest in "op-ed television." It also appealed to the increasingly vocal independent producers, who felt shut out of the PBS schedule. Marc Weiss, with his credentials as an independent producer and a media activist, had devoted his career to improving their lot.

Since its first season in 1988, *P.O.V.* has become a catchall for independently produced programs that would not fit elsewhere on the PBS schedule in the strand series, such as *Frontline*, *The American Experience*, and *American Masters*, or in one of the coveted 10 p.m. slots for single documentaries. As a practical matter, PBS programmers could now direct to *P.O.V.* those works they felt were too unconventional, likely to be controversial, or ones that deviated from the journalistic and aesthetic standards of a *Frontline* public affairs program. They also would not have to deal with these programs' independent producers, who sometimes didn't take rejection well and initiated letter-writing campaigns while charging censorship in the press. Programmers had another reason: programs have better carriage by stations if they are part of a series, and they are easier to promote because the series already have promotional networks set up.[11]

With the creation of *P.O.V.*, independent producers now had a place to go, and PBS programmers had a place to direct them. *P.O.V.* actually paid producers cash for the rights to broadcast their program over PBS and allowed them to retain their own editorial voices without having to relinquish them to the series editor. These independent producers could be more like their counterparts in Europe, who not only reached a public audience over the air- waves but were paid for their products. Although the series would run only ten to twelve weeks during the summer in the first few years, and with un- even carriage (stations would choose which programs to run and often sched- uled them outside prime time), most independents saw *P.O.V.* as a step forward in their struggle with PBS. One of *P.O.V.*'s stated missions, repeated by its executive producers in outreach meetings with independent producers around the country, was to provide a platform for voices not present elsewhere on television and in this society. *P.O.V.*'s mission echoed the original 1967 man- date for public television, a dream many independent documentary produc- ers and some station staff shared.

Since its founding, *P.O.V.* has aired more than a dozen independent films a year during its summer seasons. Top programs attract four to six million view- ers, most of them between the ages of eighteen and forty-nine, one of the harder audiences for public broadcasting to reach.[12]

With funding from the John D. and Catherine T. MacArthur Founda- tion, PBS, and the National Endowment for the Arts, *P.O.V.* is at present the only national forum for completed nonfiction work by independent pro- ducers that falls outside the well-established series of *Frontline, The American Experience,* and *Nova.* Since *P.O.V.* acquires programs that are complete or near completion, the series is more akin to a film festival that seeks to present the diversity and the best work of the independent producing community. It defines itself as "a public meeting place" where views rarely explored by the mainstream media find a home on the national airwaves.[13]

THE SELECTION PROCESS

*P.O.V.* executives, like the PBS programmers, face a huge number of submis- sions and have a limited amount of airtime to fill. Each year they receive hun- dreds of entries—a number that rose to more than five hundred in 1993—but only about a dozen of those yearly submissions will be accepted for broadcast. That means *P.O.V.* rejects about 98 percent of entries, more than those that are turned away by PBS programming.

*P.O.V.*'s rejection rate is higher than PBS programmers' because the PBS programmers base their estimates of submissions on a figure that includes a mix of query letters, proposals for programs with sample tapes, works in progress, and finished programs. As noted earlier, *P.O.V.* deals only with fin- ished or nearly completed nonfiction works. (*P.O.V.* screeners will occasionally preview programs at the rough-edit stage, a stage significantly further along than a query letter, a written proposal, or a proposal with a sample tape.)

"I know our seat-of-the-pants decision making here is that part of our role is to find people who are without power and without voice. Being without voice also means being without power in this society," P.O.V. founder Marc Weiss explained. "It's not a question so much about giving the voiceless a voice as it is about giving the American public an opportunity to hear. . . . It's important for a democratic society that there be people like independent film makers who are able to express those things and who are able to reach large numbers of people with those perspectives. The film makers speak for others in the society. They don't just speak for themselves."[14]

P.O.V. looks for clear voices and rare perspectives that also present the broad range of works created by independents: "A Little Vicious" (1991) is a portrait of a mongrel pit bull condemned to die by the state of Connecticut; "Maria's Story" (1991) profiles a Salvadoran guerrilla grandmother fighting the U.S.-backed military regime in her country; and "For Better or for Worse" (1993) presents several couples who have been together for at least fifty years.

In contrast to the PBS programmers who decide semi-independently what gets on the schedule, P.O.V. relies on outside screeners, an editorial advisory committee, and the executive producers' evaluation of programs to winnow down the candidates for inclusion. The four-stage process is much more open than PBS programmers'—and more time consuming—because it involves these outside screeners, including independent producers, who evaluate their peers' work.

First, thousands of applications—"calls for entries"—are sent out to 15,000 to 20,000 identified independent producers, including members of the Association of Independent Video and Filmmakers and other independent film organizations. P.O.V. executive producers also scout the film festivals and independent producing community for work that they think might be suitable for the series and that furthers their goal of bringing new television to the public television audience. Most of the new work, however, finds its way to P.O.V. through the series submission process.[15]

Each submission to P.O.V. is evaluated at least twice. P.O.V. staff send out each of the submitted tapes to two "prescreeners," who assess the program's potential for P.O.V. using an evaluation form provided by P.O.V. These prescreeners, who are often independent producers themselves, are asked to watch at least twenty minutes of each tape, and all of the program if they think the work is strong enough to merit serious consideration. The tapes are then returned to the P.O.V. office with the prescreeners' evaluations.

The second stage is when series executive producers read through the evaluations. They watch the works that have survived the first prescreening process, about one-third of the films originally submitted. Like their counterparts at PBS programming, they do not watch every program in its entirety unless, judging from the first ten or twenty minutes, they believe the program would be a likely candidate for the series.

"Not every film gets looked at all the way through because this is television," Weiss explained. "If I've watched twenty minutes and it's not going anywhere, and I already have evaluations from two prescreeners—I'm sitting there with the book of evaluations—sometimes I'll fast forward."

In the third stage, executive producers make a short list of about forty programs to be screened again, this time by P.O.V.'s editorial advisory committee. This committee is made up of six independent film makers and six public television programmers. The group typically meets three or four days in December or January each year to screen and discuss the strongest contenders for inclusion in the series. Two PBS programmers attend the meeting as observers but don't participate in any informal votes. The P.O.V. executives in attendance listen, quietly taking notes and trying not to signal their own favorites, and reserve the right to depart from the committee's recommendations.

"It's almost a religious thing with me," Marc Weiss said. "I am there to soak in as much advice as I can from people and really hear them. I may ask them questions. There's very vigorous discussion within the group. It's not my role to change their minds."

The process also helps prevent the executive producers' personal tastes from playing too large a role in determining what's accepted and what's not. "A lot of films that I go in thinking I really like this film, if I get strong negatives from the editorial committee, it usually goes by the wayside," Weiss said. "On the other hand, films that I'm ambivalent about which get strong positives, move up on the list. My point in setting up the editorial committee in the beginning was that one person's taste should not govern a selection like this because it has too much impact on the film makers and too much impact on the audience. . . . The series needs to cater to tastes other than my own."

The advisory committee watches most or all of each film and then discusses it. Next a straw vote is taken by the committee to indicate which films are strongly supported, but the final decision about the series's programs remains with P.O.V.'s executive producers. David Davis, executive director of the American Documentary, which oversees P.O.V, is the only person who can overrule their decisions.

"We [the executive producers] have the option of taking a film that nobody in the editorial committee likes and putting it in the series. We've done it once or twice." However, Weiss said he would never put programs on that had not at least been shown to and discussed by the editorial committee because that would undermine the legitimacy of the process.

### P.O.V.'S RELATIONSHIP WITH PBS AND THE STATIONS

P.O.V. executives enjoy good public relations with the stations. One of the reasons for this is that different station representatives from around the country participate in the evaluation process.

Another reason has to do with the way programs are packaged. Unlike other documentary series on PBS, a short interview precedes and sometimes follows each film. This personalizes the film by reminding viewers the work has been made by a real, live film maker with his or her own particular views. P.O.V. was the first national series to broadcast "video letters" from viewers, who "talk back" to P.O.V. using home-video camcorders. (This innovation was later adopted by the *Frontline* series.)[16]

Marc Weiss, P.O.V.'s founding executive producer, and his coexecutive producer, Ellen Schneider, came out of the independent producing community and have a network of friends and associations in that community's main centers, San Francisco, Los Angeles, and New York. Weiss cofounded the Association of Independent Video and Filmmakers (AIVF), and Ellen Schneider was at one time communications director of the Independent Television Service (ITVS). (Schneider has been the driving force behind *E.C.U./Extreme Close Up*, a new series showcasing the first-person accounts of the lives of a diverse array of storytellers, shot with camcorders.)[17] They also were baby boomers intent on claiming public television for their generation, a demographic group lagging behind children and seniors on the PBS map of viewers.

But the window for independent work on P.O.V. is small, and even with the institutional shield provided by the series format, several P.O.V. programs have come under attack from religious fundamentalist organizations, conservative political groups, and, perhaps the most damaging, from public television station managers themselves.

During the 1980s, independent film makers produced documentaries critical of the Reagan administration's policies toward Nicaragua, El Salvador, and Guatemala, joining the chorus of some vocal members in the U.S. Congress as well as community and religious groups who challenged those policies. When the Reagan administration escalated the nuclear arms race though "Star Wars" and the production of more nuclear weapons, independent film makers made films that expressed the concerns of the antinuclear movement, reporting vital information about the nuclear legacy and questioning official policy. (One of these films, "Dark Circle," is the subject of the next chapter.)

The conservative call to reassert "family values" coincided with the gay rights movement's efforts to expand the definition of "family" beyond the hetero-sexual nuclear family. The movement spawned many films that humanized gays and lesbians in this culture war, and several of them were broadcast on PBS's series *P.O.V.*

# Chapter 3                                    "Dark Circle"

*I felt "Dark Circle" was just, simply, telling the truth
about Rocky Flats and Diablo Canyon. I was just trying
to tell the truth.*
            —Judy Irving, coproducer and narrator

*It's more difficult to say ["Dark Circle"] falsified
anything, but it left one with the uncomfortable feeling
that this is propaganda, not journalism.*
    —Nat Katzman, former KQED station manager

The case of "Dark Circle" involved a series of decisions and choices that led
PBS and KQED/San Francisco to scuttle the national broadcast of a provocative documentary about the nuclear weapons industry in the mid-1980s. This
eighty-two-minute film was first accepted by PBS for a national broadcast in
1985. Then it was formally rejected a year later, leaving a messy trail of mis-
understandings and accusations: KQED management privately accused PBS
of inconsistency, PBS programmers quietly blamed the station for deviating
from procedures, and independent producers publicly and privately charged
PBS with censorship.

The controversy surrounding "Dark Circle" reveals how PBS programmers decide what is appropriate to send to the stations with the PBS logo and
how they manage conflicts when disagreements over a program arise. Such
decision making involves a series of judgments about the programs and the
producers. When programs have to do with social movements and include
critiques of government policies or major corporations, these judgments take
on ideological or political dimensions. As traffic cops of perspectives, the PBS
gatekeepers, as well as their associates at the local affiliate stations, become
active participants in debates about contested social issues by deciding which

1. First atomic bomb explosion, code-named "Trinity," New Mexico, July 16, 1945.
*Photo: Los Alamos National Scientific Laboratory, courtesy IDG Films.*

views of reality will contend on the airwaves, when they will be broadcast, and in what context.

The dispute over "Dark Circle" unfolded within an increasingly polarized political climate marked by the Reagan administration's escalation of nuclear weapons production and a growing grassroots movement against nuclear weapons and nuclear power. Like several other documentaries that have become controversial, "Dark Circle" was linked through its subject matter and its producers to a social movement at odds with official government policies. When PBS and KQED rejected "Dark Circle," they robbed a national public television audience of the chance to see a sympathetic portrait of nuclear victims and peace activists, an unflattering portrayal of the U.S. government and major nuclear industry corporations, and to receive information about radioactive contamination tied to the nuclear industries. (It should be noted, however, that the documentary eventually aired locally on KQED and nationally on Ted Turner's WTBS and later on the newly created PBS series *P.O.V.*)

PBS wasn't alone in containing these perspectives. In the mid-1980s, the information about radioactive contamination and illnesses at nuclear weapons plants as presented in "Dark Circle" fell outside the national mainstream media's usual framing of the nuclear weapons industry. Today, nuclear-related environmental pollution and its harmful health effects are widely recognized as part of the nuclear legacy. Facts that were once hotly contested or ignored in the mainstream media are now believed.

The "Dark Circle" case did not involve an organized mobilization of special interest groups or the direct interference by vested economic and political interests—the broadcast was derailed before these could have developed. But the way it was derailed reveals much about how decisions were made and rationalized by public television gatekeepers and how independent film makers are often removed from the decision-making process.

The case highlights the differences between the collective aesthetic and journalistic practices dominant in public television documentaries, and the practices and techniques accepted in the independent film-making community. Rather than emulating the preferred PBS style of public affairs documentaries with dispassionate narrators, certified talking-head experts from opposing camps, and little or no music, "Dark Circle" took a clear point of view, treated ordinary citizens as firsthand experts, and used editing and musical techniques uncommon in public television news and public affairs programs. Although "Dark Circle" collided with the journalistic conventions embraced by public television, it remained true in form and content to the feature-documentary tradition in the United States, a genre that encourages films with strong points of view, the use of innovative and dramatic techniques, and a willingness to address divisive issues that have not been sanctioned by the *New York Times*. In this world, success is measured by a film's dramatic impact, social relevance, and theatrical reception, rather than by its ratings and the number of public television stations that carry it.

## Program Description

"Dark Circle" was created by three Bay Area independent producers who were concerned about nuclear contamination and related issues: Judy Irving, Chris Beaver, and Ruth Landy. The film was shot at the Rocky Flats Nuclear Weapons Facility in Colorado, California's Diablo Canyon Nuclear Power Plant (then under construction), and in Hiroshima and Nagasaki, Japan. Most of the story unfolds at Rocky Flats near the facility operated by Rockwell International. The weapons plant, located sixteen miles northeast of Denver in the Rocky Mountains, produces the plutonium triggers for nuclear bombs under contract from the Department of Energy.

The opening of the documentary sets the tone for the program. "Dark

2. "Dark Circle" coproducers and codirectors (left to right) Ruth Landy, Christopher Beaver, and Judy Irving. *Photo: Copyright © Karen Spangenberg, courtesy IDG Films.*

Circle" begins with an excerpt from a 1963 film produced by National Educational Television in New York.[1] A science reporter interviews a nuclear scientist wearing thick gloves who is holding a plutonium "button" about four inches in diameter. The scientist explains that plutonium is "extremely toxic" and the maximum lifetime tolerance permitted for humans is "six-tenths of a millionth of a gram," but if it is handled carefully, it is perfectly safe. "Don't let it escape into the atmosphere," says the science reporter, "it may come back to you." A total eclipse of the sun accompanied by eerie music then appears with the title, "Dark Circle."

In a soft, intimate voice, Judy Irving recounts the history of life on the planet, a history which she says could end in the nuclear age. Using a first-person narrative, Irving describes growing up with "our friend the Atom" and conveys her concern that plutonium and the bomb can kill us through environmental contamination even in the absence of nuclear war.

Judy Irving, Chris Beaver, and Ruth Landy interview employees and residents at Rocky Flats whose lives have been affected by the plant. Don Gabel, a plutonium worker, is dying of a brain tumor caused by radiation. Lloyd Mixon, who has had several tumors removed from his body and whose farm lies six miles from the plant, describes the severely deformed hogs born with mouths so malformed they couldn't nurse. Other hogs were born dead with their internal organs outside their bodies. He shows chickens hatched with no eyes, and unborn chicks with beaks and feet so twisted that they couldn't break out of their shells. Rex Haag's daughter, Kris, died at the age of twelve of a cancer known to be linked to radiation. The Haags lived three miles away from the nuclear plant.

The film makers compare the similarities between the illnesses of these characters and those of U.S. military men like Richard "Mac" McHugh, who flew his airplane through radioactive clouds in the South Pacific in 1951 and at the time of the filming is dying of leukemia. They also show the health problems of the survivors of the bombs dropped on Hiroshima and Nagasaki, health problems that include cancer, sterility, and giving birth to children with severe defects.

The producers don't stop at these personal stories of death and disease but follow the trail of the nuclear victims back to the corporations that they believe bear responsibility for nuclear waste, weaponry, and contamination.

To show the links between the nuclear industry and the government, the producers film a private convention where weapons are sold to the U.S. military. Marketers and potential buyers socialize, and the names and logos of the corporations integrally involved in the production of nuclear weaponry flash on the screen. Irving says Bendix Corporation produces the bomb's packaging material; DuPont supplies radioactive hydrogen gas. A subsidiary of AT&T performs engineering studies. General Electric manufactures a neutron generator to ignite the plutonium trigger; Union Carbide provides enriched uranium. Monsanto makes explosive detonators. Mason and Hanger Silas-Mason assembles the bomb in Texas. Rockwell International oversees the production of the plutonium trigger at Rocky Flats.

At Rocky Flats, "the heart of the nuclear weapons complex," the film makers cover a community meeting where Dr. Marilyn Werkema, a scientist from the plant, tries to reassure local residents that the nuclear weapons facility is safe and the area around the plant is "a healthful place to live." A local resident who became a community organizer called for the meeting because she found twenty-three cancer cases among her immediate neighbors.

The producers tell the story of a mother who is trying to sell her home. She knows that anyone who might want a Federal Housing Authority mortgage must sign a Rocky Flats Advisory Notice from the Department of Housing and Urban Development acknowledging that "varying levels of plutonium contamination" exist in the soil. She fears she will not be able to sell her house.

Archival footage of atomic bomb experiments with people and animals fills the screen. Soldiers and civilians bask in the light of a nuclear bomb. From previously classified footage from a Defense Department experiment code-named "Priscilla," hundreds of pigs—some wearing special foil suits—are tied up in pens during an atomic explosion. The pigs survived the blast with third-degree burns over 80 percent of their bodies. A person would not.

The film shows antinuclear demonstrators passing out leaflets and trying to block the entrances to Rocky Flats and Diablo Canyon. Some are arrested.

Irving concludes that the scientists who build the bombs do not realize that nuclear weapons can kill those they are intended to protect. Finally, she says the experts may not be able to lead us out of the Atomic Age and into the next.

## The Producers and the Production

Judy Irving and Chris Beaver received their formal education in film making at Stanford University in the early 1970s. Both earned master's degrees there, a complement to Irving's B.A. in psychology from Connecticut College (1968) and Beaver's B.A. in government from Harvard (1970).

Irving started reading about the nuclear issue in the 1970s and hadn't seen herself as a "political" person until then. "I was nonpolitical in the '60s," she told me. "Classmates had gone South and rode buses. I didn't do any of it. I was more interested in skiing and learning European languages."[2]

In 1976, when Irving and Beaver were on location in Denver working on a film project, they picked up a local magazine with an article alleging the existence of plutonium from the nearby Rocky Flats Nuclear Facility in the city's water—water which they had been drinking all week.[3] This article planted the seed that became "Dark Circle."[4]

Irving surmised that most documentaries on nuclear power analyzed it from economic, political, or military perspectives, but she wanted to make one that personalized the nuclear issue through portraits of ordinary citizens with direct firsthand experience of the plutonium economy.

The Rocky Flats Nuclear Weapons Facility and the power plant under construction at Diablo Canyon in California were obvious locations for the film. Diablo Canyon was a relatively short commute from San Francisco and drew protesters from the Bay Area.

Rocky Flats already had a growing stack of articles from mainstream Colorado newspapers and scientific journals as well as in the peace movement press containing information about unsafe practices and radioactive contamination. Some of this information came from official government studies conducted by the Environmental Protection Agency in the 1970s.

National media coverage of Rocky Flats and Diablo Canyon was slight, although overall coverage of nuclear issues increased after the 1979 Three Mile

Island accident. During the period from 1978 to 1982 when the producers were making "Dark Circle," only six articles appeared in the *New York Times* about the Rocky Flats Nuclear Weapons facility. Most were short AP wire stories. A handful of others were published in the *Washington Post,* the *Wall Street Journal,* and the *Christian Science Monitor.* Rocky Flats did not become an ongoing news story until 1989, seven years after "Dark Circle" was finished.

The *New York Times* is arguably the most influential paper in the United States. Network television and radio news editors select most of their national stories of the day from its pages. The meager coverage of Rocky Flats during the time when the film was researched and produced indicates how marginal the story was perceived to be by the paper's bellwether news editors.

The articles that did appear in this newspaper contained shocking information. The longest article in the *New York Times* (fifteen paragraphs) was filed from Berkeley, California, by an unnamed reporter and was published on April 10, 1979.[5] It reported some of the findings of Dr. Carl Johnson, the local county health director and a professor of preventative medicine at the University of Colorado. Dr. Johnson had found that men living in the most plutonium-contaminated areas around Denver had 24 percent higher rates of cancer than those who lived in areas with no plutonium contamination in the soil. For women, the rate was 10 percent higher. The findings contradicted a 1977 report prepared by the Federal Energy Research and Development Administration that said radiation from plutonium emissions at Rocky Flats could cause only one cancer death among the 1.6 million people living in the Denver area. The Johnson study also referred to "routine plutonium emissions" from the Rocky Flats plant beginning in 1953, citing several releases of plutonium into the atmosphere in 1957, 1968, 1969, and 1974. On April 21, 1981, the *New York Times* ran a two-paragraph AP wire story about a protest at Rocky Flats by an estimated 10,000 demonstrators.[6]

The other articles reported the Environmental Protection Agency's request to perform a test to destroy PCBs at Rocky Flats, government plans to build a security zone at the plant, and how a nuclear emergency test was almost taken for real.[7]

Additional documentation surfaced in the scientific community and from groups monitoring the sites and following litigation related to Rocky Flats. Very few details of these findings surfaced in the pages of the *New York Times,* although a few morsels of information found their way into the longer articles.

In September of 1981, the *New York Times* carried an eight-paragraph AP wire story about a lawsuit that revealed a 1957 fire at Rocky Flats had sent clouds of radioactive material over Denver and contaminated the land around the plant.[8] It also mentioned a survey by Dow Chemical Company, which

3. Raye Fleming (left), antinuclear activist, from "Dark Circle." *Photo: Copyright ©*
*Karen Spangenberg, courtesy IDG Films.*

operated the plant for the former Atomic Energy Commission, that found
"high levels of radioactive material at Ralston and Semper elementary schools,
both within 12 miles of the plant."[9] A plant spokesman denied any "radioactive contamination of any consequence" at the time of the fire, and no warning was given to schools or the state health departments in the affected areas.

The 1981 lawsuit uncovered a web of government secrecy and mismanagement at the Rocky Flats plant and confirmed the activists' fears: this was
the *worst* nuclear fire and explosion to date.[10] The government told the public little or no radiation had escaped, even though an explosion blew out hundreds of ventilation filters, destroyed radiation monitors, and threw thick
plumes of black smoke into the air.[11] Daily life around Rocky Flats went on
as usual.

The lawsuit also turned up previously undisclosed research findings. In
1973, researchers found radioactive tritium in Walnut Creek, which flows into
the Great Western Reservoir supplying water to the town of Broomfield. The
next year, the Environmental Protection Agency reported that cattle grazing
east of Rocky Flats had ingested more plutonium than those on the Nevada
test site near Los Alamos, where hundreds of explosions had occurred in the
1950s and 1960s.

Although much of this information never penetrated the national media, the research and documentation supported the film makers' contention that nuclear weapons manufacturing at Rocky Flats was endangering the health and lives of ordinary U.S. citizens.

No documentary can be made without money and equipment, so shortly after returning from Denver in 1976, Judy Irving wrote a proposal to raise money for the film.

The first grant for "Dark Circle" came in 1977 from David Brower of Friends of the Earth, who gave Irving $2,500 in research funds to get the project moving. Later that year, she submitted a proposal to the National Endowment for the Arts, during the Carter administration, which approved a $35,000 grant. Soon the Film Fund gave $10,000.

The growing visibility of the peace movement and increasing public concern over the safety of nuclear reactors after the 1979 explosion at Three Mile Island drew high-profile celebrities and foundations into the peace movement. Private liberal foundations made funding for nuclear issues and the peace movement priorities in their written guidelines. "Dark Circle" fit their agendas. This cultural and media environment made it possible for Ruth Landy, Judy Irving, and Chris Beaver to raise a total of $430,000 in cash to complete "Dark Circle." Landy organized house-party fund-raisers and benefits for the film project. (She raised $40,000 in one night at a house party in New York attended by Coloradan Judy Collins and other celebrities.)[12]

The peace movement around Rocky Flats and Diablo Canyon in California spawned a pool of leaders to take part in the film. Pam Solo, a Catholic nun working with the American Friends Service Committee, who appears in the film, helped Irving and Beaver locate people to be interviewed. Solo and members of other organizations including Physicians for Social Responsibility, Abalone Alliance, Mothers for Peace, and the Nuclear Freeze Campaign provided the film makers with moral support, background, and general information about events at Rocky Flats and the nuclear power plant at Diablo Canyon in California.

Warning lights from the power industry started going on while the film makers were in production. In 1980, they were thrown out of a Rockwell International stockholders' meeting in Dallas. Public relations personnel from Rocky Flats contacted the film makers to find out what kind of film they were making.

The producers didn't hide their political beliefs about the nuclear industries. Instead, they made a film that put a human face on nuclear weaponry and contamination, and indicted the U.S. military, the Department of Energy, and the major corporations with interests in the nuclear power and nuclear weapons industries for endangering the health of American citizens.

## The Theatrical Release and the Overture
## to Public Broadcasting

In 1982, after five years in production and fund-raising, "Dark Circle" premiered at the New York Film Festival and received a standing ovation and enthusiastic reviews. Vincent Canby, film critic for the *New York Times*, described "Dark Circle" as "a well-made, extremely grim documentary look at what life holds for people in and around the Rocky Flats Nuclear Weapons Facility near Denver" and "an urgent horror story."[13]

The film began its theatrical run, garnering more reviews along the way. After the London Film Festival, it toured Britain with the sponsorship of the British Film Institute. Soon it was shown in Australia and Japan. In 1983, "Dark Circle" won nearly every major documentary prize in the United States, including the Grand Prize for Documentary at Sundance, a blue ribbon at the American Film Festival, and a "Certificate of Special Merit" from the Academy of Motion Picture Arts and Sciences. Siskel and Ebert gave it two thumbs up.

Movie theaters and college campuses throughout the country started showing the film, and sometimes the showings benefited peace groups, such as local chapters of the American Friends Service Committee.

The nuclear industry took notice. In 1983 and 1984, the American Nuclear Society, the Department of Energy, the Atomic Industrial Forum, Arkansas Power and Light, and El Paso Gas and Electric screened "Dark Circle." The Atomic Industrial Forum, a nuclear power industry lobby, described the film in 1983 as "a powerful antinuclear piece, one which makes the nuclear weapons/nuclear power connection more insidiously, more hauntingly, more jarringly than most any other film. It has received much publicity through key film critics' reviews and even a *Today Show* plug."[14]

With a stack of laudatory film reviews and prestigious awards, the producers contacted Pam Porter at KQED, San Francisco's public television station, about presenting "Dark Circle" to PBS for a national broadcast. Porter, who handled acquisitions and worked in the cultural programming department, said KQED agreed to serve as the "presenting station" to PBS and sent off a tape and letter to Barry Chase, PBS vice president of news and public affairs programming, on August 10, 1984.

A fire delayed PBS's response, but eight months later, in April 1985, Porter told the film makers that Gail Christian, who worked under Chase, said she would accept the film for a PBS broadcast without cuts at full length and that it would air at 10 p.m. on a weeknight.

The producers were delighted, but Porter told them they needed to raise money for step-up costs, publicity, and related expenses. (Step-up costs cover the expenses of putting on the PBS and KQED logos, technical evaluations, and basic promotion.) They quickly sent out fund-raising requests and grant applications. The Bingham Foundation came through with a $35,000 grant. Later, private donors contributed $10,000.

On June 28, 1985, the film makers met with Porter, who gave them a detailed budget of $9,300 for step-up costs for the PBS broadcast. On August 13, 1985, Porter at KQED formally notified Christian at PBS that the funds had been raised and requested a firm PBS airdate. Porter also informed Christian that the film makers would produce a KQED-approved introduction, or "wrap," with Representative Pat Schroeder (D-Colorado) to round out the eighty-two-minute documentary to eighty-seven minutes and forty seconds, the appropriate length for the PBS broadcast.

Porter sent the transcript of the wrap to Christian, but neither Porter nor the producers heard back from PBS before Schroeder's introduction was taped on September 6. The taping proceeded as scheduled, but behind the scenes, dissension within the ranks of PBS programming and what appeared at first to be a "turf battle" at KQED threatened to sink the broadcast.

## The Sinking of "Dark Circle"

Whether the resistance to the broadcast came initially from KQED or PBS, the PBS broadcast of "Dark Circle" was in serious jeopardy by September 1985.

"Dark Circle" had been caught in a bureaucratic mix-up between Pam Porter in cultural affairs and Beverly Ornstein, then KQED's director of current affairs. Shortly after she requested an airdate from PBS, Porter told the film makers that the "flak is flying" at KQED and the station had decided to remove its logo from the film, but that it "would support the film in every other way."[15]

Ornstein argued "Dark Circle" should have been screened by her when it was first submitted to KQED, especially given the documentary's current affairs subject matter. "It should have gone to the current affairs department rather than the acquisitions department because then it wouldn't have gotten to PBS," she said. "It would have had the same result, but it would have been much cleaner."[16]

When Ornstein found out that the film had been submitted to PBS without her knowledge, she marched in to see Nat Katzman, then the vice president and manager of KQED, to voice her objections to the program. As a work of journalism, she felt she couldn't stand behind it. "We didn't feel we could put our logo on it and say, 'This is a presentation of KQED News and Current Affairs, which is solely responsible for its content,'" she said. "The documentary didn't present on the screen sufficient documentary evidence to substantiate the conclusions alleged on the screen. The heavy-handed editorializing in the way it was edited contributed to the feeling that the documentary was driven by point of view rather than by documentary evidence and facts."[17]

The bureaucratic tangle with Pam Porter in acquisitions was more than a procedural mix-up; it indicated conflicting judgments about what is "news" and what is "advocacy" programming, the overlapping jurisdiction between "cultural affairs" and "current affairs" in cases where a public affairs topic is addressed in an unconventional, non-hard-news manner, and an ongoing dialogue inside KQED about how the station should present independently produced films with strong points of view.

For Ornstein and her boss, Nat Katzman, "Dark Circle" was a piece of advocacy film making, and both believed KQED should steer clear of it as a national program unless it could be packaged so viewers would know the film was "opinion." "It wasn't that the claims in the show were false," Katzman said. "It's that it left one with the uncomfortable feeling that this is propaganda, not journalism."[18]

Katzman's perception of the independent film makers also influenced his reservations about the film. "It was made by people who I believe were deeply committed to the antinuclear cause. I don't believe those producers would have reported it if they found that Rocky Flats was safe and everybody who got cancer smoked for fifteen years. I don't believe they would have put that in the film."[19]

Objections to the film and the film makers' credibility were soon echoed at PBS. When KQED pulled its logo, red flags went up and the entire PBS programming staff took a critical look at the film, a standard procedure before setting an airdate with shows deemed problematic or controversial but that are still candidates for inclusion in the national schedule. Christian recalls most of the staff and her boss, Barry Chase, voted against airing the film; Chase was the only one in her department who had the authority to overrule her decision. "It was almost an unwillingness on the part of the PBS staff to believe that the Rocky Flats plant had poisoned the entire community around it," she said. "They were not going to believe that this is the way we do business in America, and that meant the film makers obviously had to be wrong."[20]

Yet Christian said she had by then felt confident the film's facts were verified. As a former news director (the only PBS programmer on staff with those credentials), she was convinced the producers had done "a credible job" researching the film despite the fact that they did not have a track record with PBS. Besides, she had already accepted the film for a 10 p.m. broadcast on a weeknight.

4. Diablo Canyon Nuclear Power Plant in California. *Photo: Copyright © Karen Spangenberg, courtesy IDG Films.*

Christian believed a psychological denial prevented her colleagues from perceiving the film's merits. "PBS was just throwing up a smoke screen," Christian said. "PBS didn't want to air the film because they didn't believe it. And then they had to come back and say, 'Well, why don't we believe it?' And then they started grabbing at straws."[21]

This wasn't the message that filtered back to the producers. They had no idea that such a radical about-face had occurred. According to Judy Irving, they knew only—from Pam Porter—that the panel had a "list of questions" about "Dark Circle" requiring answers and documentation before PBS would schedule the program.

The list hadn't arrived by late September, so coproducer Chris Beaver called Gail Christian on September 30. The producers were anxious to provide PBS with additional documentation supporting the film's allegations.

Christian told Beaver, "It's the goddamn system. If KQED would put their logo on, I could give you an airdate within two weeks. The questions [the panel wants answered] are crazy. Once again public television looks like a bunch of fools. The panel was six little quakey, shaky people in a room."[22] The panel wanted documentation on how the film makers knew Rocky Flats was sixteen miles from downtown Denver and how they knew how long it took the black brant to fly from Alaska to Mexico. Christian told Beaver the panel asked about fifty questions like this before the film had run its first half hour.[23]

Christian insisted KQED was the problem because it had removed its logo. This meant KQED wouldn't stand behind the documentary and PBS would have to take the flak alone if there were a controversy or negative response to the documentary from affiliate stations, special interest groups, or irate viewers. PBS wasn't willing to do this.

Beverly Ornstein said PBS was the problem. "Why did PBS need us anyway? PBS could have put the show on with its own logo, but Chase had the same concerns about the journalism that we did so he didn't want to do it."[24]

With the presenting station backing out, Christian had to decide whether to fight for the show internally or seek a graceful way to pull the program. She did not want to give up, so she went back to Barry Chase to find ways to make the show more acceptable.

During the fall of 1985, Christian, Katzman, and KQED staff discussed several ways to make the show "acceptable" for a PBS broadcast. Various suggestions included adding a follow-up panel discussion, asking the producers to reedit the film to make it more "balanced" and "fair" to the nuclear industries. Not all the options discussed filtered back to the producers. From Pam Porter, they understood Christian and KQED management wanted them to cut the arms sequence where the corporate logos appeared because this scene was not considered "germane" to the story. Judy Irving argued that the arms sequence was "totally germane" to the story; besides, it was crucial information she wanted to get out to a national audience.[25]

According to Nat Katzman, the producers "simply didn't want to take no for an answer," and they refused to comply with requests to change the program.[26] Instead, they demanded that PBS stand by its original offer to air "Dark Circle" at 10 p.m. on a weeknight.

In early October, Pam Porter told the film makers Gail Christian found the Schroeder introduction unacceptable. She said Barry Chase and Christian were bouncing the show between them, but Nat Katzman at KQED would do what he could to get the show on the air.

Katzman recalls this period was very frustrating. He wanted PBS to broadcast the show in an "acceptable context," but he said the producers refused to change it and Chase wouldn't explain clearly why he was rejecting the show even with an introduction written by KQED. He blamed Christian for the mess: "First she asked us if we'd present the program, and of course, we said yes because we were told PBS wanted it. Then, suddenly, PBS doesn't want it, and Gail asks us to justify why we want to present it. We couldn't do it. If PBS didn't want it, Gail shouldn't have accepted it in the first place." Katzman also saw Christian as "out of step" with PBS and public television because she not only accepted the program but seemed to sincerely believe that the film was fair, a judgment he found incredible for a PBS programmer.[27]

Despite this behind-the-scenes turbulence, the film makers and KQED staff drafted national press releases, prepared press packets and ads for the as-yet unscheduled but still anticipated PBS broadcast. KQED continued to exchange letters with PBS, proceeding as if the broadcast would take place at some time in the future.

On November 5, Beverly Ornstein sent two versions of a disclaimer to Gail Christian, one slightly shorter than the other but not differing in content. Both disclaimers identified the show as a presentation of KQED, explained it was produced by three Bay Area independent film makers and that the show contained "a particular point of view" to "promote an end to the production and proliferation of nuclear weapons." It identified "Dark Circle" as a "personal statement against nuclear proliferation," an "editorial" film that "doesn't fit easily into the traditional documentary format of television journalism."

With this disclaimer, KQED agreed to act again as the presenting station and would present it with KQED's station logo after all. But the damage to the show's credibility proved harder to repair.

Meanwhile the film makers, unaware of the serious threat to the film's broadcast, went ahead and bought mailing lists and continued preparing publicity materials for the national broadcast. All this stopped when they met privately for coffee with Pam Porter outside the offices of KQED for a candid discussion about the show in December 1985.

According to Judy Irving, Porter said PBS had asked KQED to produce a half-hour pro-and-con debate to follow the showing of "Dark Circle," at a cost of $20,000, to balance the point of view of the film; otherwise PBS wouldn't air it. By this time, the film makers were furious. They felt Gail Christian was upping the ante and trying to squirm out of her original offer to air the show.

In their end-of-the-year report to supporters, the film makers urged funders (including the foundations that had contributed to the film), friends, and anyone else to "bird-dog" public television with letters and phone calls to PBS and local affiliates urging PBS to set an airdate as originally planned. The controversy spilled out to a limited public.

Word spread through the Bay Area independent community. Articles about PBS's wavering on "Dark Circle" appeared in *Release Print*, the monthly San Francisco newsletter of the Film Arts Foundation, and reached the national independent production community through the *Independent Film and Video Monthly*, the monthly magazine of the Association of Independent Video and Filmmakers.[28]

In February 1986, Christian officially withdrew PBS's offer to air the program. Despite KQED's agreement to show the film, she said, "KQED did nothing to stand behind the integrity of the film and . . . effectively hung the film makers out to dry. . . . [KQED was] just adding fuel to PBS's fire, and PBS said, 'If you won't back up the film makers, why in hell should we?' A strong station can protect any film if they want to. The station ran off and left them high and dry. . . . It was a sloppy mix-up at KQED to begin with. The film got caught in a bureaucratic nightmare, and when that happened, everything started to unravel."[29]

The film makers were basically left in the dark. Since Pam Porter was their only link to the internal discussions, the producers were excluded from talks about the film's fate that took place inside PBS and KQED. They were out of the loop. And because the film makers never received the "list of questions" from PBS—because PBS never sent the letter—they did not have an opportunity to defend the film from its detractors.

On March 17, Judy Irving and Chris Beaver sent a four-page letter of protest to Barry Chase with copies to about forty supporters, including the Bingham Foundation, which had put up $35,000 for the broadcast, and the donors who had given a total of $10,000 for the same purpose. The film makers recounted their chronology—how Gail Christian at PBS had accepted the show and then rejected it. They said the choice of Representative Pat Schroeder to introduce the show had been suggested by her, and that the introductory script had also been submitted as a courtesy.

Irving and Beaver said they had operated in "good faith" while Christian escalated the demands, at one point even suggesting to Pam Porter that the documentary be cut to an hour. The film makers demanded Chase reinstate the original offer to air the show without cuts at 10 p.m. on a weeknight. They also threatened to sue for redress and compensation for the money spent on publicity but soon backed away from this threat after realizing a lawsuit would be "too expensive."[30]

A month later, in April 1986, Chase met with KQED staff and agreed to rescreen and reconsider PBS's decision to cancel "Dark Circle." Then on May 23, 1986, he wrote a three-page letter to Nat Katzman, KQED station manager, justifying his decision to reject it. "I cannot in good conscience tell the stations that PBS recommends they broadcast this film, even with a full-scale wraparound," wrote Chase, "because to do so would be to mislead stations and viewers regarding my evaluation of it."[31]

According to Chase, "Dark Circle" lacked journalistic credibility and balancing views and used anecdotes instead of citing primary sources of information. He described the narration as "simplistic and irresponsible" because it blurred the distinctions between different forms of nuclear technology: nuclear weapons manufacture, nuclear power plants, nuclear weapons testing, and nuclear warfare. "The film's structure and narrative leave no question about where the producers stand on all these issues—they think they're all bad things—and little room for inclusion of any material suggesting that these issues may involve dispute and complexity in areas such as jobs, economics, alternative energy sources, military threat from foreign powers, etc."

Chase cited the film makers' editing of the corporate logos of nuclear weapons manufacturers with forbidding music as an example of the film's "use of unacceptably manipulative devices which are all too common in advocacy films." Finally, he argued PBS already had a long list of programs raising concerns about nuclear power. "Accordingly, given our journalistic concerns," wrote Chase, "there is too little to be gained by producing a wrap-around to justify a decision to include 'Dark Circle' in a PBS broadcast." He offered to reimburse the producers for expenses attributable directly to PBS requests (such as the taping of the Schroeder introduction but not publicity costs) and reminded KQED that the station or the producers could always distribute the show to public television stations without the PBS logo. "We prefer to husband the logo, and its warranties, for controversial programs whose combination of journalistic quality and new information warrants a PBS commitment."[32]

Seven years after writing this letter, Chase recalled the combination of factors that led him to reject the program. It wasn't solely the juxtaposition of corporate logos with the arms bazaar or the lack of a sit-down interview with the president of Rockwell International or the secretary of energy; it also had to do with how the program got to PBS. Had the program entered the system with the imprimatur of KQED's current affairs department, Chase would have felt more comfortable supporting it.[33]

Chase believed that no public television gatekeeper asked "the right questions" and that the producers themselves "didn't ask the right questions." The fact that the producers did not have a prior "relationship of trust" with PBS programming contributed to his apprehension. Chase said he might have accepted a story about Rocky Flats had the program been made by producers with whom he already had a relationship of trust, who would have asked "the right questions to the right people."

"One must make a case in a way which an audience and a gatekeeper can trust," he said. Had the show come from *Frontline* or Bill Moyers, that is, sources he felt more comfortable with because he had dealt with them over a period of time, or had the story been produced by a producer or reporter he knew and trusted, he said he might not have rejected the film.

"Gail and I probably would have shared a personal opinion that the basic thrust of the show was true, but that has very little to do with the sort of professional responsibility that you have in this position," Chase said. "You've got to get your stations to run it, and they have a right to feel safe that you've done your job; that's what you're there for, from their point of view. And they also employ you. They're also the boss. I mean there's a certain ethical responsibility one has to those people who are paying the bills."

Chase said the indirect communication between different people at KQED and PBS also created a bureaucratic mess, which he believes was a major factor in the confusion that arose about this case. He never spoke to the producers directly; that task fell primarily to Christian and his colleagues at KQED.

## Analysis of the Controversy

"Dark Circle" is not a case of blatant censorship where PBS or KQED caved in to overt or explicit pressure from special interest groups or a chorus of station managers. Nor is it simply a case of "anticipatory avoidance" where gatekeepers sought to avoid controversy. Instead it reveals a much more subtle decision-making process in which the implicit criteria used by public television gatekeepers kept a provocative, personal indictment of the nuclear industry off the national PBS schedule.

When Barry Chase objected to the film's tone and content, he expressed his perspective using language commonly understood in the public television world, "lack of journalistic credibility" and "balance," and he labeled the documentary "advocacy film making." But years later, after leaving his position at PBS, Chase verbalized the unspoken premise that underlay his reasoning: the independent producers were outsiders whom he simply didn't trust and was unwilling to take a risk with on a program that concerned national security issues.[34]

The hazards of the nuclear weapons industry as presented in "Dark Circle" are now widely acknowledged as true, having reached the media's threshold of credibility through news coverage of several lawsuits involving Rocky Flats and the Hanford Nuclear Reservation in Washington State and numerous health and environmental studies. But much of the facts about nuclear contamination were already available to reporters in the 1970s. At least ten years had passed since this information first surfaced in the scientific community, local newspapers, and in the alternative press. Chase admitted years after rejecting the program that the producers were "ahead of their time with the story."[35]

Beverly Ornstein wondered about that herself. "In the last couple of years,

I remember thinking those 'Dark Circle' people, they were right. But I fault them for the manner in which they presented the evidence. It was presented in a highly charged manner, which made it more difficult given the fact that it was new information. The alarmist presentation made it harder to just deal with the facts."[36]

Chris Beaver was exasperated. "Everybody agreed plutonium got out of the Rocky Flats plant. The next question was, how dangerous is plutonium and what effects can we see? If you know these effects, then what is your responsibility as a journalist?" he said. "KQED and PBS abdicated their journalistic responsibility and their moral responsibility. They wouldn't even listen to our evidence. Not to engage in the dialogue is to be willfully blind—willfully blind in terms of a hazard to public safety and well-being.

"Once you've dug as deeply as we did, you make judgments and reach understandings that are impossible to set aside. Our vindication in subsequent news articles was not a fortunate coincidence. We knew the story."[37]

SKEPTICISM ABOUT "DARK CIRCLE" 'S SUBJECT MATTER

In the "Dark Circle" case, the depiction of the independent producers as wide-eyed radicals not to be trusted and the charges of advocacy film making shifted the dispute over the film away from the hazards of the nuclear weapons industry to the journalistic credibility and character of the producers. Chase, Katzman, and Ornstein were not the only ones who were skeptical about the film makers and their film's message. As media critic Mark Hertsgaard observed during the Reagan years, mainstream American journalists generally didn't take seriously the claims of the grassroots nuclear freeze or disarmament movements.[38] Condescension permeated this coverage and served to perpetuate rather than question the nuclear status quo.

"Dark Circle" rode the tide of the antinuclear movement and was released within months of one of New York City's largest peace demonstrations in the summer of 1982. Millions attended antinuclear protests in the United States and in Europe, and the movement became so large the media could no longer ignore it. However, the mainstream U.S. media portrayed the nuclear freeze movement as "a group of sincere, well-meaning but hopelessly simpleminded individuals" whose ideas were "naive to the point of irrelevance."[39] This media context reinforced the skeptical eye cast on "Dark Circle" and its producers by decision makers at PBS and KQED.

POWER STRUGGLES AND IDEOLOGICAL CONFLICTS

In tugs-of-war, those with the most power win. Chase had the power to enforce his judgment not only because he had the ultimate bureaucratic authority but also because most of his colleagues, including KQED's Nat Katzman and Beverly Ornstein, shared his rationale and perspective. They inhabited the same cultural world with its shared meanings and beliefs about what is an appropriate way to treat a public affairs topic and what is an appropriate program for the stations to receive. Together, they reinforced the boundaries of what is suitable for broadcast in the public television world and what isn't.

Gail Christian's unwillingness to recognize and maintain those boundaries placed her on a collision course with her boss and others in the public television system. She was the only one at PBS or KQED who came right out and said that "Dark Circle" was not fit to air because it portrayed the major corporations as callous and showed that the U.S. government colluded in endangering the health and lives of its citizens. The documentary's critics rather appealed to the mainstream media and standards of balance and journalistic credibility to discredit the program. This language reinforced the dominant media perspective on nuclear issues and the peace movement in the 1980s.

The charges of propaganda and countercharges of censorship highlight the different worlds their occupants inhabit as well as their different intended audiences. It was not difficult for PBS to call "Dark Circle" a propaganda film, nor for the producers to call PBS a censor. All documentaries embody implicit value judgments that can be disputed by anyone with the clout to be heard. (Even the most innocuous film about desert mice in Arizona presumes certain values about the nature of deserts and lives of rodents, in addition to their worthiness of viewers' attention.) The case of "Dark Circle" shows PBS had the clout to be heard, much more clout than the independent producers and their supporters inside public television.

The film makers did speak to their own audience with the tools they had. Their audience was their friends, supporters, and fellow members of the independent production community centered primarily in the Bay Area and in New York. When their show was rejected, they leveled a charge of censorship. They mobilized a small campaign in which their supporters wrote letters and made phone calls to PBS to try to change Chase's decision. They also publicized their "censorship" in the independent producers' press, focusing attention on the ideological role of public television gatekeepers and adding another case to the list of provocative, award-winning independently produced documentaries rejected by PBS. But these acts and the clout of the independent community proved no serious challenge to PBS.

Chase had his own primary audience: KQED and the other PBS affiliates. He didn't need other votes besides his own to enforce his decision. And he did not want to lend the PBS logo to a film he wouldn't stand behind. He said he wouldn't be able to honestly defend it if stations were faced with a time-consuming controversy over the film or got flak from nuclear interest groups accusing PBS of airing propaganda or from conservative groups upset over federal support for public television.

### "DARK CIRCLE"'S UNCONVENTIONAL MEDIA FRAME

In "Dark Circle," the portrayal of the peace movement, the role of the U.S. government in nuclear weapons manufacturing, and nuclear industries fell outside the conventional media frame at PBS and the national media.[40] Chase's frame divided the nuclear industries into various technologies and addressed each one separately, rather than emphasizing the interconnections between them.

The national news media—as exemplified by the handful of articles in the *New York Times*—did not cover the Rocky Flats story closely, nor did they give significant space to the peace movement. Because these stories had not reached a national media threshold, the PBS programmers were less likely to believe the film makers' depiction of Rocky Flats.

The "Dark Circle" case unfolded while a grassroots campaign against nuclear power and nuclear weapons' production was gaining momentum. National and homespun organizations picked up the antinuclear banners while the Reagan administration escalated the production of nuclear weaponry, justifying it with the rhetoric of the Cold War.

While the Reagan administration saw itself battling the Soviets abroad, its supporters waged unofficial war in the media at home. During the mid-1980s, organizations like Accuracy in Media criticized public broadcasting for its "left-leaning antenna" and set the groundwork for a campaign to turn up the heat on politicians to cut funding for public television altogether. President Reagan appointed conservatives to the board of the Corporation for Public Broadcasting, and his allies frequently attacked the Public Broadcasting Service as a bulwark of Democratic liberals.

Yet nowhere in the debate over "Dark Circle" did fear of offending the Reagan administration or a possible retaliation against public broadcasting arise overtly in writing or in interviews. Nor was there any evidence of direct interference by the nuclear industries, although Chase expressed concern that "Dark Circle"'s depiction of the nuclear industries' logos was unfair and manipulative.

### "DARK CIRCLE"'S UNCONVENTIONAL STYLE OF PRESENTATION

Most independent films are not produced specifically for public broadcasting. They are shown in theaters and festivals, and sometimes air locally on

PBS affiliates. They receive recognition and awards in the documentary and entertainment communities, and their style of aesthetic presentation and storytelling must be sufficiently compelling to hold a movie audience. Because theatrical films often require a different mode of presentation than television documentaries, a program like "Dark Circle" can win a shelf of film awards but still not be accepted for a PBS broadcast.

What is standard form for PBS documentaries is only one of several possible forms for independent documentaries. The "Dark Circle" producers deviated from the dominant public television documentary convention at the time by using a first-person narrative rather than an omnipresent third-person narrator to tell the story. They did not do formal, sit-down, "talking heads in chairs" interviews with representatives from the nuclear industries and the U.S. government. Instead the film makers showed these representatives expressing their views out of their offices or at public hearings. They integrated government and corporate opinions into the fabric of their nonfiction storytelling by presenting a distillation of the official perspectives. This way the film makers portrayed the officials as players in a drama rather than authorities who somehow stand outside it.

The film makers also vehemently resisted efforts to dilute or compromise their program, displaying a pluckiness common in the independent film-making community. They exemplified the commitment to "tell the truth as I see it" that runs deep in the U.S. independent documentary tradition as well as the conviction to use film as an instrument for social reform and change. The film makers saw themselves as providing important information to the viewing public about the interconnections within the nuclear industries and getting out the word about the unintended victims of nuclear weapons.

Sociologist Todd Gitlin describes a devil's wager for social movements in relation to the mass media. If they stand outside "the dominant realm of discourse," they will be "consigned to marginality and political irrelevancy" and the movement will likely be ignored. If they gain credibility by playing by the conventional political rules, the movement will lose its oppositional edge and its issues will be treated as reforms. At best, these reforms will be incorporated into programs acceptable to political authorities.[41]

The producers of "Dark Circle" faced this dilemma: tone down the documentary to exclude the material indicting the major corporations in nuclear industries, or lose a chance to reach a national audience over PBS. The producers chose "telling the truth" as they saw it. Eventually, their documentary did air over the national PBS airwaves on *P.O.V.*, a series inaugurated after their original rejection. But before it did, it aired on Ted Turner's WTBS and the cable station Bravo, and the national media legitimized the Rocky Flats story.

## Ted Turner, P.O.V., and the Rocky Flats Story

In the summer of 1986, shortly after PBS decided not to broadcast "Dark Circle," the producers sent fifteen cassettes to Ted Turner (through his secretary, his then-fiancee Jane Fonda, and even a sympathetic couple who had dinner with the maverick TV mogul).[42] That fall, Ted Turner decided to air the program uncut as a presentation of his series *Better World Society*, and WTBS spent $60,000 on publicity. The cable network advertised in *TV Guide* and *USA Today* and garnered the highest ratings on WTBS for a documentary to date. Most reviews were laudatory, but television critic John Corry of the *New York Times* said the film "plays like propaganda."[43]

Turner gave "Dark Circle" the green light once the film makers were successful in getting the film to him and he had taken a look at it. "Dark Circle" aired with no editing and little packaging on WTBS because Turner, as CEO of the Turner Broadcasting System, had the freedom to air what he wanted. He was not subject to the same pressures that PBS programmers were. He did not have to worry about irate affiliate stations upset because he broadcast a program that "deviated" from mainstream journalistic norms and conventions. Furthermore, none of his advertisers and investors were going to pull the plug on him for airing a lone documentary critical of nuclear weapons. Turner also shared the film makers' concerns about nuclear power, and through his *Better World Society* series, he was committed to advocacy programs that sought to make a more peaceful future.

PBS programmers operate in another universe. As a "service" organization, they are answerable to local stations who look to them to provide national programming their local viewers would like to see. The programmers themselves are restrained by their colleagues higher up in the PBS bureaucracy who make judgments about programs, mindful of the political and journalistic mainstream and their individual careers. Moreover in 1985, PBS didn't have a venue for point-of-view programs.

In 1988, the cable channel Bravo aired "Dark Circle," and the same year the producers submitted the show once again to PBS—this time to their friend Marc Weiss, the founder and executive producer of the new independent documentary series *P.O.V.*, a series dedicated to showing works "with a strong point of view." Weiss accepted the show for *P.O.V.*'s 1989 series and scheduled it for August 8 in between the anniversaries of the bombings of Hiroshima and Nagasaki.

Prior to scheduling the show for broadcast, Weiss sent the producers a list of fourteen questions from *P.O.V.* and PBS requesting source and verification of several facts mentioned in the narration. Chris Beaver provided the information in a memo written December 30, 1988, roughly eight months before the broadcast. PBS then gave *P.O.V.* the green light in January 1989 to air the show. The series paid the producers $24,600 for the right to broadcast the documentary.

Most of the major newspaper reviews tied to the *P.O.V.* broadcast encouraged viewers to tune in to the film while describing it as biased and dated. The *Washington Post*'s Tom Shales wrote that the film is "unbalanced and proud of it."[44] *TV Guide*'s Art Durbano recommended that viewers watch the "shrill, one-sided and often amateurish quasi-documentary about a subject that nevertheless deserves serious public scrutiny."[45] Longer reviews mentioned the earlier dispute with PBS.

On the day of the broadcast, *USA Today* featured an interview with Judy Irving in which she recounted how PBS had wanted the film makers to cut the show to an hour, eliminate a nuclear weapons arms bazaar sequence and the nuclear weapons manufacturers' logos. She charged these elements made PBS "nervous" because General Electric, Rockwell International, and AT&T—the companies that built the hydrogen bomb—were also major underwriters of public television programming. Irving accused PBS of having tried to censor the film. In a sidebar with the interview, PBS's Barry Chase defended the earlier rejection and dismissed Irving's suggestion that politics motivated PBS's decision to not air "Dark Circle" as "insulting" and "without evidence," citing how PBS had aired "The Death of a Princess" years before despite a boycott threat from an oil company.[46]

When "Dark Circle" aired on *P.O.V.*, the conservative media watchdog group Accuracy in Media was ready. Reed Irvine, editor of *AIM Report*, devoted an entire issue to criticizing "Dark Circle" as "another PBS propaganda atrocity." AIM charged PBS with aligning itself "with the radical environmentalists who are putting pseudo-scientific scare stories at the top of the left's new political agenda."[47]

Irvine echoed several objections previously made by Barry Chase. He criticized "Dark Circle" for failing to distinguish between "civil and military uses of nuclear energy," for the use of anecdotal evidence, and for having "the intellectual sophistication of the placards displayed by noisy antinuclear demonstrators." Irvine cited Rockwell's radiation monitoring program at Rocky Flats and nuclear industry studies affirming that nuclear power is safe. He also used the article to blast *P.O.V.*[48]

Not wanting AIM to go unanswered, Marc Weiss of *P.O.V.* asked Chris Beaver to prepare a written response to AIM's attack. Beaver provided a twenty-page memo.

PBS's acceptance of "Dark Circle" for *P.O.V.*'s 1989 season wasn't as risky a move as it would have been for PBS a few years before the Rocky Flats story had gained national attention. The broadcast took place in a different media context and within a niche created by PBS specifically for independently produced documentaries with strong points of view.

By August 1989, the *New York Times* and other major newspapers had begun following the Rocky Flats story. In all, the *New York Times* published ten articles about the Rocky Flats Nuclear Weapons plant between January and August 8, 1989, the date of the *P.O.V.* broadcast of "Dark Circle." This exceeded the number of articles the paper had published on the subject during the five years when "Dark Circle" was in production.

Timing benefited the broadcast. Two months before "Dark Circle" was scheduled to air, the *New York Times* reported on June 6 that seventy-five agents from the FBI and the EPA had raided Rocky Flats in search of evidence that federal environmental laws were being broken at the plant. The FBI's 116-page affidavit charged Rockwell International and the Department of Energy with violating several environmental laws by incinerating hazardous waste, polluting local water supplies, and knowingly making false claims that Rocky Flats was in compliance with environmental laws.

On June 21, *Times* correspondent Matthew Wald wrote a feature about the economic impact of Rocky Flats on Colorado's economy. A few weeks later, stories appeared about workers contaminated at Rocky Flats, unsafe working conditions, and more mismanagement.

On September 12, 1990, "Dark Circle" won a national Emmy in broadcast journalism for "Outstanding Individual Achievement in News and Documentary." Barry Chase looked on as *P.O.V.* accepted the award on behalf of the producers, who said they could not afford the plane tickets to the ceremony. With this award, PBS had a total of ten Emmys for the 1989 season, the same number as CBS. They tied for first place.

The film makers' credibility was vindicated. Judy Irving and her coproducers based their research on evidence that was already present in official documents from several civil lawsuits against Rocky Flats, published scientific reports, and stories in regional newspapers. Although it took years for this information to filter out to the public through the *New York Times*, placing the blame for the nuclear victims' fates at the feet of corporations like Rockwell International and the U.S. Departments of Energy and Defense was by 1990 within the bounds of the expressible.

## Postscript

Ironically, what proved troublesome to PBS and KQED in 1986 proved beneficial to the producers. "The controversy broadened the appeal of the show, and it's still being shown," Irving said. "Now I realize if it had aired at 10 p.m. on a weeknight, it probably would have been buried. I learned you can get a tremendous audience through controversy."[49]

Gail Christian drew a different lesson. "In my ten years at PBS, 'Dark Circle' was one of the couple of times where I felt really beaten. Maybe I was the person who felt like a fool for staying there. I think 'Dark Circle' was one of the films that made me realize that this couldn't go on forever."[50] She left PBS in 1989 in the wake of another battle over an independently produced documentary, "Days of Rage: The Young Palestinians."

# Chapter 4

# "Days of Rage: The Young Palestinians"

*This business of who gets responded to, in what manner,
and what issues are allowed on the air is really quite
interesting because it really does have to do with who's
powerful and who's weak, and who cares.*
      —Gail Christian, former PBS programmer

Independent producer Jo Franklin-Trout could not be dismissed on any of
the grounds used by Barry Chase at PBS to discredit the producers of "Dark
Circle." She had a relationship of trust and a proven track record with PBS,
and she created documentaries that conformed to the service's standards of
journalism and style. Nevertheless, the controversy that erupted around
Franklin-Trout and her documentary, "Days of Rage: The Young Palestinians,"
was unmatched by any other controversy in 1989. This chapter examines what
happens when a journalist with pedigree credentials and an insider relationship with PBS takes on one of the hottest, most divisive political and human
rights issues of her day.

The story of the "Days of Rage" controversy—the who, what, where, and
how—also clarifies the symbiotic relationship between PBS, public television
stations, and powerful special interest groups that can and do exert influence
on whether PBS broadcasts a program, and in what context.

As in the "Dark Circle" case, PBS programmers were divided about the
program's suitability for broadcast as a "stand alone" program. A majority of
programmers believed the issue was "fairness," which raised the philosophical
question of how much influence the eye of the beholder has on the perception of the accuracy of the facts in a documentary. A documentary can "have
all the facts right" yet still be considered "inaccurate."

5. Palestinian youths in the Intifada. *Photo: Courtesy Pacific Productions.*

On September 6, 1989, the Israeli-Palestinian conflict spilled onto American public television in a two-and-a-half-hour special called "Intifada: The Palestinians and Israel." The special was built around Franklin-Trout's ninety-minute documentary, "Days of Rage." The national broadcast followed several months of meetings, letter-writing campaigns, and protests by pro-Israeli Jewish-American organizations and Arab-American groups sympathetic to the plight of the Palestinians. Eventually, viewers saw "Days of Rage" packaged between two specially produced six-minute videos presenting an Israeli perspective on the Intifada and a follow-up panel discussion tilted in favor of the program's critics.

Pro-Israeli groups charged PBS with airing Palestinian propaganda by broadcasting "Days of Rage" in any context; Arab-American groups and independent film makers charged PBS with censorship for attempting to neutralize the voices of the Palestinians by setting them in a broader context.

"Propaganda" and "censorship" are trigger words, tactical weapons on the rhetorical battlefield. The seven-month public controversy over the film was another chapter in the ongoing conflict in the United States between supporters of Israel and supporters of Palestinian rights, and it generated the largest splash in the press to arise from PBS's efforts to address the Palestinian issue.[1]

The timing of the program and controversy coincided with growing frustration among Bush administration officials about the nonresolution of the Israeli-Palestinian issue. Since the Intifada began in December 1987, the Israeli government had stepped up its security measures in the occupied territories. Armed Israeli settlers continued to move into the West Bank despite U.S. threats to cut off aid to Israel, which receives more U.S. aid than any other country.

Pro-Israeli, Jewish-American organizations increasingly found themselves on the defensive in the media and at the highest governmental levels. Waning American support for Israeli policies in the territories and reports of Israeli human rights violations in Gaza and the West Bank tarnished the Israeli government's generally favorable media image as a U.S. ally in a troubled region, a democratic society surrounded by hostile Muslim countries. Palestinians were gaining ground in the domestic propaganda war as the images of stone-throwing youths highlighted decades of frustration under the twenty-two-year Israeli occupation and the Palestinians' demand for their own state.

## Program Description

The cast of characters in "Days of Rage" includes dozens of Palestinians and several Israelis. Comments from the following people are among those that weave throughout the program: Michael Posner, executive director of the Lawyer's Committee for Human Rights; Major General Yehoshafat Harkabi, former director of Israeli Military Intelligence; Dr. Meron Benvenisti, former deputy mayor of Jerusalem; Oded Evan from the Israeli Embassy in Washington, D.C.; Daniella Weiss, executive director of Gush Emunim; Samia Khoury from the Women's Relief Organization; Dr. Nabil Jabari, a dentist and president of Hebron University; Major General Mattiyahu Peled, retired from the Israeli Defense Forces.

"Days of Rage" opens with tense music as several Israeli soldiers carry away a young Palestinian man. Viewers hear a number of perspectives on the Intifada, which sets up a dramatic tension. A human rights attorney describes the occupied territories of Gaza and the West Bank as "a powder keg waiting to explode." An underground leader of the Intifada, his face hidden by a scarf, describes the Israelis as oppressors who cannot destroy what is in the mind of the oppressed. A Palestinian woman says, "We have nothing more to lose." An Israeli settler with an American accent says he understands the Palestinians would like their own state but does not think it should be in so sensitive an area as the West Bank. An Israeli woman suggests the Palestinians create a state for themselves somewhere in the Arab world, but not anyplace where it would touch or endanger Israel. A retired Israeli general says the Intifada has united the Palestinian community and made the people ready to sacrifice themselves for their freedom. A Palestinian schoolgirl says, "We're at the point

of no return. We're not going to stop until we get what we want: a Palestinian state."

Over images of Palestinian youth throwing rocks at Israeli soldiers, Jo
Franklin-Trout begins her narration: "The Palestinians in the occupied territories demand a state in exchange for recognizing Israeli's right to exist, and
vow to continue the uprising until a solution is reached." On camera, she continues: "Now months into the rebellion that has rocked Israel and the territories, the search for a solution escalates and many feel the situation has
reached a turning point in history. Tonight we take you inside the territories
for a look at the realities that led to the rebellion and for a look at the young
Palestinians behind it, a new generation very different from the old, ready to
take history down a very different path: who they are, what they are, what
they want, and how they intend to get it, and what end to the crisis now seems
possible."

With archival footage, Jo Franklin-Trout recounts a brief history of the
conflict. She describes the influx of Jewish settlers in the area since the turn
of the century, and how the British who took over Palestine in 1917 tried to
straighten out conflicting promises made to Jews and Arabs during World
War I. She also describes how the British issued the Balfour Declaration urging the creation of a national Jewish state, but one that wouldn't hurt the
civil rights of the Arab community. British troops tried to effect a balance,
but riots ensued and coexistence proved futile. Franklin-Trout says the rise of
Hitler accelerated immigration as Jews fled Europe, and partition became inevitable. In 1947, the British left Palestine and the United Nations took over,
voting to partition Palestine into Jewish and Arab states. When Israel pro-
claimed itself a state in 1948, Arabs were enraged. War broke out and left
the state of Israel in place of most of the area that had been Palestine. Hundreds of thousands of Arabs were displaced into refugee camps, believing their
stay would be temporary. Franklin-Trout says Israeli troops, anticipating an
attack from Egypt and Jordan and in the 1967 "Six Day War," moved to oc-
cupy Gaza and the West Bank of the Jordan River, land populated by one and
a half million Arabs living in small towns, on family farms, and in old Arab
cities including Hebron. Egypt and Syria attacked Israel in the 1973 Yom Kip-
pur War, but Israel remained in firm control of the occupied territories.

Palestinians featured in Franklin-Trout's program uniformly describe Israel as an "occupier" and repeat their call for a Palestinian state as the only
solution they see to the situation. All feel degraded as human beings by the
Israeli presence. Several tell stories of family members killed or beaten by Israeli soldiers. Since the Intifada began in December 1987 after Israeli soldiers
killed four people in Gaza, thousands of Palestinians have been arrested or

detained for months in prison as "security offenders," often without charges being filed against them. The film describes a police state where 10,000 Palestinians live in detention camps. Academics, doctors, journalists, human rights activists, lawyers—anyone the Israeli authorities suspect is or could potentially be a leader of the resistance is arrested without charges and jailed for six months for "the safety of the public." Some are deported. Dr. Jabari, president of Hebron University, says he received death threats when released from detention from people who identified themselves as members of the Mosad, the Israeli secret service.

Franklin-Trout's film shows Palestinians living in densely populated, poverty conditions without adequate plumbing or sanitation. She says over 650,000 people live in the Gaza strip, a territory five miles wide and twenty-eight miles long. An extended family, with as many as ten people to a room, lives in one house. Another family lives in the rubble of a house that had been bulldozed by the Israelis because one of the boys living there confessed under interrogation to throwing a Molotov cocktail. The house is in shambles, but the owner cannot rebuild it without the required permits the Israeli authorities refuse to grant.

Oded Evan, an Israeli diplomat, defends the use of collective punishment in the form of bulldozing of houses: "We feel that this is some sort of signal to those who are active in these subversive activities. There is a price that you pay, and we also hope the family involved will prevail on those individuals not to resort to these subversive activities." He also says the refugees are not citizens, and therefore they are not entitled to political rights. Human rights attorney Michael Posner charges that collective punishments, such as the bulldozing of houses or putting an entire village under house arrest to punish the community for the actions of individuals, violate the Geneva Convention. He says the Israeli government wants to control political as well as violent activities. Retired Major General Peled describes the Israeli measures as "draconian" and says the Israeli government's "iron fist" approach escalated with the rise of the Intifada.

In Franklin-Trout's film, the Israeli government appears to control the population through a combination of armed force, bureaucratic rules, and psychological intimidation. Palestinians can be arrested if they are caught without their identification cards, and soldiers can confiscate the cards until detainees do what the soldiers demand: pick up stones from a demonstration or scrub away anti-Israeli graffiti. Dr. Meron Benvenisti, former deputy mayor of Jerusalem, fears that Israel could eventually become a "master race democracy," with only Jews in charge of the government and Arabs having no political voice.

A European doctor working in the occupied territories reports the systematic beatings of teenage boys by Israeli soldiers. Another doctor describes how the soldiers interfere with the treatment of patients by delaying the ambulances' access to the injured or by setting up checkpoints on the roads to the Palestinian hospitals. The doctor describes the soldiers' use of American-made rubber bullets, some of which explode inside the body causing extensive internal damage. One doctor says there are only nine hundred hospital beds in the Gaza territory to serve the needs of the 650,000 people in the territories, a quarter of the number necessary for a population of that size. While official Israeli figures on the first five months of the Intifada put the casualties at 1,200, the doctor estimates the number is over 20,000.

Franklin-Trout says the Intifada is the younger generation's answer to the failed tactics of their parents and grandparents. Some Palestinians draw parallels between Hitler's treatment of the Jews and the Israeli's treatment of the Palestinians. A Palestinian student says, "The same as Hitler did to them, they do the same thing. They bury the Palestinian people now, they shoot the women and men. They impose curfew and make the area a military area."

The film maker interviews a youthful leader of the Intifada, who describes how the underground network plans protests, strikes, and other activities sometimes right under the noses of the Israelis in Tel Aviv. In the occupied territories, they communicate with each other through whistles, symbolic clothing, and other means. The Palestinian community shelters and supports the youthful rebels.

Franklin-Trout describes how some young leaders, inspired by Gandhi's example, have implemented nonviolent strikes, boycotts, and protests to bring the economy to its knees. Some villages strive to become self-sufficient like the Israeli kibbutzim so they are not economically dependent on the Israelis for their basic needs.

She also visits an orphanage to interview a psychiatrist, who assesses the psychological damage of the war on the children who have seen death up close. A little girl describes seeing her father shot in front of her house during the Muslim holiday of Ramadan. "He was standing in front of the house calling my brothers into the house. The soldiers thought he was telling them to attack, so they shot him in the heart. Three bullets."

Samia Khoury, a Palestinian woman in her fifties with the Women's Relief Organization, wonders about the effect of the conflict on the Israeli youth and soldiers. "It's a tragedy occurring on both sides." She says security for Israel will come with justice for the Palestinians.

The documentary ends with retired Major General Peled calling for the creation of a Palestinian state in the West Bank, Gaza, and East Jerusalem,

6. "Days of Rage" producer-director Jo Franklin-Trout interviews an underground leader of the Intifada *Photo: Courtesy Pacific Productions*.

and for direct talks between the PLO and Israel. This is the only way he sees out of the conflict.

## The Producer and the Production

Unlike several other independent film makers who produced documentaries on the Palestinian issue, no one at PBS could attack Jo Franklin-Trout for lacking journalistic credentials. A senior reporter who covered the Middle East for *The MacNeil/Lehrer NewsHour*, Franklin-Trout had credibility within public television not only through her work for *MacNeil/Lehrer* but also because she had produced three major and highly successful series for PBS prior to her ninety-minute documentary on the Intifada. She lived in the Washington, D.C., area and had the geographic advantage of being able to cultivate and maintain her relationships with other major journalists and the gatekeepers at PBS programming.

Franklin-Trout was also part of the community of influential national journalists, a circle that included ABC anchor Peter Jennings; Phil Geylin, head of the editorial board at the *Washington Post*; Anthony Lewis, columnist of the *New York Times*; and Jack Nelson of the Washington Bureau of the *Los Angeles Times*, and political figures like Jody Powell, former aide to Jimmy Carter. These were relationships built over years. She was a consummate insider.

The first series that Franklin-Trout produced was called *Saudi Arabia*, and it was broadcast in three installments in 1981. Two years later, PBS aired another three-part series, *The Oil Kingdoms*, on the Persian Gulf states of Kuwait, Oman, Qatar, Bahrain, and the United Arab Emirates. In 1986, PBS aired her four-part series *The Great Space Race*.

Franklin-Trout was a savvy marketer. She sold copies of her programs to universities, museums, and high schools throughout the world, and international broadcast rights. Her documentaries made money. She also served as a consultant on the Middle East to the U.S. State Department.[2]

While producing the three series, Franklin-Trout developed an ongoing, working relationship with PBS programmers Barry Chase and Sandy Heberer. Over lunch and face-to-face meetings, the three would discuss her current projects and possibilities for future ones. She had access to Chase and Heberer as well as their respect. Since she had extensive experience and contacts covering the Middle East, Franklin-Trout recalls Chase suggested she develop a series on Iraq and Syria, two of the least covered countries in that area.

"There was a relationship of trust, and we hadn't encountered any situation where [Jo Franklin-Trout] tried to distort anything," Chase said. "I characterized her series on Saudi Arabia as sympathetic, but I was sympathetic to it having to be sympathetic—you don't get access [to some of these countries] unless you're perceived to be sympathetic, especially after 'Death of a Princess.'"[3]

PBS programming provided her with a $20,000 research grant to develop the Iraq-Syria series, but after putting together a proposal and budget, Franklin-Trout believed it would be too costly to produce.[4] She turned her attention to the one major story in the Middle East that she and several of her journalist colleagues believed had not been adequately covered on PBS or in other U.S. media: the Palestinian situation. As with her other programs intended for a national PBS broadcast, Chase and Heberer knew about this project from its inception.

"It wasn't high on their agenda," Franklin-Trout recalled. "I could pick up from the innuendos that this wasn't one of their favorite avenues that I'd gone down. . . . I think they didn't think I'd do it."[5]

Franklin-Trout tried to raise money for the production from the same corporate underwriters that had supported her earlier series. She found they were uniformly reluctant to underwrite a program on a topic as controversial as the Palestinian issue.[6] Then she decided to pool the money she had made from the very profitable sales of videocassettes from her earlier series on the Middle East.[7] These funds, accumulated over years, financed the production of "Days of Rage." After she finished the program, Franklin-Trout worked out a distribution deal with the Arab-American Cultural Foundation to cover the left-over postproduction costs. Based on the finished program, the foundation paid Franklin-Trout $30,000 in 1989 for the right to distribute cassettes of "Days of Rage" after the PBS broadcast.[8] This brought the total cash budget for the program up to $180,000.

Jo Franklin-Trout completed "Days of Rage" in September 1988 after taping the program over the summer while the images of rock-throwing Palestinian youth continued to make headlines around the world. She showed a rough cut of the documentary to Sandy Heberer and another programmer in August 1988. "When they saw the rough cut, everybody was quite nervous. There was no disputing any of the facts, figures, or information."[9]

Sandy Heberer called Franklin-Trout after the screening and told her she had some problems with the documentary. "In the first rough cut, there was not a current Israeli spokesperson, and we immediately noticed the lack of that," Heberer recalled. "Jo is a very candid person, and I believe she said this was indeed still a work in progress and that this concern could be addressed quickly."[10]

Franklin-Trout remembers discussions where Heberer asked her to incorporate interviews with more Israelis to balance the story. She recalls the discussions in these terms: "They said every time a Palestinian said, 'We have a problem,' I should put in an Israeli who said, 'No, here's why it's not a problem.' And I said, 'Oh, come on, that's not the only form of acceptable journalism. The title of the film is 'Days of Rage: The Young Palestinians,' and the opening says 'this will explore who the Palestinians are, what they're all about, and what they want and why they're waging the Intifada.' And to have this Ping-Pong ball, going back and forth—it's an intellectually dishonest form of journalism."[11] Franklin-Trout recalls PBS programmers were also concerned about the historical part of the program. "They wanted me to put in more about how the Jews who came to what had been viewed as Palestine came because they had been having such a hard time elsewhere," she said, "I said, 'Okay, but I don't think it's necessary.' The rest of the revisions I said, 'Forget it.'"[12]

After several discussions, Gail Christian and Sandy Heberer of PBS programming negotiated a few revisions in the historical sequence, but Franklin-Trout refused to make other significant changes. PBS also had the program fact-checked to make sure the documentary did not contain inaccurate information.[13]

Steve Emerson, author and then an investigative journalist at *US News and World Report*, was among those who received a call from PBS. He said Barry Chase asked him for a pledge of confidentiality, which he refused, citing his role as a journalist. Emerson recalled Chase told him something "didn't

smell right" about the financing and asked if he had any background on
Franklin-Trout. Back in 1982, Emerson had questioned the financing of her
series on Saudi Arabia, which he believed "wasn't appropriate," but after doing a little digging in his files, he said he told Chase, "I don't have anything
on this lady."[14] He asked to preview the documentary, but PBS would not release it to him.[15]

Gail Christian said she saw the film when it was almost at the fine-cut
stage, and she doesn't recall having had major problems with the documentary, nor does she remember requesting significant revisions of the film. "When
we saw it, the staff had no problems with that film. They said it was clearly
presented as a point-of-view film. There's no way anybody looking at this film
could be misled into thinking it was anything other than what it is—a look
at the Intifada." Some programmers liked the documentary less than others
and expressed concern that some stations would have a lot of trouble with it,
according to Christian. She said all programmers agreed that it should air.[16]

Chase agreed to the broadcast because he said the program was professional and well made, but it wasn't the film he had anticipated. "I expected a
sympathetic ear to the plight of the Palestinians," he said. "What I felt we
got in 'Days of Rage' was leading questions and an advocacy piece that was at
times over the edge. It was a view of the Intifada, a provocative view of the
Intifada. Where it fell down was in its evident lack of impartiality on certain
issues and selective choices, but everybody makes these decisions. . . . We put
it on because it provided a point of view not well provided before."[17]

The PBS programmers knew the program would make the affiliate stations nervous, so they decided from the beginning that it would have a host,
a presenting station, and a follow-up panel discussion. They did not want the
program to go out without a "wrap" because this could give viewers the impression that the program met PBS journalistic standards for balance and fairness within the body of the program. They also knew the program would be
controversial because programs on the Palestinian issue had a record of generating a great deal of controversy by groups on both sides of the issue.[18]

During the winter of 1989, Jonathan Kwitny at WNYC/New York ar-
ranged with Gail Christian at PBS to present "Days of Rage" to the broadcast
system, a common practice when dealing with independently produced documentaries on public affairs topics.[19] Kwitny, a former *Wall Street Journal* reporter, agreed to host the program and already had begun seeking out panelists
for a follow-up roundtable discussion. Kwitny reportedly contacted the Israeli
Embassy for suggestions on whom to invite to participate on the panel to represent an Israeli point of view on the Intifada. The *Los Angeles Times* reported
Kwitny even sent the Israeli Embassy a copy of "Days of Rage," an act Kwitny

7. Israeli soldiers stand guard in the occupied terrotories. *Photo: Courtesy Pacific Pro-ductions.*

has denied.[20] Although it is unclear how the embassy received a copy of the program, Jewish-American groups supportive of Israeli policies received bootleg copies of "Days of Rage" in the spring of 1989.

On March 20, PBS notified affiliate stations that PBS would broadcast "Days of Rage" on June 5 with WNYC as the presenting station. Franklin-Trout set about preparing publicity materials and contacting television review-ers. She had just finished setting up an interview with television critic Howard Rosenberg of the *Los Angeles Times*, when she received a call from Gail Chris-tian at PBS informing her that WNYC had backed out of its role as the pre-senting station. PBS would not air the program without a wrap, so unless another affiliate station would agree to produce the follow-up discussion and present the program to the system, "Days of Rage" would not air with the PBS logo.[21] Franklin-Trout said Christian told her PBS was pulling "Days of Rage" off the schedule.[22]

PBS decided to cancel the show because the sponsoring station withdrew its support. On March 26, six days after PBS announced WNYC would present the documentary, Chloe Aaron, the newly appointed vice president of the sta-tion, announced WNYC never intended to present the show. She chided sta-tion staffers and Jonathan Kwitny—whose program, *The Kwitny Report*, she canceled citing lack of funding—for overstepping their bounds by giving PBS the impression that WNYC would sponsor the program.[23] According to

Kwitny, there had been a "genuine disagreement."[24] According to Christian, Aaron also called other PBS affiliate stations, warning them that broadcasting "Days of Rage" could damage Aaron's ability to raise money in the New York market.[25]

Franklin-Trout told Howard Rosenberg about PBS's cancellation of the broadcast, and she recalls he "went off the wall." She said he felt PBS had a terrible history on the Israeli-Palestinian conflict, and that he often thought about writing about it. This was his opportunity.[26]

## Involvement of the Media and Special Interest Groups

The "Days of Rage" controversy first gained national attention on April 22 when Rosenberg wrote an article with the headline "PBS Backs Away from Palestinian Documentary." Rosenberg, whose column is syndicated in more than six hundred newspapers, described "Days of Rage" as "a powerful, well-made program that conveys a message expressed in fragments on newscasts but never before presented on American TV as a documentary-length statement without a rebuttal. It's a catalogue of Palestinian horror stories, of broken bodies and broken villages, of deep emotional scars, of squalid refugee camps, of collective punishment, of charges of Israeli brutality."

Rosenberg reported Franklin-Trout's charge that public television was "afraid" to broadcast her show and recounted WNYC's refusal to sponsor it. He suggested Chloe Aaron decided to withdraw the program because she feared the show would undermine WNYC's fund-raising efforts since New York is home to 1.7 million Jewish Americans. This raised the thorny question of whether public television is more beholden to pleasing subscribers and sponsors than to its commitment to use the medium as a forum for diverse views on controversial topics.

The Rosenberg article also alerted special interest groups, who then started marshaling their troops to promote or cancel the broadcast. On April 24, 1989, the American-Arab Anti-Defamation Committee sent out an "Action Alert" urging members to contact PBS affiliate stations to lobby for the original airdate, June 5, the twenty-second anniversary of the Israeli occupation of the West Bank and Gaza. Pro-Israeli groups, who had by now received bootleg copies of "Days of Rage," began strategizing and soon received a rhetorical gem from Chloe Aaron.

Jeremy Gerard, *New York Times* television critic, was the first to quote WNYC's Chloe Aaron's explanation for canceling "Days of Rage." Aaron told Gerard, "It's one-sided. It makes no mention of how the Jews got to Israel, no mention of the Holocaust, no mention of how the Palestinians treated the

Jews nor how Arabs treated the Palestinians. It's a pure propaganda piece that I'd compare to Leni Riefenstahl's 'Triumph of the Will.'"[27]

Aaron's assertion that the documentary was "propaganda" resounded throughout the controversy; all subsequent articles and reviews echoed or addressed it in one form or another. It fueled articles and op-eds in city newspapers as well as in the Jewish-American and Arab-American press. Aaron's comments also gave the first public signal to the grassroots, pro-Israeli, Jewish-American groups, who began to protest plans to broadcast the program nationally or in their local areas. Aaron's charge that "Days of Rage" was "pure propaganda" sent shudders through PBS and the affiliate stations, who braced for pressure from local viewers.

The charge of propaganda led Arab-American groups and some commentators to countercharge "censorship." On May 23, Fairness and Accuracy in Reporting, a media watchdog group, picketed the offices of WNYC to protest Chloe Aaron's "political censorship."[28] *New York Times* columnist Anthony Lewis also entered the fray. In an op-ed titled "Fear of Freedom," Lewis criticized Aaron's decision and rhetoric, arguing the "fear of genuine freedom to express a strong point of view has drained a powerful medium of much of its informing potential. . . . We shall see whether public television has the backbone needed for freedom."[29]

## Countdown to the Broadcast

After Howard Rosenberg's article appeared, WNET/New York announced it had agreed to sponsor "Days of Rage" and scheduled an airdate with follow-up discussion for Wednesday, September 6. The controversy began to take on new life as proponents and opponents of the broadcast focused their attention on WNET.

WNET and PBS faced a sticky dilemma. PBS could not cancel the broadcast because this would appear to be giving in to pro-Israeli pressure, and besides, PBS had already announced that the program would air. The embarrassment of PBS withdrawing the program altogether would be especially awkward since prominent groups and commentators had already lined up on opposing sides framing the dispute as "propaganda" or "censorship." PBS and WNET could broadcast the "Days of Rage" as is, but then they would be vulnerable to criticism by pro-Israeli groups for airing "propaganda."

"There was never a politically right answer, which is one of the things that both independents and stations never seemed to understand," Chase said, who recalled tossing and turning at 4 a.m. as he struggled to find an answer to the dilemma. "Either way, you were screwed."[30]

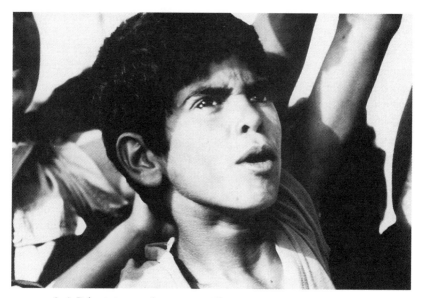

8. A Palestinian youth in protest. *Photo: Courtesy Pacific Production.*

Christian remembers facing the prospect of being a traitor to the system since PBS is a subscription organization that survives on the dues paid by the member stations. "The stations never want to be in a position of rejecting a program at their level. They want the program to be rejected by PBS so if someone calls up and says, 'Why didn't you air x, y, or z,' they can say, 'PBS rejected the program and didn't offer it to me,'" Christian said. "So what happens is, the heat comes in from the larger stations to PBS saying, 'I'm going to suffer a big financial loss if you put your name on this program.' That was the case of 'The Young Palestinians.'"[31]

The question facing broadcasters was not *whether* to air the program, but *how* to broadcast it. Finally, WNET and PBS hit on a solution. A hint of the compromise came on May 29 when Richard Hutton, WNET's director of public affairs programming, told the *New York Times* that "Days of Rage" was "one-sided" but performed a service in "permitting the Palestinians of the Intifada to express their views." He said WNET's job was "to 'neutralize' the documentary's weaknesses and shore up its strengths."[32]

PBS and WNET wanted to broadcast "Days of Rage" in a format that attempted to strike a balance between irreconcilable perspectives and interest groups, and be consistent with public television's stated commitment to the intelligent viewer. "If you believe, as public television must and does, that people are intelligent enough and over time will receive news from different sources so they can make informed decisions," Chase said, "then you trust them to see a work that is not perfect."[33]

The same day WNET announced it would broadcast "Days of Rage," Walter Goodman, who had received a preview copy of the documentary, published the first detailed review of the documentary, shaping the perception of the program for viewers and subsequent reviewers. Goodman compared "Days of Rage" unfavorably with the documentary "Arab and Jew: Wounded Spirits in a Promised Land (1989)." ("Arab and Jew" was based on a Pulitzer Prize–winning book by former *New York Times* Israeli bureau chief David K. Shipler.) In contrast to the glowing review of "Arab and Jew," Goodman described "Days of Rage" as "a tract for the Palestinian cause," where Palestinians are presented "as victims of a brutal occupation and heroic fighters in a war for liberation. . . . Chloe Aaron's charge of 'pure propaganda' is uncomfortably close to the mark."[34]

Goodman didn't limit his criticism to the program but also questioned Jo Franklin-Trout's credibility. He described the producer as "an advocate for the Palestinians" who "arouses suspicion," while Shipler "earns a viewer's trust."[35]

By June, three months before the scheduled broadcast, the various players lined up as follows:

—Jo Franklin-Trout, Arab-American groups, the Association of Independent Video and Filmmakers, and progressive Jewish groups criticized PBS/WNET for caving in to pressure from pro-Israeli groups by refusing to air the program on its own, without the WNET wraparound;

—PBS, WNET, and affiliate stations, including KCTS/Seattle and WPBT/Miami, acknowledged "Days of Rage" was "one-sided" but thought it should still be shown with balancing material and a panel discussion, and "let the viewers judge the program for themselves";

—WNYC, organizations that defended Israeli policies in the occupied territories, major Jewish-American groups, and individuals who believed the documentary was "propaganda" and should not be broadcast in any form.

That summer, Palestinian and Israeli groups turned up the heat on PBS, WNET, and affiliate stations. They mobilized supporters to promote, halt, or modify the national broadcast of "Days of Rage."

The pro-Israeli groups were the best organized through their network of national and local Jewish-American organizations. They held meetings with executives at WNET, PBS, and affiliate stations to express their anger about the broadcast of "Days of Rage" and called for its cancellation.[36]

The American Jewish Committee, the Anti-Defamation League of B'nai B'rith, and the Committee for Accuracy in Middle East Reporting in America (CAMERA) prepared detailed written critiques of the show and sent them out to their local activists to follow up at affiliate stations.[37] They urged local members to meet with the management of PBS affiliates to express concern about the broadcast and to phone and write letters about public television's anti-Israeli programming.[38] (It was left up to individuals to decide whether or not to cancel subscriptions.)[39] They put forth a consistent line of argument charging "Days of Rage" with historical inaccuracy and bias, and labeled the show "propaganda." They also encouraged other stations to follow WNYC and Chloe Aaron's example by refusing to carry the program.

In New York, a dozen Jewish leaders and businessmen headed by Dr. Ken Kelner, the national vice president of the Zionist Organization of America, met with WNET president William Baker and other WNET senior executives to urge the cancellation of the broadcast.[40] During this two-hour meeting, Baker allegedly admitted that "Days of Rage" was not journalism, described it as "seriously flawed," and insisted WNET was not granting it credibility.[41]

Delegation members responded that propaganda could never be adequately balanced and that the need for a panel discussion only demonstrated how biased the documentary was. After the meeting, Kelner called on the Jewish public to "flood Channel 13 and PBS with their outrage over this plan to defame Israel and the Jewish people" and provided readers with the address and phone number of WNET.[42]

WNET also met with Faris Bouhafa and Kate Seelye of the American-Arab Anti-Defamation Committee to reassure them that WNET stood behind "Days of Rage."[43]

WNET's compromise was announced on July 20. By then, WNET had received nearly 2,500 letters, 70 percent protesting the planned broadcast. Many of the letter writers threatened to cancel their subscriptions, a potentially significant loss to the station since 28 percent of WNET's $100–million budget was then coming from subscribers.[44] In an unprecedented move, the station management decided "Days of Rage" would not be shown on its own followed by a panel discussion as originally planned, but instead WNET would produce two six-minute video segments that would cover Israeli perspectives of the Intifada. These would be shown before and after "Days of Rage" to provide alternative views to those expressed in that documentary. PBS gave WNET $150,000 (nearly as much as it cost to make "Days of Rage") to fund the panel discussion and the bookend videos.[45]

Jo Franklin-Trout said she received "hundreds" of threatening, anonymous phone calls over the summer of 1989 both at her office and her home, where she lived with her family. She said PBS and WNET also refused to let her see how her film was being packaged. She felt very strongly that the proposed packaging with specially produced "pro-Israeli" videos was "intellectually dishonest." Franklin-Trout declined an offer to appear on the follow-up panel.[46]

Arab-American groups and the Association of Independent Video and Filmmakers charged WNET and PBS with watering down the show and trying to neutralize its impact without really canceling it.

Pro-Israeli activists at the local levels mirrored the lobbying efforts in New York. They prepared responses to any charges of bias and propaganda that might come from their local communities. They sought to mitigate the damage to their image and attempted to find ways to broadcast "Days of Rage" that would not leave them open to charges of airing pro-Palestinian "propaganda," on the one hand, or "caving in to" pressure groups, on the other, even with the WNET packaging of the film.

By September 1989, "Days of Rage" had become a lightning rod for public opinion on Israel, and the Palestinians and pro-Israeli groups kept up the pressure. In late August, the Anti-Defamation League of B'nai B'rith sent copies of a letter by Michael Posner, the director of the Lawyer's Committee for Human Rights, to local activists and public broadcasters. The human rights attorney, who appears in the film, now said he wanted to formally dissociate himself from the program because the film "fails to present a full or balanced examination of the current human rights situation in the West Bank and Gaza."[47]

On September 3, the *Palm Beach Post* reported a local synagogue had sent a petition with 295 signatures to WNET protesting the broadcast and describing "Days of Rage" as "hate-mongering and misdirected propaganda against Israel."[48] The *Detroit Free Press* reported WNET had received 4,000 letters about the show, including three hundred subscription cancellations. While generally quiet on programming disputes, Bill Moyers told a reporter, "If you knew half the story of the mean-spirited, threatening attack on Channel 13 because we're carrying this—first from Jews and then, after Channel 13 began to repackage it, from Arabs—you'd understand why public television, caught in the middle, depending upon public strings, leaves a lot of territory unexplored."[49]

The final assault on "Days of Rage" came a week before its scheduled airdate. Steve Emerson, whom Chase had consulted earlier, wrote an article in the *New Republic* that sought to derail the broadcast.[50] The *New York Times* reported Emerson's charges on August 31, a week before the scheduled broadcast.[51] In these articles, Emerson alleged "Days of Rage" was funded by Arab money and produced in "close cooperation with an Arab organization headed by a friend and adviser to PLO Chief Yasir Arafat." If true, PBS would be obliged to cancel the broadcast since the funding of the program would be in violation of PBS funding guidelines. (PBS guidelines prohibit financing of programs by those with a direct interest in the editorial slant or content of the film.) He also identified Jo Franklin-Trout as a board member of the Arab-American Cultural Foundation.[52]

Emerson's article set off a wave of new reports in the press, which resounded inside PBS programming. The allegations of bias and tainted funding put Jo Franklin-Trout on the defensive. She admitted joining the board of the foundation, but she said this was six months *after* she completed the film—a chronology disputed by Emerson. He also accused PBS of being lax by failing to check into the film's funding earlier.

PBS responded with a public statement explaining that funding guidelines did not prohibit independent producers from selling postbroadcast rights, but PBS agreed to investigate the case.

Gail Christian remembers Franklin-Trout's funding situation was unusual for an independent producer. "In my entire ten years at PBS, I may have seen one other film with that kind of funding," she said. "To have a producer say, 'I don't have any underwriters. This money came out of my pocket,' there's a good chance half the people in the room are going to snicker because no one's going to believe that story."[53]

Christian also defended Franklin-Trout against her colleagues' skepticism by citing PBS's previous relationship with her: "My position was, 'This is a producer who has done . . . other series for you, and you have a relationship with her. Why would you suddenly decide to call your producer a liar? Was she lying on the other . . . series?' We accepted her . . . other series. We accepted her sources of funding on those, and I have no reason not to believe her this time. And I certainly can't believe it because somebody said she was a bag lady for the Saudis."[54]

## The Broadcast                    .

Emerson's charges and the vocal protests did not stop "Days of Rage" from airing on September 6, nor discourage an estimated 5.9 million viewers from tuning in. PBS added a scroll at the beginning and end of the special acknowledging the allegations about questionable funding made by Emerson in the *New Republic* but also stating that it hadn't been able to verify them.

Affiliate stations added their own introductions and disclaimers. At KCTS/Seattle, the station president, Bernie Clark, appeared on camera to introduce the program. He acknowledged that "Days of Rage" presented "an extremely pro-Palestinian viewpoint, at the expense of ensuring fair treatment for the Israeli point of view." He also explained KCTS's public rationale for airing the program: that "understanding is best advanced by exposure to a full range of issues and opinions; that is why 'Days of Rage' is being presented with additional material that provides necessary context. This additional material will examine the Intifada and provide the Israeli point of view."

Like several other stations, KCTS also added a notice, which crawled across the bottom of the screen, giving a KCTS phone number for viewers to call if they would like to comment on the program. Staff monitored the telephones to answer questions and tabulate responses to the program. (In the end, about five hundred people called KCTS. Eighty percent of the calls were positive, 10 percent were negative about "Days of Rage," and another 10 percent criticized the "packaging" of the program.)

The program began with the station's disclaimer, followed by former assistant secretary of state Hodding Carter, who introduced the WNET special "Intifada: The Palestinians and Israel." He told viewers "Days of Rage" was "one particular view of the conflict" and said the United States had a commitment both to the State of Israel and to "the principle of self-determination." Then he introduced the first six-minute video, which presented Israeli views of the Intifada.

The video described the twenty-two-year Israeli occupation of the West Bank and Gaza as a fact of life for many Israelis and noted that about 70 percent believed it should continue for security reasons. A body on the street covered by a white cloth, burned-out vehicles, and several dead bodies from a bus hijacked by a Palestinian were shown to justify the Israeli fears of "Palestinian terrorism," which "raise memories of Auschwitz and Treblinka."

The narrator said threats from Arab leaders precipitated the 1967 war, and that the occupation of the West Bank was Israel's response to Jordanian attacks from that area. Israel, a country of five million people in a geographic area smaller than New Jersey, had hostile Arab neighbors that threatened "to throw Israel into the sea." The video showed an American hostage, the Ayatollah Khomeini, and marches by Muslim fundamentalists. The narrator concludes by saying that Israeli fears of attack explained their occupation of the territories.

Hodding Carter returned to tell viewers they "won't hear those Israeli concerns expressed" in "Days of Rage." He said the film had been criticized for "not putting hard questions to advocates of the Palestinian cause, and that the Israelis presented in the film were from "one extreme or the other," but not the Israeli mainstream. He said its broadcast had been strenuously protested but that it reflected "opinions rarely heard or seen at length by Americans."

He said these views were "discomforting," but if true, could be "oddly encouraging" because they suggested a movement away from the "historic call for the destruction of Israel and toward coexistence."

"Days of Rage" ran its full ninety minutes, was followed by another video representing an Israeli perspective, and a panel discussion.

The pro-Israeli video showed Israelis attending a human rights demonstration and a counterdemonstration organized by Jewish fundamentalists. The narrator underscored how the Palestinian human rights issue was argued publicly in Israel.

An Israeli man worried about the moral decline of Israeli soldiers in the occupied territories; a woman urged viewers "to see the whole story," of Arabs spitting on Israeli soldiers and throwing stones, and said, "Sometimes those stones kill."

The narrator said the Intifada's strikes and violence had persuaded Israelis that Palestinian nationalism would not go away, and that two of three Israelis believed negotiations with the Palestinians were inevitable within five years. The challenge was to keep the lid on the violence.

An Israeli soldier said nobody wanted to shoot a fourteen-year-old kid, but Ehud Olmert, the minister of Arab Affairs, explained that Israel was fighting a war.

To address the issues of Israeli soldiers' use of "unnecessary force," the video pointed out that more than seventy soldiers and officers had been brought to court for these offenses, including two colonels who were discharged from the military service. Four soldiers were tried for beating an Arab to death in the Jabalya refugee camp, were convicted of brutality, and sentenced to six to nine months in jail, a penalty some Israelis thought was too lenient.

The deportations, people held in prison without being charged, the demolition of houses—the narrator said these practices had been condemned by international investigations, but Israel's "open society makes these abuses easier to monitor than in other countries."

The panel discussion included questions raised by Hodding Carter that echoed many of Barry Chase's original reservations about "Days of Rage," and it provided a forum for groups opposed to the broadcast. Carter began by asking each of the five panelists to characterize the Intifada. Then he asked them to comment on "Days of Rage" itself: "Is this the kind of journalism you ought to demand in a subject this complex? Is it a good piece of work?" He followed up by asking if the documentary, in their opinions, was a work of advocacy journalism, and if so, whether it should be shown on public television.

Seymour D. Reich, chairman of the Conference of Presidents of Major American Jewish Organizations, described the Intifada as the work of Palestinian terrorists and called the program "pure propaganda," whose showing "does not serve a purpose." He said the program was not a documentary because it did not show both sides of the issue and it did not address Israel's security needs. He also stressed that Israel was a democracy that wanted peace. All the Palestinians presented in "Days for Rage" wanted to live side by side with Israel, supporting the two-state solution, but Reich said some Palestinians still called for the elimination of Israel. "Advocacy journalism has a place on television," he said, "but pure propaganda on television does not serve a purpose."

Alan L. Keyes, former assistant secretary of state and later a Republican presidential primary contender, said the Intifada was part of a moral and political warfare to delegitimize the Israeli government and U.S. policy toward Israel.[55] It deflected attention away from Arab neglect and irresponsibility in dealing with the Palestinians. He felt "Days of Rage" was "only powerful for the ignorant" because it "falsified history" and "lies to the viewer." He felt strongly that the historical sequence omitted the role and responsibility of Arabs.

James Zogby of the Arab-American Institute called the Intifada an insurrection by Palestinians who "grew up under a cruel occupation." He referred to forty years of Israeli propaganda and said that the program finally let Palestinians tell their story and why Palestinian children were rebelling. He maintained that the program should have aired in June and that it was an "insult" to the Palestinians, Americans, and viewers to have a discussion after the program.

Richard Murphy, a former State Department diplomat, and Walter Ruby, a journalist for the *Jerusalem Post*, both said "Days of Rage" was unbalanced and partial but also compelling. Murphy said one knew from the title that the program presented a Palestinian viewpoint, and if one kept that in mind, the program was "very striking." Ruby said the Intifada has been a transforming event for Israelis and Palestinians, but he was bothered by the "unrepresentative" Israelis interviewed. He said Franklin-Trout interviewed Israelis from the extreme right and extreme left, but that most Israelis were somewhere in the middle—frightened for their own security and for Israel's.

## The Press Reaction

On September 6, the day of broadcast, the *New York Times* devoted several articles to the controversy. Walter Goodman described "Days of Rage" as "loaded" but having "special value" in bringing the perspective of Palestinians to the public. He acknowledged the WNET additions had the effect of "softening" the impact of Franklin-Trout's film and that these additions "inevitably tilt in Israel's direction since they are offered as antidotes to the even more assertively pro-Palestinian material." Jeremy Gerard gathered comments from media commentators Ben Bagdikian and Martin Gottlieb, who found the use of the disclaimer "problematic" and a "cop-out."[56]

The *New York Times* also carried two opinion articles side by side under the headline "'Days of Rage'—Journalism or Propaganda?" One was by Jo Franklin-Trout and the other by Steve Emerson. In "It's a Fair, Honest Film," Franklin-Trout expressed amazement at the "different set of editorial standards" by which critics judged her film; reiterated that the events portrayed in the film had been fully documented by the U.S. State Department reports on human rights; and denied that the Arab-American Cultural Foundation had funded the film.

In "Financed by Arab Money," Emerson called for PBS to cancel the program pending an investigation of the film's funding, and asked, "Why is PBS afraid of the truth?"

Most of the reviews in the nation's other newspapers were critical of "Days of Rage," reciting the charges that the film was one-sided and that the "justifiable fears" of the Israelis were not addressed. Some struck a moderate course by adding that the film was still valuable in presenting a view rarely heard on American television.

Other reviewers, like Robert Goldberg of the *Wall Street Journal*, didn't stop at panning the film but also attacked the producer. Goldberg reiterated that the film was "warped" but added that Franklin-Trout's work was "intellectually slipshod," "heavy-handed," and filled with "soggy thinking."[57]

The *Washington Post*'s Tom Shales dismissed "Days of Rage" as "baldly biased and lopsided, a movie made to plead a cause rather than to explore a crisis." He also criticized it as a work of "deliberate deception" and concluded with a final salvo: "If Jo Franklin-Trout ever had serious credentials as an independent journalist, she has now turned them in for a career in public relations."[58]

Scott Pendleton of the *Christian Science Monitor* gave "Days of Rage" a favorable review and chided the packaging of the film, which "doesn't so much balance it as sink it." He said the whole two-and-a-half-hour program should be wrapped "with a documentary on the media power of the pro-Israel lobby."[59]

*Seattle Times* television columnist John Voorhees praised "Days of Rage" as an important film and recounted how "nervous-nelly PBS" was supposed to show the program earlier but panicked when the film was accused of being one-sided. He applauded both the documentary and the follow-up discussion, and concluded, "The semantic rows, charges and counter-charges that erupt during the panel's discussion make it abundantly clear why "Days of Rage" needed to be made and shown."[60]

All the television critics' verdicts were inextricably linked to the controversy. The controversy became the story upstaging the chorus of Palestinian voices presented in "Days of Rage." Significantly, the pro-Israeli groups succeeded in deflecting attention away from the political issues posed by the Intifada and overtly tried to color reviewers' interpretations of the film. By repeating that "Days of Rage" was "pro-Palestinian," "propaganda," "poor journalism," "biased," "skewed history," and filled with "distortions," most of the reviewers and WNET ultimately gave credibility to the framing put forth by pro-Israeli groups.

## Analysis of the Controversy

PBS programmers often rejected programs on the Israeli-Palestinian issue because they believed the story had already been done (and usually cited *Frontline*), they didn't trust the producer's journalism, and the producer didn't have the clout to protest a PBS decision. But these hurdles didn't keep Jo Franklin-Trout's program off the schedule. She was an insider with prior journalistic experience at PBS, she had contacts among influential journalists in the national media, and she couldn't be easily dismissed by PBS programmers as a wide-eyed, radical film maker with little experience and low technical standards. Besides, Chase felt the story was worth presenting: "We put it on because it provided a point of view not well provided before. That doesn't mean it was *the* correct point of view. It was a piece of the puzzle. Unfortunately in television, only one thing comes out of the box at once."[61]

### PACKAGING THE PROGRAM

PBS stood up with WNET, albeit on wobbly legs, against stations and interest groups that tried to kill the broadcast altogether. The two institutions hit on an uneasy compromise that didn't satisfy any of the parties entirely: they devised a unique packaging for the program that diluted the film's message.

The questions asked by Hodding Carter in the panel discussion expressed many concerns initially raised by Barry Chase, and they led the discussion down a path that sought to neutralize the views expressed in the film by contextualizing them. Panelists challenged the historical portion of the film as slanted and noted its "failure" to include moderate voices from the Israeli population. The video wraparounds and the panel discussion produced by WNET and broadcast with the PBS logo, however, made Franklin-Trout's feature-length documentary on the Intifada more acceptable to public television gatekeepers.

Heberer looked back on the decision to air it. "Tough decisions are tough decisions, but when you decide to schedule something, it's because you believe there is merit in the broadcasting of this piece, and we continued to believe that."[62]

Jo Franklin-Trout, media critics, and defenders of the film questioned whether the packaging—the videos, introductions, and follow-up discussion—were "responsible journalism." Do viewers need to be told by the host or local affiliate station president that a documentary is "pro-Palestinian" and contains "falsehoods" if they are "intelligent" enough to "make up their own minds"?

PBS's (and KCTS's) answer was "yes." Years later, Heberer defended the decision to air the film as PBS had. "In the end, the film still needed additional context," she said.[63]

The packaging of "Days of Rage" was an uneasy compromise for Chase and Heberer, the end result of Chase's nagging reservations about the film and the coercive persuasion from interest groups whose concerns were reinforced by stations such as WNYC and WNET. PBS revealed itself to be vulnerable to intimidation by organized pro-Israeli groups and station managers, and a weak forum for perspectives some organized interest groups consider unworthy of expression.

A CONTINUING ISRAELI-PALESTINIAN CRISIS

Timing played an important part in the program becoming controversial. The Israeli-Palestinian issue was ongoing at the time of the broadcast, and American political leaders were deeply divided. The Bush administration was growing impatient with the Israeli government's refusal to negotiate an end to the conflict. U.S. public opinion seemed to be shifting. The political stakes in the battle to spin public opinion on Palestine were high in 1989 as pro-Israeli groups, such as the American Israel Political Action Committee, organized to keep U.S. aid flowing into Israel.

Jo Franklin-Trout didn't break a new story and her documentary didn't present information that wasn't already available in the mainstream print media. The New York Times and other papers were covering cases of alleged Israeli brutality and human rights abuses in the territories during 1988 and 1989. The U.S. State Department's 1988 annual report on human rights stated there had been "a substantial increase in human rights violations" as a result of Israel's response to the Palestinian uprising, and it criticized Israel's actions.[64]

The next year's report on the human rights situation in Gaza and the West

Bank substantiated many of the fact-claims about deportations, arrests without charges, and other human rights violations depicted in "Days of Rage." For example, it reported that Israeli soldiers continued to violate the rights of Palestinians in the occupied territories, causing "unavoidable deaths and injuries." It also reported "a significant increase in violence caused by Palestinians directed at other Palestinians." Israeli military authorities regularly entered Palestinian houses without search warrants. These forced entries resulted in "beatings, destruction of property and arrests," the report said. "In 1989, 88 Arab houses were demolished and 82 were sealed by the Israelis 'for security reasons.'" According to the report, Israeli soldiers or settlers killed 304 Palestinians during 1989, and the Palestinians killed thirteen Israelis in the territories. Palestinians killed 128 other Palestinians for real or perceived collaboration with the Israelis.[65]

Israel, which is still receiving more U.S. aid than any other country, has long enjoyed a special status in the Middle East as the only democracy and U.S. ally in the region. But with the Intifada, the mainstream American and international press began to cover the repressive measures taken by the Israelis in the occupied territories: the bulldozing of houses, the deportations and arrests of Palestinians.

Franklin-Trout's critics did not want this information amplified by the public television broadcast. But a few years after the "Days of Rage" broadcast, even the Israeli government was ultimately forced to recognize the legitimacy of the Palestinian grievances when it opened direct negotiations with the PLO in 1993. The conflict remains unresolved.

### CONTRASTS BETWEEN "DAYS OF RAGE" AND *FRONTLINE* DOCUMENTARIES

The underlying questions posed by the "Days of Rage" case (and the "Dark Circle" case) are: Who gets to be a journalist? Who can speak on the divisive issues of the day? What factors influence these decisions? The answers come into focus by contrasting the status and work of Jo Franklin-Trout and that of *Frontline*.

Some topics invite controversy, and during the 1980s, two such topics were the Palestinian issue and the abortion issue. David Fanning and his series had been a target of some of the same organized groups that criticized "Days of Rage." These groups noted that his bias was evident because he had revisited the Palestinian issue more often than any other topic. The *Frontline* series had produced several documentaries on the Israeli-Palestinian conflict from its first season in 1983, but none of its documentaries evoked as strong an organized reaction and as much press attention as "Days of Rage."

During the ten years between 1983 and 1993, *Frontline* produced six documentaries on the Israeli-Palestinian issue: "Israel: Between the River and the Sea" (May 16, 1983), "The Arab and the Israeli" (November 13, 1984), "Retreat from Beirut" (February 26, 1985), "Israel: The Price of Victory" (June 2, 1987), "The Faces of Arafat" (February 27, 1990), and, notably, "Journey to the Occupied Lands" (January 26, 1993), which was the only documentary that resulted in a lengthy internal investigation.[66]

None of the *Frontline* documentaries was packaged with a PBS-commissioned wraparound because such packaging was not deemed necessary; the series format provided its own package. Fanning, as executive producer, had also built a solid track record with PBS and a relationship of trust with Barry Chase and the other PBS public affairs programmers over the years. He had the confidence of the public television system behind him, and he received funding from it. He was not as vulnerable to charges of tainted funding and usually did not have to defend his work in public: public television public relations staff did that for him.

When pro-Israeli groups, such as CAMERA, attacked *Frontline* for its "pro-Palestinian bias," they could not catch and sustain the attention of the national media in the anti-*Frontline* campaigns. This meant that their complaints against *Frontline* programs did not spread far into the public arena, unlike the attacks against Jo Franklin-Trout's film.

Franklin-Trout was an easier target because public television gatekeepers had underscored their ambivalence about the program by packaging it and spoke publicly against it. Franklin-Trout's film also presented Palestinians of the Intifada to viewers before PBS gatekeepers, and vocal, pro-Israeli interest groups, were willing to accept them as legitimate players on the world media stage. Therefore, some saw PBS as a vehicle for propaganda, while others saw it as caving in to special interest groups and as a censor.

## LEGITIMIZING THE PALESTINIAN PERSPECTIVE

"Days of Rage" was on the cutting edge of changing public perceptions, and by being on PBS even in its packaged state, the system helped legitimize through representation the perspective of the Palestinian youth. Despite the wraparounds, the program offered viewers an opportunity to hear the voices of the Intifada. Whether they chose to listen was another matter.

When the controversy erupted over "Days of Rage," it did not directly foster dialogue on the Palestinian issue in the press. Rather, critics questioned Franklin-Trout's credibility and her journalism, though her facts had been fact-checked by PBS.[67] "Days of Rage" opened up debate about the Intifada indirectly by introducing viewers to some of its members. It presented the raw voices of the Palestinian youth, even though the show's packaging had also become a story in itself.

"History has borne out everything the film had to say," Franklin-Trout said. She believes PBS would have canceled her program if she had not "turned every screw" and brought every element of pressure to bear. "I didn't have the intention of burning my bridges at PBS, but when we got into the process, that's what it came down to: either back off and disappear, or burn my bridges at PBS."[68]

## Postscript

After the broadcast of "Intifada: The Palestinians and Israel," PBS announced several changes. Gail Christian, who had accepted "Days of Rage" for national broadcast, resigned "to pursue other interests."[69] PBS completed its investigation of "Days of Rage" and found no evidence to support Emerson's charge that guidelines had been violated. PBS did, however, agree to review its underwriting policies, reviving an old debate about underwriters and their interest in programming. PBS also announced it was creating an internal council to review "controversial" programming, a move raising concern that PBS might shy away from such point-of-view programming in the future.[70]

Public television set about repairing its relations with the pro-Israeli groups upset by the broadcast of "Days of Rage." On November 30, the *New York Times* reported PBS would broadcast "A Search for Solid Ground: The Intifada through Israeli Eyes."[71] An unnamed WNET executive told the *New York Times* that no attempt would be made to offer a Palestinian perspective on the film, but that the documentary would be followed by a short panel discussion. This film was in progress during the height of the protests about "Days of Rage."[72]

A week later, Walter Goodman broke the story that Uriel Savir, the Israeli consul general, had helped raise $382,000 the preceding June for "A Search for Solid Ground" by introducing the film makers to four New York businessmen active in Jewish causes. Goodman commented, "This is pledge week on WNET. . . . Either the packaging of the first documentary was too much or the packaging of the second is too little. Can that have anything to do with the number of Palestinian contributors to New York's public station compared with the number of Jewish contributors?"[73] But when "A Search for Solid Ground" aired on January 16, 1990, no funding disclaimer appeared with the show because PBS was convinced the businessmen had put up their own money, just as Jo Franklin-Trout had.

Franklin-Trout did not burn her bridges with PBS entirely. After "Days of Rage," she went on to write *The Wing of the Falcon,* a love story set during the Persian Gulf war, and a screenplay based on the novel.[74] She worked as a consultant for the U.S. State Department and with the U.S. military during the Persian Gulf war and is developing a PBS series about "people who changed the course of history in the twentieth century."[75]

# Chapter 5                              "Tongues Untied"

*I am a black, gay man. I made the work from that*
*perspective. There is no debate about whether my life is*
*right or wrong. It is right—period! . . . My life is of*
*value and so is the life of my community.*
                    —Marlon Riggs, independent producer

The ten-week *P.O.V* series, true to its mandate, has often been a showcase
for films by independent producers that embody perspectives from the margins of mainstream American culture and journalism. These film makers frequently express the concerns of various social or political movements of their
time, such as the peace and gay rights movements, and the campaigns against
U.S. foreign policy in El Salvador. They are, in the words of *P.O.V.* executive producer Marc Weiss, "poets, prophets and pamphleteers."[1]

Of all the provocative programs shown on *P.O.V.* since its first season in
1988, none has proved more controversial than "Tongues Untied," a video
essay by a gay, African-American film maker, Marlon T. Riggs (1957–1994).
The case underscores the role of independent producers in giving expression
to unorthodox and unpopular views. "Tongues Untied" presented ideas and
perspectives many people were unwilling to hear, in a form programmers were
unwilling to accept.

The "Tongues Untied" case became a point of reckoning for programmers,
station managers, *P.O.V.*, and PBS. It highlighted a struggle within public television over its reason for existence and its role in a heterogeneous and changing society. Programmers and managers had to reexamine their understanding
of and commitment to public television's original mandate "to give voice to
the voiceless." They were openly divided and sometimes confused about their

9. Director Marlon Riggs with poet Essex Hamphill in "Tongues Untied." *Photo: Ron Simmons, courtesy Frameline, Inc..*

programming responsibilities in their respective communities, torn by conflicting allegiances and obligations.

How programmers and station managers handled "Tongues Untied" measured their courage or timidity in the face of their many conflicting priorities. Programmers who rejected the program often justified their decisions by appealing to their own and their communities' standards of what is "decent" and what is "obscene." Others came to the defense of the program by articulating their understanding of public television's mission as a noncommercial alternative that takes risks by broadcasting provocative, innovative programs. The "Tongues Untied" case revealed which programmers saw public television as primarily a vehicle for educational programming and which viewed it as a provider of alternative programming committed to reflecting the diversity of perspectives in American society.

Public television's mission had become increasingly cloudy—even irrelevant to some programmers—in the years since it was first articulated in poetic, Great Society prose in the mid-1960s.[2] Inside public television stations and at the annual PBS meetings in the early 1990s, hallway chats about "Tongues Untied" evolved into soul-searching and sometimes angry discussions about the definition and relevance of public television's original mission given the dependence of stations on viewer contributions and other funders—such as corporations and state or local governments—and a desire to maintain good relations with the local community. Georgia Public Television knew firsthand how high the stakes were: the state politicians threatened to cut all funding to the state's public broadcasting service if it ever dared to air a program like "Tongues Untied" again.

At the national level, public television was under attack by conservative interest groups and politicians, who pressed Congress to cut off or curtail federal funding for public broadcasting, citing programs like "Tongues Untied" as "obscene" and "promoting a gay life-style." Groups such as Donald Wildmon's American Family Association and conservative critics in Congress turned their spotlight on PBS as another publicly funded institution they felt had strayed from the morally acceptable path.

## Program Description

A viewer advisory appears on the screen: "The following program contains explicit language and images. Viewer discretion is advised." Then comes the introductory tease which sets the tone for the program. Marlon Riggs, who produced, directed, and edited the film, snaps his fingers with other African-American men to a jazzy beat. The following words, one at a time, fill the screen, white letters on black: "Black men loving black men is *the* revolutionary act." Next a black hand slaps the Jerusalem Bible and an extreme close-up of the preacher's mouth shouting, "Abomination! It's an abomination!" Viewers see grainy, black-and-white images of a black man being assaulted by several men as voices chant, repeating this poem:

> Anger unvented becomes pain
> Unspoken becomes rage
> Released becomes violence.
> Cha-cha-cha . . .

Marlon Riggs speaks into the camera: "I was blind to my brothers' beauty—now see my own." The poem-chant continues, then the *P.O.V.* interview with Marlon Riggs begins.

Riggs says it was hard for him, as a director and producer, to step from behind the camera to stand in front of it. But rather than trying to find and persuade someone else to talk about their experience of being black and gay and having HIV, he decided that he had to put himself on the line, personally and professionally, to tell this story.

After the interview, the film begins with the hypnotic chant "brother to brother" over a slow-motion, black-and-white montage of African-American men talking, playing basketball, hanging out together. Riggs, naked, dances slowly in darkness, arms obscuring his face.

Riggs uses dance, music, poetry to passionately tell his compelling story of searching for acceptance in a society with racist whites who stigmatize him for being black, and antigay blacks who stigmatize him for being gay.

Riggs underscores the homophobia in popular black culture by presenting clips of comedian Eddie Murphy telling "fag jokes." Pacing back and forth on the stage, Murphy says, "Faggots aren't allowed to look at my ass while I'm up here. That's why I keep moving. You don't know where the faggot section is." Riggs shows a scene from Spike Lee's film *School Daze*, with a circle of aging African-American men chanting, "Fag, fag, fag, fag, punk, punk, punk, punk" at an unseen, rival fraternity.

Riggs describes growing up feeling like an outsider, a "punk," in his own community. He went to a white school where he was one of two blacks. "Nigger go home" graffiti greeted him there. Other African-Americans called him an "Uncle Tom" for going to the white school for smart kids. Viewers see close-ups of mouths chanting a chorus of hostility: "Uncle Tom," "motherfuckin' coon," "punk." Assaulted by these names, Riggs says he ran deep into his self to find a stillness where he felt safe.

While still a teenager, Riggs says he was beaten up and left in the street for being black and gay. A white man with green-gray eyes rescued him and became a close friend. Although they never touched, Riggs fell in love. Viewers hear Roberta Flack singing "The First Time Ever I Saw Your Face" as the camera zooms in on a portrait of this young, blond white friend.

Later Riggs moved to San Francisco but felt "like an invisible man" as an African-American gay because most of the images portrayed in gay media were of beefy white men. He felt no solace immersed in a world of "vanilla" and says his experience was not unique. A black gay man tells how he avoided the gaze of another black gay man on the street, an avoidance marking an unwillingness to face the common, painful feelings of exclusion in the white gay mecca.

"I don't know why but I'm feeling so sad," Billie Holiday sings as the camera rests on a black transvestite, pensive and waiting. Another, a streetwalker, waits for love and a date as Nina Simone sings "Love Is the Color of My True Love's Hair."

A fundamentalist preacher and a black power activist break the hypnotic trance of the music with the banter of "abomination" and "sin." Rejected by voices in the black community criticizing black gays as "faggots" who are "undermining the family" and are "part of the problem," Riggs brings home the hatred he says is felt by black gays from the African-American community. A black activist asks, "Where does his loyalty lie? What is he first: black or gay?"—questions Riggs says are absurd. Black gays feel isolated, stigmatized, and mute, a silence that resounds in a duet of poetic verse read by Riggs and the poet Essex Hemphill.

> Silence is my shield
> It crushes.
> Silence is my cloak
> It smothers.
> Silence is my sword
> It cuts both ways.
> Silence is the deadliest weapon.
> What legacy is to be found in silence?

"Tongues Untied" is committed to ending the silence about being black and gay. A doo-wop quartet sings, "Hey boy, can you come out tonight?" A gay rights parade with banners—"Silence = Death" and "Black Men Loving Black Men Is *the* Revolutionary Act"—ties the struggles of African-American gays to the civil rights movement of Sojourner Truth, Frederick Douglass, and Martin Luther King, Jr., a lineage Riggs says gives him strength to battle "the ticking time bomb" in his own blood: HIV. The faces of friends and people he has known flash on the screen, African-American men, most in their thirties, dead from AIDS.

Riggs ends the program with his own self-acceptance and a march. "I was mute, tongue-tied, burdened by shadows and silence. Now I speak and my burden is lightened, lifted, free."

## The Producer and the Production

Marlon Riggs was born into a military family in Fort Worth, Texas, in 1957.[3] Educated in American history at Harvard University, where he graduated with honors in 1978, and with a master's degree in broadcast journalism from the University of California at Berkeley (1981), where he later became a tenured professor, Riggs brought pedigree academic credentials and a direct, yet poetic and lyrical approach to his work on the African-American and gay experience. The producer, whose parents expected him to be a preacher, became an articulate and vocal leader in the independent producing community, an activist who testified before Congress about public broadcasting's poor funding

10. Marlon Riggs. *Photo: Janet Van Ham, courtesy Frameline, Inc.*

and treatment of independent producers as part of the battle to create the
Independent Television Service.[4]

Riggs first gained national attention as a producer in 1987, when "Ethnic Notions," a one-hour documentary analyzing 150 years of racial stereo-
typing of blacks in American culture, aired on PBS.[5] He approached this
painful and taboo subject with an analytic and unapologetic tone, showing
viewers how popular culture both shapes and reflects public attitudes. The racial stereotypes of the "Mammy" figure, the "Brute," the "Pickaninny," and
"Sambo" evoked strong reactions within the black community, and some black
leaders criticized Riggs's program, fearing it would stir up memories of a racist
past better left forgotten.[6] But "Ethnic Notions" won Riggs a national Emmy
and other awards when it aired nationally on PBS. It also received numerous
awards at film festivals.

In 1991—the same year as the "Tongues Untied" controversy—Riggs completed a sequel to "Ethnic Notions," a feature-length documentary titled "Color Adjustment," that followed up the same typology of racist portrayals and conflict of African-Americans in the television age. The documentary traced forty years of race relations in the United States through the lens of prime-time television programs. This film, coproduced with Vivian Kleiman, opened P.O.V.'s 1992 season and garnered several of television's highest documentary accolades, including the George Foster Peabody Award.[7]

These two major works were relatively accessible to a general audience, and they grew out of Riggs's own lived experience as an African-American and his study of U.S. history, but neither film explicitly focused on another level of the producer's identity: his homosexuality.

Riggs turned his creative attention to his experience as a black gay man when, in December 1988, he spent several months in the hospital battling kidney failure. At that time, he learned he was HIV-positive.

Riggs had pondered a new video project on being black and gay nine or ten months earlier, and had begun taping what he thought would be a fifteen-minute video screened in gay bars.[8] Riggs had even applied for some funding, but the video had not gelled in his mind until, gazing up from his hospital bed at the television talk show *Geraldo*, he began to spin images in his mind, and the scenes and poetry came into focus.[9] They culminated in the fifty-six-minute "Tongues Untied," which he shot and edited in four months in 1989.[10]

"This piece came out of a very desperate drive and need on my part, partly because I'd been very, very ill earlier in the year and had a strong sense of my mortality, not knowing what would happen next and realizing that I had certain gifts as well as a number of means that most people didn't," Riggs told Robert Anbian, editor of *Release Print*, a newsletter of the Film Arts Foundation. (This is an organization of film and video makers based in San Francisco.) Riggs continued:

> I knew how to do this work. It's like the opportunity was presented to me as well as the insight that I may not be here in order to continue this, or to put it off and wait till a better day, a more convenient time when my career was more established and this wouldn't threaten it in any way. I realized I had to go for broke. I was really very desperate, adrenaline-rushed, intensely energetic to do this, without thinking about distribution and fundraising and so forth. I didn't think about fundraising, I thought I'd try two or three places that I hoped might be amenable to this, but I'm not going to bother to convince others or wait years and hope that somebody will finally realize that this is a worthwhile subject to explore on film or video.[11]

Riggs knew he wanted to involve a community of artists, dancers, musicians, and poets whose lives mirrored the experiences he was hoping to translate into video, so he decided on a collaborative approach involving the dance, music, and life stories of other black gay men combined with his own first-person narration, rather than writing a self-absorbed monologue that he believed would have little appeal. Inspired by the publication of several black gay anthologies in the mid-1980s, Riggs wanted to bring this poetry into his video and sought a way to visualize it. Soon he realized he could not convey its spirit in a traditional documentary form, such as that used in "Ethnic Notions," and still be true to the poetry. He sought a new form that would express the feel and perspectives of the poetry and reflect his experience and that of his friends in the black gay community.

Riggs also did not want to have to *explain* gayness or blackness to a general audience. He intended the work specifically for black gay men, such as the members of Gay Men of African Descent or Black Gay Men United. He said that this choice freed him to speak frankly and passionately in the film and "not fear alienating an audience that may not understand the terms, or the rage or the degree of sexual attraction."[12]

The producer had some apprehension about how his intended audience would react to the film, just as he had when he finished "Ethnic Notions," which some black leaders felt was too strong:[13]

> I was putting things out on the table that a lot of people feel very uncomfortable putting out there for public viewing. I knew there were certain things that might get me in trouble with a particular kind of black gay leadership which is middle class, educated, more polished, wanting to present an image that's more accessible and amenable to the public. But I knew I would deal with frankly obscene language, that I would show drag queens who were not elegant and beautiful and pretty but who were street and low, if you will. I knew I would deal with interracial relationships, black/white relationships which a number of people within the black leadership find troublesome.[14]

He also faced a visual challenge with his new project since his topic was about sexuality.

> I wanted to show how people touch, and the touching. I didn't want to show pornography. I wasn't interested in showing erect genitalia and winking anuses and so forth. You can find those things in your local video store. I wanted to show two black men touching tenderly, romantically, and sexually . . . an image that I had never seen and which would confirm an experience for a number of people.[15]

Riggs made "Tongues Untied" for $8,000 cash from two small grants: a $5,000 Western State Regional Arts Fellowship (from funds that came from the National Endowment for the Arts but were administered regionally) and $3,000 from the Film Arts Foundation. Riggs also received $32,000 in donated in-kind services for production and postproduction at the journalism department of the University of California at Berkeley where he worked.[16] The credits list him as producer, director, editor, and primary photographer.

While teaching classes at Berkeley's School of Journalism, Riggs had access to state-of-the-art cameras and postproduction equipment, and he lived in the San Francisco Bay Area, where he had a circle of supportive friends, organizations, like the Film Arts Foundation, and professional colleagues.

Although he had enjoyed a previous relationship with KQED/San Francisco—which had provided postproduction facilities so he could complete "Ethnic Notions"—Riggs did not make "Tongues Untied" with public television in mind. He made it because he felt he was running out of time and wanted to make a vital statement to his gay black brothers and the black community at large before it was too late.

## Initial Reactions and Submission to P.O.V.

Riggs was surprised when "Tongues Untied," completed in 1989, attracted audiences outside his intended audience. The documentary (which had been transferred to film) was screened around the world at film festivals in Edinburgh, Copenhagen, Dublin, Montreal, and Melbourne. Viewers and critics received the documentary with praise. The film won many prestigious film awards in the U.S. and abroad, including "Best Documentary" at the Berlin International Film Festival, and "Best Independent/Experimental Work" from the Los Angeles Film Critics, a Blue Ribbon at the American Film and Video Festival, "Best Documentary" at the New York Documentary Festival, and "First Prize—New Visions" from the San Francisco International Film Festival. Prior to its broadcast on P.O.V., it was shown without controversy on the BBC, Barcelona Television (Spain), and three local public television stations: KQED/San Francisco, KCET/Los Angeles, and WNET/New York.[17]

In March 1990, when the film opened at the Castro Theater in San Francisco and was shown at the Pacific Film Archive in Berkeley, Peter Stack at the *San Francisco Chronicle* described "Tongues Untied," in his review of March 16, as "propelled at times by a beautifully articulated anger . . . a movie that is lucid and provocative, full of issues that force painful schizophrenic emotional struggles for black gays." Valerie Soe, writing in *Artweek* on March 1, called the program "a stunning and innovative piece which breaks cultural barriers, challenges formal conventions, and questions the meaning of gender roles, video and life in one big poetic, celebratory melange." Karl Bruce Knapper in the March *Bay Area Reporter* wrote he hadn't realized "just how starved I was for some validation and affirmation of my existence."

Marc Weiss, executive producer of *P.O.V.*, first saw the documentary on WNET in June 1990 as part of "Gay Pride Week" and soon contacted Riggs about submitting it to *P.O.V.* for a possible national PBS broadcast. Weiss recalled the program appealed to him because "it's an extraordinary and brilliant film" with "a perspective that is available nowhere else on television" and that "absolutely fits the core mission of *P.O.V.*, which is to provide a platform for voices which are unheard elsewhere on public television."[18]

Weiss asked Riggs if he would consider offering PBS stations an edited version of the program, eliminating a few of the words and images some station managers and programmers would find objectionable, but Riggs refused, feeling this would destroy the integrity of his work. Weiss urged Riggs to submit the program to *P.O.V.* with the understanding that it would not be cut or edited if it were accepted for broadcast by the series.[19]

The process for accepting "Tongues Untied" was like that for other *P.O.V.* programs, except that the editorial advisory committee gave more time and attention to it, knowing it would be controversial with station programmers and viewers because of nudity, language, and subject matter. It was one of the handful of documentaries that the committee of six representatives from PBS affiliate stations, six members of the independent producing community, and two PBS observers watched together in its entirety. When the committee met early in 1991, Weiss said a majority in the advisory group agreed fairly quickly that "Tongues Untied" should be on *P.O.V.*, even without cuts. Three representatives from the stations dissented.[20]

"A couple of them said, 'We would not be able to show this in our market, and therefore I cannot in good conscience support its broadcast.' But I think all of them said, 'It's a very powerful piece of film making.' Nobody said, 'What a terrible film this is,'" Weiss recalled.[21]

He said the question was not *whether* the program would be put on but *what would happen* when it was put on. Discussion then turned to how *P.O.V.* could make the strongest case for the program when everyone on the advisory committee knew some stations would not carry it because of the language and imagery, and that some interest groups and individuals would attack them for putting it on.[22]

Weiss also contacted Mable Haddock, executive producer of the National Black Programming Consortium (NBPC), and asked her organization to copresent the program to the system. The NBPC, created to promote programs by African-American producers, had awarded "Tongues Untied" the organization's top prize in 1990. Not only would the copresentation add to the program's credibility, but Haddock agreed to mobilize support for it in the black community. This proved a difficult and trying task.[23]

The National Black Programming Consortium had been deeply divided about giving "Tongues Untied" its top documentary award but awarded it ultimately because, according to Haddock, it was "well-produced, innovative, compelling, and because it looked at a part of the African-American community that hadn't been looked at before and had the potential to bring in new audiences." This early warning that the documentary would generate strong reactions in the African-American community put Haddock on alert, but she was not fully prepared for the homophobia she discovered there. When she approached ten major African-American organizations for endorsement quotes for the program, none of them wanted their names associated with it.[24]

"I've been a woman all my life. And a black all my life, but when people found out I was supporting this program—I thought I knew hate, I thought I knew sexism and racism, but the hate—you could just feel it. It was palpable. People would call me and say, 'You must be gay, too, that's why you're supporting this.' They had a real problem with my saying that we have a problem in our community about this," Haddock told me. "Everyone was saying—you know, what white people say about black people: 'I like them. Some of them are my best friends. I have them in my family, but I'm really uncomfortable.' . . . What we say to them is, 'You can come to my picnic as long as you don't flick your wrist,' so we have a very subtle way of putting people in their places."

The subject matter of "Tongues Untied" also opened old wounds in the African-American community, which made it harder for that community to support it. "It was really about domination and slavery," Haddock said. "During slavery, black folk were portrayed as sexually promiscuous, so that breeds a very conservative thinking about sex because we're reacting to what we've seen a dominant community thinking about our sexuality. We haven't been really free to explore sexuality because we were portrayed as the 'bitches,' the 'big bucks'—breeding—so it opens up that whole kind of thing. . . . The issues of sexuality in our community are really undealt with, and that includes homosexuality."

Haddock herself was not exactly thrilled that *P.O.V.* chose to showcase a work about black, gay homosexuality—its first major work by an African-American in the series—especially when so many other issues plagued the black community, such as crime, poverty, drugs, and lack of housing. But she accepted *P.O.V.*'s invitation to copresent because she believed the issues raised in the documentary needed to be dealt with in the black community. She felt that supporting its broadcast was the right thing to do.

Anticipating that some stations would have difficulty scheduling the program and that the program would be controversial, the editorial committee and *P.O.V.* executives discussed how to prepare stations for the broadcast. Weiss wanted the stations to give the program "a fair shot" and to understand why *P.O.V.* was scheduling it. He also knew that "if they show it, there are going to be people attacking them."[25] So Weiss, the *P.O.V.* staff, and the advisory committee formulated the following strategy to prepare the stations for "Tongues Untied" and to provide them with a defense of the program.

In March 1991, *P.O.V.* announced that "Tongues Untied" had been scheduled for a July 16 broadcast at 10 p.m., and on the advice of the advisory committee with its PBS observers, Weiss sent out letters to the stations letting them know about two "preview feeds" of the show—one in March and another in April—to make sure every programmer at the 281 stations in the system that carried *P.O.V.* had a chance to view the program, discuss it, and decide whether or not to carry it.

As a standard procedure, PBS also sent the stations a very detailed memo listing when and where swear words or nudity appeared.[26] "It's like a list of every 'objectionable' word that appears in the film as well as every image that might offend—'partial nudity here, two men kissing there,'" Weiss said.[27] The memo also listed where the word "fuck" was used, and how many times.

Weiss understood some program managers simply read the memo and rejected "Tongues Untied" on that basis without even previewing the film. He said many more of them not only watched the film but had station staff look at it, too. Some even invited their own community advisory committees or other select citizens to preview the film and discuss whether or not to air it.

In May, a month before the press realized what was happening, Weiss conducted an informal poll of the top fifty stations and found out that at least a dozen stations would not air the program.[28] Weiss said various reasons were given for this decision: Some stations believed their audiences would be offended by the program's language and nudity. Several program managers were personally offended by the documentary. Others liked it personally but felt they could not air it in their particular communities because they feared local pressure from the film's critics if they did.[29]

## The Press Coverage of *"Tongues Untied"*

The "Tongues Untied" controversy unfolded publicly when the daily newspapers began covering the story on June 8, 1991. Between that date and August 8, 1991, more than three hundred items appeared in the nation's daily newspapers, including feature stories by reporters, articles by syndicated columnists, interviews, editorials, and published letters to the editor. The specialized gay and conservative press also presented feature stories on the controversy, but coverage of the controversy in the African-American community was notably muted.[30]

Much of the debate about "Tongues Untied" took place in a decentralized fashion in the pages of local newspapers, where reporters interviewed station representatives and sought to characterize the debate with newsworthy leads. The chronology of the coverage fell into four basic phases: first, the breaking of the story in Florida and Georgia; second, the escalation of the controversy with the entry of Donald Wildmon's American Family Association and other organizations into the fray, as well as heightened media participation and coverage at the local level; third, the reviews around the time of the broadcast and the broadcast itself; and fourth, the fallout from the broadcast in the state of Georgia and for *P.O.V.*

### PHASE I: THE STORY BREAKS

Paul Lomartire, staff writer and television critic at the *Palm Beach Post*, wrote the first feature story. It contained information that shaped subsequent accounts. With the headline "Explicit PBS Film on Black Gays Could Reignite NEA Controversy," Lomartire's June 8 article was also among those that soon reached the desk of the Reverend Donald Wildmon. The article summarized the film and opened with a newsworthy angle: that "Tongues Untied" might be the next battleground over NEA funding of the arts because *P.O.V.* and Marlon Riggs were both recipients of NEA funds, and because the program depicted black, gay life. Lomartire's story gained wide exposure when it was carried in other newspapers syndicated through the *New York Times* wire service and Cox News Service.

Lomartire recalled first hearing about "Tongues Untied" in May, when he received a phone call from a programmer at WXEL/Channel 42 in Florida's West Palm Beach. Having reviewed other *P.O.V.* programs, the reporter was able to obtain a preview cassette from the series. After viewing the program, he interviewed Marlon Riggs and also Marc Weiss, who told him he was "blown away" by "Tongues Untied" when he saw it on WNET/New York the previous year. "It is probably the riskiest of all the films we've shown," he said to Lomartire. "It's certainly risky in the current climate given last year's attacks on the National Endowment for the Arts. And in terms of content, gay men, which frequently have been the target of the right, sure it's something that's risky to some degree. And we are funded by the NEA. This season it's $250,000 (of the total $1.1 million *P.O.V.* budget.)"[31]

When Lomartire learned from Weiss that the film was funded in part by the NEA, he confirmed this with the endowment, and he realized the film could be "the next battlefield for funding." His telephone call was the first to alert the NEA public relations department to the matter.[32]

"That was basic reporting," Lomartire recalled. "If I had not gotten a call from the local station and I had not seen it and the NEA funding wasn't a part of it, I'm not sure I would have written about it at all."[33]

Then the reporter began calling stations around the country to find out if they planned to carry the documentary. His article quoted unnamed public television programmers who described the work as "abrasive" and "reprehensible," as well as several others (identified by name) who were refusing to air the film. The story about the divisions among public television stations took shape.

Lomartire described the program as containing "sexual street language rarely heard on television, as well as full frontal nudity and drawings of male genitals."[34] He reported that WPBT/Miami and WXEL/West Palm Beach had agreed to broadcast the documentary, and he said WPBT did so "without any internal debate."[35]

Lomartire wanted Riggs to have a chance to respond to the station critics, so he asked Riggs why he refused to allow *P.O.V.* to offer an edited version to the stations.[36] "If you blipped and beeped you'd have blips and beeps from the beginning to the very end," Riggs explained. "It defeats the purpose and places us again within that closeted, silent, shameful space that too many gay men and lesbians, black and otherwise, inhabit in this society."[37] Riggs told Lomartire the editing would simply have sanitized the film's message for a predominately white TV audience, and he didn't want to do that.[38]

Lomartire asked Riggs about the public television programmers who told him the film "violates community standards." Introducing a theme that was heard again and again in the coming months, Riggs responded, "Whose community? When people say community standards won't abide by such a work, they're reflecting their myth of what that community is about and not the tremendously diverse community as it exists." As for the sexual images, nudity, and language, which some programmers found "too blunt," Riggs told

Lomartire, "We still remain very adolescent as a nation about how we confront and understand and attempt to analyze sexuality. We prefer our myths. We prefer romantic illusions and we prefer silence." That silence, he said, perpetuates "the hatred and loathing that the majority culture feels" toward gay men and lesbians.[39]

Lomartire also quoted programmers from Wichita, Milwaukee, and Nashville who rejected the program, citing local economic pressures and legal concerns about airing "pornography" or "indecent programming." One felt this was a no-win situation and was surprised PBS and *P.O.V.* thought "they could get away with putting that show on across the country." Another said, "Sure, PBS sends out a nice packet saying this is why we think it should be on the air, but that doesn't cut it with the person who calls and says, 'Never again will I support your station with money or anything else.'"[40]

Lomartire told me his editors rarely allow a story to run fifty-five column inches, and he fought to keep Riggs's quotes from being edited down or deleted.[41] While he wanted to be fair and be sure the film maker's position was in the text, he said his editors were attracted to the story because it was, potentially, a "hot story." Lomartire also noted the six weeks between his story and the July 16 airdate gave critics of the program time to organize.[42]

A second article published in the South picked up on Lomartire's themes. Gary Yandel at the *Atlanta Constitution* reported his local station's decision to broadcast the program on July 16. Like Lomartire, Yandel framed his article in terms of the film becoming another controversy about NEA funding because it received NEA funds and contained sexually explicit language and images.

Yandel quoted spokesperson Caroline Kowalski of Atlanta's public television station, who said she was sure the program would irritate some people, but that it wasn't her station's job to be a moral censor. "It's our job to present films and TV programs that depict the wide set of perspectives and to alert people to the fact that it is very hard stuff and definitely not suited to children and adolescents. They should use their own discretion. If they're offended by it, turn it off."[43]

On June 13, news began to spread of a revolt within the public television ranks when articles appeared announcing that at least seventeen of the top fifty public television stations had decided not to broadcast "Tongues Untied" and that eleven more were planning to air it on a delayed basis.

Among those that decided not to broadcast the program were stations in Houston, Milwaukee, Denver, Portland (Oregon), Memphis, Nashville, Dayton, Kansas City, Oklahoma City, Norfolk, and South Carolina Educational

Television, whose program manager, Mimi Wortham-Brown, explained, "We think a majority of our audience would find the show unacceptable."[44]

Stations in Los Angeles, where "Tongues Untied" had aired the previous year, and the Cleveland and Chicago stations scheduled the program at 11 p.m.—an hour later than its PBS feed—while Miami and Seattle chose to bury the show in the middle of the night, at 1 a.m. and 3 a.m., respectively.

Weiss and then-director of communications Ellen Schneider put forth *P.O.V.*'s message that "Tongues Untied" was part of public television's mission. Weiss defended the program in the news reports. "The ability for a filmmaker to be both angry, poetic and humorous is very unusual. It raises fundamental questions, not just about society's attitude toward blacks and gays, but numerous questions about people's search for identity. There's no way we couldn't show it."[45]

### PHASE 2: THE ESCALATION OF THE CONTROVERSY

THE AMERICAN FAMILY ASSOCIATION VERSUS THE NEA AND PBS. The controversy entered a new phase when the Reverend Donald Wildmon, president and founder of the Tupelo, Mississippi–based American Family Association, attacked the program as part of his ongoing campaign against the NEA. Wildmon had read the earlier newspaper articles on the program but had not viewed it. "All I know is what I've read about it," he told the *New York Post*.[46] The reverend based his knowledge of the program on descriptions, specifically Lomartire's, that appeared in newspapers. On June 20, Wildmon sent out a press release criticizing the film and condemning the NEA for funding it.[47]

"For two years most of the American public have known of the debate over some kinds of art being funded with tax dollars by the NEA," said Wildmon in his press release. "However the number of taxpayers who have been able to actually see any of the art in question has been extremely small." He announced PBS would broadcast "Tongues Untied," produced by "a black homosexual," on July 16 and urged Americans to watch the film "and see for themselves how their tax dollars are being spent."[48]

On June 21, the press reported that Wildmon denounced the documentary for its "sexual street language rarely heard on television, as well as full frontal nudity and drawings of male genitals." While admitting he had not seen the film, he criticized it, using Lomartire's one-sentence description of the program verbatim. Wildmon also sent word out about "Tongues Untied" to association members through the *American Family Association Journal*, his organization's monthly newsletter with an estimated circulation of 325,000.[49]

When Wildmon began to use "Tongues Untied" as a weapon in his ongoing war with the National Endowment for the Arts, the NEA, PBS, the advocacy groups People for the American Way and FAIR, and Marlon Riggs responded immediately. The NEA battle was spilling over into public television, and its defenders were ready.

The NEA fired off a statement June 20—the same day as the American Family Association press release—citing the millions of Americans who have daily access to endowment-sponsored productions and pointing out that only a handful of its 90,000 grants had become controversial in the endowment's first twenty-five years. The press release praised "Tongues Untied" for exploring "a contemporary issue in a meaningful way" and cited the film's "critical acclaim" by listing its awards.

People for the American Way, founded by Norman Lear, jumped to defend the show against Wildmon and other conservative critics of "free expression." Arthur J. Kropp, president of the 290,000-member advocacy organization, called Wildmon "a power hungry demagogue" who is trying to "take the choice away from the American public so he can be the arbiter of taste in this country."[50]

"Don Wildmon clearly thinks the American public is going to reject this film, and the NEA with it," Kropp said in his widely quoted press release. "What Don Wildmon is going to learn is that the American public is a good deal more open-minded than he is."[51]

PBS's Mary Jane McKinven, who was then working in PBS corporate relations, defended the program as "a response to public broadcasting's mandate to reflect the diversity of American society, including points of view rarely seen on television." Like the film's other defenders, she cited the program's "critical acclaim" and told reporters a viewer advisory would precede the film.[52]

Marlon Riggs also sent out a letter to his supporters urging them to contact PBS and their local affiliates and give them this message: that public television should "demonstrate leadership in becoming a forum for *enlightened* public discussion on questions of racial/sexual identity," that it should "take risks" even if this meant offending the mainstream, and that its mission was "to be an alternative to commercial television, not an imitator, and thus to honestly represent America's rich cultural, political, and not least, sexual diversity."[53]

Right after the first volley from the American Family Association, *P.O.V.* executives strategized privately about "how to get out front" in framing the debate. They had the advantage of having seen the film, and most of its non-public-television critics had not. Ellen Schneider predicted viewers would applaud the chance to learn "about issues they know nothing about: homophobia

within the black community and racism within the gay community."[54] Weiss
explained later that *P.O.V.* "kept trying to shift the debate over to what are
the American values that justify putting a show like this on the air."[55]

The lines in the sand were now drawn. While *P.O.V.*'s Marc Weiss and
Ellen Schneider and PBS's Mary Jane McKinven defended *P.O.V.* and affirmed
the award-winning film, which was, in Schneider's words, "an important example of what point-of-view filmmaking is all about," many public television
station managers and the Reverend Donald Wildmon and his supporters saw
it as an obscene work that flew in the face of "community standards" and
"decency."[56]

As stations' decisions to air or not air "Tongues Untied" became public,
the National Endowment for the Arts issued a strong public endorsement of
the documentary on June 26 and confirmed that the grants for both *P.O.V.*
and Marlon Riggs's proposal had been approved by the chairman of the NEA,
John Frohnmayer. FAIR, the media watchdog group, issued a statement criticizing the public television stations for refusing to air it.[57]

Two days later on June 28, the *Washington Times* reported Reverend
Wildmon planned to send letters to "every senator and congressman," urging
them to watch the program when it aired on Washington, D.C., stations
WETA and WHMM on July 16. The reporter pointed out that a House hearing on whether to reauthorize funding for the Corporation for Public Broadcasting was scheduled for July 17, the day after the broadcast of "Tongues
Untied." This underscored how the debate over public funding for the arts
now included the debate over public funding for public television.

Representative Matthew Rinaldo (R-New Jersey), the ranking Republican who sat on the telecommunications and finance subcommittee, said he
was "outraged" by press reports on the program's content and predicted the
show "could well raise an issue during consideration of legislation to reauthorize the Corporation for Public Broadcasting."[58] This was music to Donald
Wildmon's ears as he turned his attention to public television: "We're notic-
ing that they are showing an inordinately high number of programs dealing
with homosexuality. . . . We do not think the government should be endors-
ing the homosexual lifestyle."[59]

Riggs was unavailable for comment during the first phase of the controversy because he was in Ireland attending INPUT, an international public television conference where "Tongues Untied" was being screened, but once he
was back home in Oakland, California, at the end of June, he was again available for telephone interviews with the press.

And so Marlon Riggs, *P.O.V.* executives Marc Weiss and Ellen Schneider, and PBS's Mary Jane McKinven continued their efforts to defend the film as consistent with public television's mission while several station managers dissented and hostile voices in Congress and the conservative religious community tried to use "Tongues Untied" to challenge public funding for the arts and public television.

THE LOCAL ANGLES. By the end of June, the debate about "Tongues Untied" was taking place among interested citizens in their communities, in the pages of local newspapers, and in most public television stations all over the country. Like the public television system, the conversation was decentralized. The local stations became the focal point where critics and supporters of "Tongues Untied" converged. They also became the place where programmers and station managers chose either to reaffirm public television's commitment to diversity or to yield to other obligations.

Newspaper reporters followed up on the story in their areas by interviewing station managers or programmers at their local public television affiliates. Some wrote features about how the decisions were made and how the local community reacted to them.

The press coverage of "Tongues Untied," both local and national, led from two basic angles: the attacks on the program's NEA funding by Donald Wildmon, and the number of stations refusing to carry it.[60]

The station managers and programmers who chose to reject the program consistently cited its sexual and racial language, visual imagery taken from pornographic magazines, the belief that the film was "patently offensive" for their communities and "inappropriate for broadcasting into the home." Some pointed out that certain words in the program—such as the "f-word"—couldn't even be printed in the newspaper, and decried the show as "poorly produced." Even while they refused to broadcast the show, some, like Nebraska Educational Television, sought a middle ground by inviting members of the community to see the program at their stations at special screenings.

Station managers and programmers who scheduled the program argued that the documentary was part of public television's mandate to be an alternative and to air perspectives not commonly heard elsewhere. Some advised those likely to be offended by the program to simply "switch the dial."

The stations' responses as portrayed in the press spanned a wide spectrum of opinion. On one end were station executives, like Jack Dominic, the senior vice president of the Cincinnati station, who defended the decision to air the program, citing a reluctance to be a "censor." On the other end were those who felt ambushed by *P.O.V.* and PBS's decision to send them a

program that violated their communities' standards for decency. In Dominic's
words:

> It's not for me or our station to be deciding what people watch and
> don't watch. That isn't to say that we would run absolutely anything
> that came along. I looked at the program. Is it difficult to watch? Yes.
> Does it have some very hard-hitting material? Yes. Would I want my
> six-year-old child to watch it? No. On the other hand, should it have
> a forum? Yes. And one of our purposes is to provide a forum for a
> variety of different points of view, whether we agree or disagree with
> them. If we're going to air the series, then darn it, we're going to air
> the series, and we're not going to start to pick and choose based on
> what we dislike or like or what the audience can handle. We will air it
> at 10 p.m. and there is an on/off switch on the TV set. One of the
> things that public TV does is allow [viewers] to get a window on what
> exists and it's not always what we would like to exist, but we're better
> citizens for it because we know they exist.[61]

Fred Flaxman, vice president and general manager of Southern Oregon
Public Television in Medford, expressed the opposite view. In a letter to the
editor, he defended his decision not to air "Tongues Untied" because the "repeated use of vulgar words and frontal nudity violates the sense of decency
and good taste" in his community. He wondered if his critics would be upset
if he refused to televise castration, diarrhea, or close-ups of vomiting or def-
ecating. "Would that be called 'censorship' too?" he asked. Flaxman said he
had to draw the line and resented being called a "censor." He aimed his anger at PBS: "Any network that distributes a program that is rejected by 200
of its affiliates is doing something wrong. Wasting our valuable time, for one
thing. Wasting our money for another. Embarrassing us from coast to coast.
Losing vital public financial support. Alienating countless viewers in those
communities that choose to run the program. . . . It is time that PBS adhered
to some broadcast standards of its own."[62]

Other broadcasters, such as Tom Dvorak, program manager at the Milwaukee station, told reporters the film "doesn't really even help the gays and
lesbians in defending their rights because it's presented in such an offensive
manner. A viewer in a general audience would be totally offended."[63] Maynard
Orme, president of KOAP in Portland, categorized much of the film as "pornography" and explained, "This film does not treat black homosexuals in a
dignified way—they treat each other like slaves, like a meat market."[64] Quotes
like these gave ammunition to the film's critics.

When confronted with these reactions by reporters, Weiss acknowledged
the film "makes some people uncomfortable" but defended the film as "a very

strong piece" about an important subject. Like Weiss, Ellen Schneider understood that the program put stations in "a difficult position," but stressed to reporters that "challenging programming" that expresses alternatives views is what *P.O.V.* and public television are all about. "I'm disappointed that some individuals feel that's not the mission of public television, and that audiences can't themselves make up their own minds about what they want to watch. . . . If people would see the film, they'd understand that it's not about dirty words, not about body parts: It's a search for identity."[65]

Leaders in the gay community in Milwaukee and other cities where the PBS affiliates chose not to air "Tongues Untied" called on gays and lesbians to withhold contributions to the stations.[66]

Meanwhile, stations that rejected the program tried different ways to handle it in their communities. KOAP/Portland made plans to set up a private screening for viewers who wanted to see it. At KUHT/Houston, where the general manager said language would be a problem with his audience, a local art museum decided to show it independently of the station.

Occasionally, reporters told how their local stations had involved community advisers in their decisions. For example, a reporter at the *St. Petersburg Times* reported that three women and one man who served on the community advisory board of WEDU/Tampa Bay had watched the film and decided unanimously that it was "patently offensive for this community." They advised the new station manager, Stephen Rogers, against airing it.[67] He complied with their recommendation.

Newspapers throughout the country wrote articles in direct reponse to their local stations' decisions about broadcasting the program. For example:

*In Maine*, the statewide Maine Public Broadcasting declined to air the program. The *Maine Times* published a feature article, "You Can't Say That on Television," and reprinted Essex Hemphill's poem "Nowwethinkaswefuck." According to Robert Gardiner, general manager of WCBB/Lewiston, the word "fuck" was spoken thirty-four times. "It's not the subject matter at all. It's the profanity," he told the *Maine Times*. "I'm mad at the *P.O.V.* series producers for not working with Marlon Riggs to make it acceptable."[68]

The article included *P.O.V.*'s response. Ellen Schneider stressed, as in many other interviews, that *P.O.V.* accepted the program on Riggs's condition that it air uncut, and that "public television should be taking a leadership role in promoting diversity and tolerance. Ultimately, Marlon Riggs's film is about tolerance, understanding and learning to live with differences. Television is an excellent forum for this film. Hatred endures because of a simple lack of communication."

*In Detroit*, the *Metro Times* created a forum for Marlon Riggs and Robert F.

Larson, general manager of WTVS/Detroit, who refused to air the program. Riggs wrote an open letter to Larson accusing the station manager of "censorship" for refusing to air "Tongues Untied." Larson wrote a response, and the clash between the two articulated the conflicting themes.

When he learned WTVS refused to broadcast "Tongues Untied," Riggs described it as "yet another sad example of public television's knee-jerk avoidance of controversial programming." He accused the station of becoming an accomplice in a form of repression—"silencing not just my voice but the voices and visions of diverse, nationwide communities."[69]

Larson replied that WTVS rejected his program because "many of the words and images" were "unacceptable for broadcast television." He was exercising his "responsibility as a steward of the signal."[70]

In Seattle, the local affiliate, KCTS, chose to broadcast "Tongues Untied" at 3 a.m. The Seattle Post-Intelligencer did a feature about how the station arrived at its decision.[71] The program manager at KCTS had screened the show with selected staff, including some gay staff. They had another screening with fifteen people from outside the station, many of whom were African-American and several of whom were gay men.

Then-station manager Tom Howe objected to the language but approved airing the program at 3 a.m. because he felt it would be a time "when it was least likely to be inadvertently seen."[72]

A prominent Seattle black minister worried the film would make the public malign black males more than they already do, but he did not want to censor it. A black gay man felt affirmed by the program. A black KCTS board member believed the language and nudity were too explicit for KCTS and felt the show was degrading to African-American men. He opposed broadcasting the program and thought the 3 a.m. time-slot was "a reasonable compromise." A public radio news host empathized that a community-supported station wouldn't want to run the risk of having viewers cancel their subscriptions. One of the two KCTS advisory board members thought the program was unprofessional and amateurish and should be rejected on those grounds. But the other found it very rewarding and moving; she suggested it be shown at 10 p.m. with a panel discussion and believed not only that the station would be "courageous" to show it, but also that viewers would learn from it. A gay leader said the program was a "golden opportunity" for the station to make a progressive step forward—although the step was quite tiny since the show would air at 3 a.m. A KCTS producer did not like it because women were referred to as "bitch" and "ho," and as a black woman, she was bothered because "here was another dysfunctional black male on television." The airtime was, for her, a good compromise. A black gay artist said seeing the film "was like Christmas," affirming of his reality and "incredibly positive."[73]

In addition to articles and letters in the newspapers, the controversy generated editorials and columns. Journalists expressed viewpoints ranging from outrage at stations for "censoring" the program, reprimanding them for abandoning public television's mission, to those who described the program and dutifully reported the stations' reasons for not broadcasting it, citing "community standards" and "indecency" charges, occasionally mentioning subscribers. In general, the reporters echoed the framing of the controversy as put forth by the groups involved in it: "free speech/censorship" versus "community standards/indecency."

Steve Bornfeld of the *Times Union* in Albany, New York, applauded WMHT's decision to air the program as "a responsible move under the right circumstances." He wrote that every programmer who backs away from the documentary abdicates his or her responsibility to provide viewers with "enlightened and provocative fare."[74] David Zurawik of the *Baltimore Sun* applauded *P.O.V.* for "stirring things up and making people think."[75]

An editorial in the *Chattanooga News-Free Press* condemned the NEA for "using your federal tax money to finance indecency," PBS for disseminating "obscenity," and WTCI/Chattanooga for scheduling "the obnoxious program."[76]

In an editorial titled "Prim Public TV," the *Charleston Gazette* accused the two public stations, Morgantown and Charleston-Huntington in West Virginia, of "becoming public censors," condemning those stations for "taking away viewers' right to decide what they'll watch."[77]

Not all the newspaper coverage framed the controversy over "Tongues Untied" as about censorship, free expression, or obscenity. Peggy McGlone of New Jersey's *Star-Ledger* suggested that *P.O.V.* "values controversy for its own sake" and interpreted the refusal of stations to carry the program "as a sign of success" that the work is too challenging for many of its outlets. She depicted the program as "disjointed," "offensively on the attack," and "held together by anger and self-pity." She argued it was a case where a program's politics had been mistaken for artistry, and the controversy about it had upstaged the work.[78]

Several papers gave Riggs an opportunity to defend his work by publishing interviews with him. Riggs told John Martin of the *Providence Journal-Bulletin* that he wasn't surprised by the public reaction to the film because the United States has historically been "hysterical about sexuality."

He also answered the "community standards" argument made by programmers to reject his program. "There's no one 'community' in any community," he said. "There are gay, lesbian and bisexual people everywhere you go. When (broadcasters) claim to be upholding a community standard, it is a standard of who they are, not, in fact, of the community they serve."

As for the use of "street language," Riggs said that language is spoken everywhere in American life, "from the bedroom to the board room," in the White House, and even at public television stations. He said many public broadcasters are on "the wrong side of history" by choosing to suppress and censor rather than allow frank and full discussion around the issues of being black and gay.[79]

In USA Today, Riggs asked, "How often has America become hysterical about honest explorations about sexuality?"[80]

The Atlanta Constitution carried an article Riggs wrote responding to criticisms of the film. He deplored the film's detractors, who damned the film without seeing it and who sought, in his words, "to silence any expression that challenged their authority and status in society." He said the "community standard" his critics wanted to defend was their own "heterosexist, male and largely (though not exclusively) white."[81]

PHASE 3: THE NATIONAL PRESS AND THE BROADCAST

As the July 16 broadcast approached, national television reviewers and columnists weighed in on the program and the controversy around it. Reviews in the Washington Post and the New York Times generally praised "Tongues Untied." All the articles referred to the Wildmon attack, most mentioned that Marlon Riggs was HIV-positive, and indicated that a number of PBS affiliates had refused to air the program.

The national critics echoed many of the themes of local critics throughout the country. The difference was that their reviews were syndicated more widely, with the exception of Paul Lomartire's.

TV critic Howard Rosenberg of the Los Angeles Times said the broadcast of "Tongues Untied" on PBS reminded him of "the way a submarine periscope surfaces amid heavy battleships in enemy waters." He pointed out The Love Boat had more sex and the daily soaps were more "sizzling." The main difference was that the touching in "Tongues Untied" was between men. "The film isn't pornographic," Rosenberg wrote, "the charge is." He put stations that refused to air the program on "the wimp list" and wrote that the list affirms a depressing irony inside public television: that many inside the public television system do not know that "its mandate is to challenge viewers, not sedate them.[82]

James Kilpatrick, columnist for Universal Press Syndicate, condemned the NEA for funding "grossly offensive 'art'" like "Tongues Untied." Relying on a description of the film by the editors of the conservative publication *Human Events*, who described the film as containing "unimaginable foul language, racial slurs, homosexual lovers kissing and full frontal nudity," Kilpatrick reprimanded John Frohnmayer, NEA chairman. "The producer of 'Tongues Untied' has every right to make his film," he said, but he doesn't have the right to make it "at public expense."[83]

Walter Goodman of the *New York Times* defended Riggs's use of street lingo, nudity, and love scenes. "If ever there was a program where such elements are justified, this is it." He said Riggs "tends to overdo" and that some of his romantic imagery is silly but at the same time "innocently touching." He mentioned Riggs was HIV-positive and the flap with Donald Wildmon and the NEA.[84]

Valerie Helmbreck of the Gannett News Service described the program as "visually moving" but the poetry as "grating, sort of like the high-pitched whine they put on the telephone to let you know it's off the hook." She said Riggs "strives for understanding through knowledge," and that he makes "a leap of faith that his audience will be able to handle the information."[85]

Jon Burlingame of the United Feature Syndicate said the program was "daring in the context of mainstream broadcast television," but he suspected it would not interest viewers outside Riggs's original, intended audience of black, gay men.[86]

As noted earlier, many of the stations that broadcast the program did so on a delayed basis, ranging from 11 p.m. to 3 a.m. Some stations, like WNIT in South Bend, Indiana, refused to air the program but invited interested viewers to attend a special screening of the show at the station's studio.[87] Others, like WNEO-WEAO in Kent, Ohio, ran the program with a "viewer warning" across the bottom of the screen during the broadcast.[88] Georgia Public Television aired "Tongues Untied" at 11 p.m., July 21, with an added cautionary announcement before and after the program, and a "viewer discretion" crawl that appeared every five minutes during the broadcast. The program prompted 926 phone calls and 349 letters.[89] The Dallas station aired the program at 11 p.m. on July 16 and encouraged callers to express their views by writing letters to be forwarded to *P.O.V.*[90]

In the end, a little more than 60 percent of the nation's viewers—those reached by the 174 PBS stations of the 284 who normally carry *P.O.V.*—had an opportunity to see "Tongues Untied."[91]

### PHASE 4: THE FALLOUT

The immediate fallout from the program in the state of Georgia came a few months after the broadcast when the state legislature threatened to cut its

funding to Georgia Public Television in retaliation for the system's broadcast
of the program. The crisis was triggered by the Georgia Council on Moral and
Civic Concerns, a conservative Baptist organization, which urged the faith-
ful to put notices in their denominational newsletters to protest the broadcast. Baptists were advised to complain to GPTV's board of directors and to
tell their state senator and representative that taxpayer money should not be
going toward programs they found offensive.[92]

On August 27, Dr. J. Emmett Henderson, executive director of the Georgia Council on Moral and Civic Concerns, wrote his own letters to members
of the Georgia state legislature protesting Georgia Public Television's broadcast of "Tongues Untied." The letters cited the "over $6 million" state con-
tribution to GPTV and urged members of the House and Senate "to
communicate with the management of GPTV to discourage the showing of
this or any similar film that promotes immorality, perversion and attacks the
religious beliefs of any citizen."[93]

On October 17, GPTV executive Richard Ottinger faced an angry chorus of legislators when he was summoned—with a few hours' notice—to a
meeting of the House Appropriations Budget Subcommittee to answer for his
decision to broadcast "Tongues Untied." The former football coach listened
to Terry Coleman, the chairman of this subcommittee, tell him that he
"screwed up" and displayed "poor judgment" by airing the show.[94] "We have
heard from our constituents," the chairman said. "This [program] is contrary
to the social mores of this state."[95]

Other House leaders, like House Majority Leader Larry Walker, asked
Ottinger, "Do you think this film reflects community standards in this state?
What about cannibalism? Do you think that needs to be shown?" House
Speaker Tom Murphy accused Ottinger of having "abandoned" the philoso-
phy of GPTV as "family-oriented."

The House budget subcommittee was to allocate $6.1 million to GPTV
for the next year, which amounted to 42 percent of the total budget of the
state's public television system. A cut in those funds would have been,
in Ottinger's words, "devastating." But Ottinger defended his decision to
air "Tongues Untied" by arguing that public television has a duty to reflect
the diversity of the society. As he told the Macon Telegraph, "This gave people
a choice, if they were interested, to learn something about that part of our
population."[96]

Ottinger also apologized for offending hundreds of people. He promised
to try harder to "make sure that community tastes and standards are not violated." He said a slight majority of calls about the program were favorable—

470 supported the decision to air it, while 456 opposed the decision. Of the 320 letters he received, 92 percent condemned the decision to broadcast the program, but he said most of those letters appeared to have arisen from an organized campaign, and most of the writers said they had not seen the program.[97]

House Speaker Pro Tem Jack Connell (D-Augusta) threatened to cut the state's funding if GPTV departed again from "family" programming by having more programs like "Tongues Untied." "In my opinion, the consensus of the committee was if they [GPTV] continue that [shows like "Tongues Untied"], they may find their funding in jeopardy."[98]

In the end, Georgia Public Television did not get its funding cut in 1991. And three years later, Ottinger was honored by the Corporation for Public Broadcasting with a special "Lifetime Achievement Award." He was only the second recipient of this award in CPB's twenty-five-year history.[99]

Unlike the funders of GPTV, those of *P.O.V.* gave the series votes of confidence. New grants came in from the National Endowment for the Arts ($250,000) and the John D. and Catherine T. MacArthur Foundation ($1.65 million), which renewed its funding for three years.

The FCC received "substantiated" indecency complaints against three public television stations that broadcast the program on July 16. The complaints were filed against WFYI in Indianapolis, WGVU in Grand Rapids, Michigan, and WGVK, its satellite station in Kalamazoo. Both of the people filing the complaints—John Price, an attorney representing anti-indecency groups, and Irv Bos, who said he had been involved in antipornography efforts—were appalled by the language. Price charged WFYI with violating the Communications Act. Bos said the program was "obscene," "terribly anti-black," the subject matter was "totally out of line," and the program "made me sick." He said public television was supposed to be educational, but that this program "was far from educational."[100]

The magazine *Human Events* decried 1991 as "a disappointing year for conservatives." Editors reported that an amendment to cut the NEA budget by 5 percent sponsored by Representative Cliff Stearns (R-Florida) lost narrowly by a vote of 228 to 196 in the House, and an earlier bill to abolish the NEA was defeated 361 to 66. Efforts were now directed at trimming the NEA budget in the Senate Appropriations Committee in mid-July.

The American Family Association, in conjunction with Senator Jesse Helms and his supporters, failed to cut funding for public broadcasting in the spring of 1992, even though they cited "Tongues Untied" as an example of public television's "indecent" programming. But they did succeed in passing guidelines for the broadcasting of so-called indecent programs: twenty-four-hour public television stations could broadcast such programs only between midnight and 6 a.m., and those stations that shut down at 12 a.m. had to air them after 10 p.m.

This was just the beginning. Soon after the Republican Party gained control of both houses of Congress in 1994, House Speaker Newt Gingrich endorsed the efforts of the Christian Coalition and other conservative groups to eliminate the funding arm of public television and radio, the Corporation for Public Broadcasting.[101] In 1995, congressional efforts to defund and privatize public broadcasting culminated in bills to phase out government funding altogether. Among the reasons for this action, Senator Larry Pressler (R-South Dakota), chairman of the Senate Commerce, Science, and Transportation Committee, and Jack Fields (R-Texas), chairman of the House Telecommunications Subcommittee, cited the failure of PBS's National Programming Service to ensure "balanced coverage" of controversial issues.

The threat to government funding for public television shook the system at its foundation as station managers, series editors, and the national PBS and CPB leadership cobbled together answers to probing questions about alleged bias and lack of balance in public affairs programming, programming decision procedures, allocation of funds, bias in oversight committees, and personnel practices. The high profile of the public broadcasting bill provided a forum for interest groups and individuals to voice concerns to the body that held the government purse strings, and it ensured that the conservative critiques of programming and financing would be taken seriously by the public television community. It also served as a clarion call to public television's defenders, who wrote letters and rallied to the defense of the system, citing the value of its signature series: *Sesame Street, Nova,* and *Nature.*

## Analysis of the Controversy

### THE CHALLENGE POSED BY THE SUBJECT MATTER

"Tongues Untied" was the cutting edge of the black gay rights movement on public television, unfiltered by middle-class niceties associated with sympathetic, human tragedy stories on gays with AIDS who were usually white. The film presented a challenge to programmers because it didn't fit that mold. "Tongues Untied" celebrated black, gay love and sexuality without shame. Close-ups of hands on bodies, men kissing, and erotic poetry framed images and words of love and passion to an undifferentiated public, a view into a world unknown to most heterosexuals and to white gays.

The debate over "Tongues Untied" wasn't overtly about homophobia; it was about change. "Community standards" change as social attitudes change. It was a scene from an ongoing struggle between the black gays and a mixed camp of Americans: the proponents of "traditional family values" as understood by the American Family Association and Christian conservatives, as well as others who were offended by nudity and language. It was part of a culture war. It was the first—and so far the *only*—program about the experience of being black and gay on public television.

The debate was de facto a litmus test on homosexuality. What some saw as "an aberrant lifestyle," others saw as a predetermined, genetic reality that could no more be changed than the color of one's skin. Each position led down a different path—one toward banning the program as a way to "contain" the spread of homosexuality, and the other toward acceptance of black gays as any other marginalized minority. Like Jews, blacks, communists, and others before them, the gay movement was stigmatized by the right wing in a culture war.

THE IMPACT ON PUBLIC TELEVISION PROGRAMMERS AND MANAGERS
"Tongues Untied" challenged programmers and managers to reexamine their definition of and commitment to the mission of public television as a service reflecting the diversity of U.S. society. How they handled that program measured their courage as programmers in the face of their perception of their communities' reactions, and also their commitment to the public television ideal as a forum for voices unheard elsewhere, and their willingness to allow a producer like Riggs to define his own self-image.

The explanations for the programming decisions not to broadcast echo the rationale of commercial stations, where community popularity and reaching the widest possible audience are the primary business. But public television is supposed to be different. PBS is supposed to take risks and offer viewers alternative glimpses of reality unseen elsewhere on the television screen. Refusing to broadcast a program because it lacks wide audience appeal defeats the purpose of public television.

Almost a year after the broadcast of "Tongues Untied," Jennifer Lawson, PBS vice president of programming, defended "Tongues Untied" before irate station managers at the 1992 PBS annual meeting in San Francisco. "PBS is not responsible for homophobia or racism," she told them. Most of a morning's general session was devoted to discussing "Tongues Untied." Public broadcasters fingered the press for putting them in an awkward position by asking if they were airing the show when they had not yet decided what to do. One station manager said the chairman of his station board ordered him not to broadcast "Tongues Untied" because it would make it too hard for him to raise money in the corporate sector. A station producer defended airing the program because "that's what diversity is all about." An African-American producer looked around the room and asked, "How can we talk about diversity when most of us here are white, middle-class, and male?" Another bemoaned a shortage of gay films on public television so that when "Tongues Untied" came around, viewers weren't ready for it because they weren't familiar with the gay community.

## PUBLIC TELEVISION'S IDENTITY CRISIS

The "Tongues Untied" case points to a crisis within public television over its reason for existence and role in society. The debate about it invited soul-searching. Public television station managers were openly divided over whether to air the program. Those who were defiant about not broadcasting the show saw the controversy as an opportunity to disagree with PBS and side with the program's critics in their communities. Some seemed confused about their responsibilities to their communities, especially when they saw their choice between being a "pornographer" or a "censor."[102]

As Patricia Aufderheide observed in her thoughtful article on the press coverage of "Tongues Untied," newspaper reporters typically "projected a welter of obligations onto the system but didn't use the controversy to probe the reasons for public television's various and sometimes contradictory obligations."[103]

The press, however, had a pivotal role in the controversy by frequently framing the debate in terms of public television's mission to take risks. Press accounts often quoted the argument of the documentary's advocates, who relentlessly and consistently framed the work as part of public television's mission.

Overall, the coverage expanded the debate about the mission of public television to a general audience, exposed the rifts among station managers about public television's proper role in society, and revealed the fragile economic dependence of stations on their communities.

## FINAL THOUGHTS

Marlon Riggs saw "Tongues Untied" as a documentary that "tries to undo the legacy of silence about black gay life. It affirms who we are, what our existence is in all of its diversities, and that we are of great value to our community and ourselves. What I wanted to do with 'Tongues Untied' was to start the dialogue, and preserve our lives in a form that people can see and address, not only now, but in years to come. People will see that there was a vibrant black gay community in these United States in 1989."[104]

For social movements that haven't reached a threshold of credibility in the mainstream media, being heard and defining one's image on one's own terms is a political act. This is what Riggs did. Knowing that silence and invisibility walk hand-in-hand, Riggs made a film where he took an active role in shaping the description of the black, gay experience. He wasn't "polite," and he didn't apologize.

For *P.O.V.* and independent producers like Marlon Riggs, the case showed the challenges of using the medium to bring marginal perspectives to a diverse public over public television. The controversy was about who was going to define the black, gay experience for the viewing public and allow it to be seen.

The discussion about "Tongues Untied" was not a direct discussion about the experience of being black and gay in America any more than the debate about "Dark Circle" was about the nuclear weapons industry. The press and internal public television debate about "Tongues Untied" was framed in terms of "indecency" and "censorship"; "Dark Circle" about "journalism" and "propaganda." Regardless of its portrayal in the media, the program itself offered millions of viewers an unprecedented opportunity to gain insight into the black, gay experience.

PBS, *P.O.V.*, and the station managers who chose to broadcast the program, even in the face of vocal opposition as in Georgia, did not back down. They hung tough, along with the NEA. However, the way the public television system is currently organized, there is very little to protect stations from taking heat from organized groups of subscribers or major funders, especially when the funder is the government.

Groups such as Donald Wildmon's American Family Association came right out and said the program promotes "a gay life-style" and that they did not want their tax dollars supporting it. They organized in Congress to trim the finances of the Corporation for Public Broadcasting and succeeded in winning symbolic and real changes.

No programmer who rejected the program rejected it by appealing to public television's mission. Conversely, no manager who aired it described it as "indecent" or "pornographic." The users of the terms "indecency" and "censorship" rationalized their decisions from these basic perspectives. The terms led some to reject the program, others to air it, but how they initially perceived the issues justified their decisions.

The public television executives who explained their rejection in terms of "indecency" and the fear of violating "community standards" made judgments about who constitutes their community, whose voices are relevant, and in this case, how homosexuality should be portrayed on public television. (For Donald Wildmon, any portrayal of homosexuality as "normal" is abhorrent, even the highbrow *American Playhouse* productions "The Lost Language of Cranes" [1992] and "Tales of the City" [1994].) Black, gay men were not part of the public television community, and many public television gatekeepers chose to reinforce their symbolic exclusion.

While the "Tongues Untied" controversy was unfolding during the summer of 1991, another one was brewing over *P.O.V.*'s scheduled broadcast in August of another film dealing with gay issues: "Stop the Church," a short documentary about an ACT-UP protest against the Catholic Church. Independent producers and gay groups felt *P.O.V.* was backing down from its own commitment to diversity when it agreed with PBS's decision to pull it from the national schedule. This case, explored in the following chapter, shows how "Tongues Untied" had a chilling effect on the system.

# Chapter 6                    "Stop the Church"

*If the Catholic Church is an easy target, it's certainly not
a permissible one.*

—Robert Hilferty, video activist

In the "Tongues Untied" case, the proponents and opponents of the program on homosexuality were clearly identified, and the consequences for stations going ahead with the broadcast were anticipated well in advance. Faced with threats to withdraw subscriptions and to cut funding for public television and the National Endowment for the Arts, PBS, P.O.V., and the NEA stood firm and stood together.

But a month after the "Tongues Untied" broadcast, PBS chose to cancel another video from the gay rights movement as a preemptive measure before any threats of public protest could arise. The video, "Stop the Church," presented a view of the Catholic Church from the perspective of ACT-UP, the AIDS Coalition to Unleash Power, an AIDS activist organization. "Stop the Church" became the sacrificial lamb that PBS and P.O.V. offered to the stations after the trauma of "Tongues Untied," and it showed once again the difficulty of programming works from the social margins.

Jennifer Lawson and other programmers at PBS, along with David Davis of the American Documentary (the tax-exempt corporation that produces and oversees P.O.V.) and P.O.V.'s Marc Weiss, explained the decision by saying they felt they had insufficient time to prepare the stations for another program that promised to be controversial so close on the heels of "Tongues Untied." Weiss feared a second controversy right after "Tongues Untied" could jeopardize P.O.V.'s future with the stations.

When PBS, without opposition from P.O.V., pulled "Stop the Church"

11. ACT-UP protest at St. Patrick's Cathedral in New York, from "Stop the Church."
*Photo: T.L. Litt, courtesy Frameline, Inc.*

from the August 1991 schedule, the immediate result was a month-long controversy in the press.

## Program Description

The twenty-four-minute video, "a Robert Hilferty Inquisition" produced by
Alter Ego Productions, begins with a montage of religious paintings, Hector
Berlioz's "Dies Irae" (Day of Wrath), and a whispering chant, "What's the
Catholic Church?" The music comes to a halt with the title, "Stop the
Church," and the screeching sound of brakes, car horns, and urban traffic.

Someone asks, "What *is* the Catholic Church?" and various answers are
given. Negative statements about the Catholic Church outnumber the positive ones: A man evokes an image of his mean third-grade teacher; another
says, "It's a communion, a oneness with everyone." Others describe the Church
as "arrogant, sterile, retrograde, and blind," "hypocrisy and hatred," "homopho-
bic," and an anachronistic institution "that practices ritual sacrifice on the
bodies of gay men, lesbians, women, and people of color." A nonpracticing
Catholic reveals she is frightened by the "fundamentalist wing" of the Catholic
Church, which she says has taken over. Finally, a man jokes, "Do you know
anybody who likes the Catholic Church, besides Catholics?"

Tom Lehrer's "The Vatican Rag" introduces New York's Cardinal John O'Connor and the Catholic Church. Priests genuflect, parishioners finger rosaries, and ushers collect offerings, all in time to the music:

Get in line in that processional
Step into that small confessional
There the guy who's got religion'll
Tell you if your sin's original
If it is try playing it safer
Sip the wine and chew the wafer
Two, four, six, eight
Time to transubstantiate.

Then the camera moves to an ACT-UP organizing meeting. "Either the Church is alive and well in this room, or it doesn't exist at all. We are the Church. We have the innate authority to criticize that fat cannibal!" a woman exclaims, the camera panning to a poster of the cardinal.

The following words appear white against a black screen: "O'Connor lobbies to ban safe sex education and the availability of condoms in public schools. HIV infection among teenagers is rapidly increasing." Another reads, "O'Connor encourages anti-abortion groups to block access to women's health-care facilities and he aggressively campaigns against abortion rights."

In a crowded meeting hall, people discuss the Catholic Church and activists' proposed action on December 10, 1989. Some feel uneasy about openly opposing the Catholics. "I can't believe the stupidity I'm hearing in this room," says a woman who has worked with Catholics on Central American solidarity causes. "Three priests were killed this week in El Salvador!" Another opposes disrupting a religious service and is "1,000 percent" against protesting inside the church. "We wouldn't want them busting into an ACT-UP meeting and celebrating mass in the middle of us," he says.

Despite these concerns, the group eventually decides to go ahead with a demonstration and a disruption of the mass, justifying this action on two grounds: that O'Connor "promotes violence against gays by his stands on birth control and sex education," and that the Church is a political institution that supports right-to-life groups and opposes AIDS education and safe sex.

With a blueprint of St. Patrick Cathedral's floor plan on the wall, organizers plan a "die-in" in the central aisle to begin a few minutes after the service starts. Protesters, dressed as church volunteers, will hand out fliers nearly identical to church programs with "Welcome to St. Patrick's Cathedral" and a drawing of the church printed on the outside. But when parishioners open the program, they will find a fact-sheet on ACT-UP, AIDS, and O'Connor.

A woman explains the media strategy: "We communicate *through* the media, not *to* the media. *Use* the media to get to the people whose attention we've grabbed with our event." A graphic artist discusses different mock-ups of posters with blown-up pictures of O'Connor and the slogans "Stop This Man" and "Stop the Church." As others prepare signs with the slogans "Curb Your Dogma" and "O'Connor: Public Health Menace," the sacred music of the Hallelujah Chorus from Handel's *Messiah* begins, bridging the poster makers with a montage of the December 10 demonstration: police barricades and protesters, a demonstrator held aloft and dressed as the "Flying Nun," and a "Keep Abortion Legal" sign. A parishioner wonders if the demonstration is about abortion and is puzzled when told it's about AIDS. She says the protest is "the pits. I don't think much of it."

The music continues as police haul off on stretchers protesters who have sat down in the street. Someone dressed up as the Virgin Mary holds a baby Jesus statuette in one hand, and in the other a sign that reads, "This Mary Preaches Freedom." A huge streetwide banner, "O'Connor: Public Health Menace," marches forward, as the Hallelujah Chorus ends.

Inside the cathedral, O'Connor begins the service. Activists quietly lie down in the cathedral's central aisle as he continues, parishioners seemingly oblivious to the "die-in" action. Then protesters begin disrupting the service. One stands up in the back, blowing a loud whistle and shouting, "You're murdering us! Stop killing us! We're not going to take it anymore! Stop it!" Some parishioners look bewildered, some pray and ignore the protest, trying to continue with the service as if nothing were amiss. O'Connor, sitting, rests his head in his hand.

Police line the aisle and begin to carry out protesters on stretchers as the organ plays and parishioners sing a hymn. (The press later reported that the police carried out 134 demonstrators.)[1] In a silent moment when the music ends, an activist shouts, "O'Connor, you're a bigot!" Another, lying on a stretcher, yells, "We're fighting for your lives, too!" The organ music resumes.

O'Connor addresses the congregation. "I always feel anguish when I meet people who hate for whatever reason. It is terribly destructive for those who hate. We must never respond to hatred with hatred but only with love, compassion, and understanding."

As parishioners leave, they tell the camera, "I don't approve of such goings-on in a holy place." Another calls the demonstration "blasphemous," and a parishioner quips, "If they behaved themselves, they wouldn't get into this mess." Another says, "This Church continues to teach what it's taught for 2,000 years . . . [that] sodomy and abortion are evil." A young man leaving says he thought the demonstration "was pretty good."

Sacred music plays over the demonstration's media coverage: news head-lines, the front covers of *New York Newsday* and the *Daily News*, a *Time* maga-zine article about the protest at St. Patrick's Cathedral.

As the credits roll, a woman's voice-over sums up the event from ACT-UP's perspective: "I think it was a huge success. What it did was get the is-sues into the public conversation. That was our aim, not to change people's minds in the hierarchy of the Church, not to make people think something in particular. But to start the conversation. Get these issues talked about and that's what we did."

## The Producer and the Production

Robert Hilferty is a video activist who joined ACT-UP in 1987, two years after his lover died of AIDS.[2] When he learned ACT-UP was going to have a demonstration against O'Connor at St. Patrick's Cathedral, he decided to make a video about it. He wanted to depict "how the organization plans something and show all the discussions that went into it," he said. "I also wanted to make a historical documentary on what was to be ACT-UP's most radical action."[3]

Hilferty is a gay man, the son of a Catholic father and Jewish mother. He grew up in New Jersey and New York and attended the Regis School, a prep school in Manhattan, where he had "a very positive experience" study-ing with Jesuits who "encouraged free and creative thinking." He said his teachers gave him "lots of confidence." Later he studied music at Princeton University and learned film making by working on his own projects and those of his friends, and as an assistant to the director Robert Altman on *Tanner '88*.[4]

Hilferty did not want to make a film that spoke only to the converted. "I was reacting to video activism," he said. "The bulk of what I saw were home movies made primarily for activists to kind of giggle and pat themselves on the back. In other words, there was no effort to communicate to an audience larger than it. . . . I wanted to make a work that was not compromised, and that also had an ability to communicate.

"It's universally agreed upon that going in to a church is politically in-correct, is inappropriate. I know that. That's why I made the film."

Hilferty made "Stop the Church" with $4,000 of his own money. He chose not to emulate the aesthetics of the conventional public television documen-tary with its dramatic lighting, "stately zooms," and steady tripod shots. In-stead, he shot his guerrilla video with a Hi-8 camcorder, did not use a tripod or lights, and began shooting six weeks prior to the December 10, 1989, protest.

"The economics of the Hi-8 camera made it possible for me to shoot it,"

Hilferty said. "Also the smallness of the camera and its sensitivity to low light situations made it possible for me to capture the group and also sneak into the church."

Shooting without special lights, a tripod, or a crew, Hilferty was able to capture images without attracting unwanted attention. So did his ability to tell a lie. In the church during the "die-in," a plainclothes policeman approached Hilferty when he pulled out his camera. "He asked me if I was doing surveillance for the Police Department. And I answered yes, and he didn't touch me," Hilferty recalled. "That's why I got the good footage that I did get . . . because I got the bulk of the most dramatic action."

Hilferty also used music and art to make a statement. "I opened the film with Hector Berlioz's 'Dies Irae'—which is the most famous trope in Church history, where God judges man and all hell breaks loose," he said. "I was basically making the statement that in terms of gay men, gay people, and women, Catholic Church history is one of exclusion and judgment."

In addition, he chose work that was produced by Christian artists and musicians he said were gay: Handel, Caravaggio, Leonardo da Vinci, and Michelangelo. He wanted to make a statement about gay invisibility.[5]

"I'm an honest film maker," he told me. "I still don't pick sides for you. I just simply show you how events flow from the point of view of the activists, but you get to pick whether or not this was appropriate."

## Acceptance by P.O.V., Cancellation by PBS

When Hilferty finished the video, he transferred it to film and entered it in film festivals. It was shown at the Berlin Film Festival, won the best documentary award at the Ann Arbor Film Festival, and was also screened at the Whitney Museum of American Art and other venues. He submitted it to P.O.V. in 1990 so it could be considered for the series's 1991 season.

In February 1991, P.O.V. notified him that his film had been accepted and would air along with several other short-format works under the title "Short Notice." Hilferty received a contract and eventually a check for $10,000, but he noticed no publicity appeared about the show from P.O.V. "There was always a sense they were walking on eggshells from the beginning, I have to admit," Hilferty recalled. "There were articles coming out about gay works on P.O.V. and not once was mine mentioned. So I knew something was up."[6]

Hilferty didn't know what else was going on at P.O.V. during the spring of 1991. Executive producer Marc Weiss said the problem with "Stop the Church" had less to do with content and more to do with timing, and regrets he did not handle matters differently.[7] He said *P.O.V.* had not put "Short Notice" on the schedule until February, which was after the full-length programs had been selected. But by March, Weiss and *P.O.V.* staff were already gearing up for "Tongues Untied" and were getting swamped taking care of station relations regarding that broadcast. "Stop the Church" simply fell through the cracks.

At PBS, Glenn Dixon, then the director of news and public affairs programming, had approved the inclusion of "Stop the Church" in *P.O.V.*'s summer schedule, *months before* the "Tongues Untied" controversy. Dixon didn't anticipate the program would become controversial until there was a flap over "Tongues Untied."[8] He didn't flag the show—indeed nobody did—until it was already in the schedule.

With programs believed to be controversial, *P.O.V.* normally sends letters and previews to stations with lots of information about the program, including sample letters that can be used by stations if they receive angry responses from viewers. But Weiss said he overlooked this procedure with "Stop the Church." "Tongues Untied" just took up too much time.

On August 12, two weeks before it was scheduled to air on *P.O.V.*, PBS announced it was pulling "Stop the Church" from the national schedule. PBS sent out a statement saying it "[finds the program] inappropriate for distribution because its pervasive tone of ridicule overwhelms its critique of policy. In addition, it does not meet PBS's standards for quality."[9] The film "does not reflect the kind of quality PBS has come to stand for," PBS spokeswoman Mary Jane McKinven told reporters.[10] John Grant, PBS vice president for scheduling and programming administration, said PBS first was alerted to the program when a PBS programmer received a phone call from an unnamed affiliate station executive in the Midwest who complained about it. The call came two weeks before PBS made a public announcement canceling the program and a month before the scheduled airdate.[11] Then Grant, Jennifer Lawson, the executive vice president of programming, and other PBS staff took a look at the film. Lawson, in consultation with her staff, chose to cancel the film.

Grant told reporters this cancellation was "a judgment call, a very subjective judgment call. . . . Our decision has nothing to do with the attack on the church in this program. It has nothing to do with the fact that it was made by an AIDS activist group. It is really the tone and the ridicule that we found inappropriate for broadcast."[12] He also said PBS was not pressured by the Catholic Church or any outside groups to withdraw the film.[13]

David Davis, executive director of the American Documentary, told the *Los Angeles Times,* "I felt another controversy at this time would break [stations'] backs and undermine their confidence in '*P.O.V.*'"[14]

In August, when Hilferty learned his film was canceled, he told *P.O.V.* staff he was not going to take the news passively. "I said to *P.O.V.*, 'You know, you're going to have to tighten your seat belts, because I'm well connected, and I'm not going to sit around for the next two weeks waiting for a broadcast that's not going to occur and sulk in my apartment. As soon as I get out of this office, I'm pressing buttons.'"[15] The film maker went to the press, and as the story broke, the press also came to him.

By the time PBS announced its cancellation of "Stop the Church," the affiliate stations had already received promotional materials on the program and had put it in their schedule as part of *P.O.V.*[16] (*P.O.V.* replaced "Stop the Church" with "Binge," a confessional video about a woman's weight problems.) PBS sent the stations a notice about the cancellation the same day the press heard about it, and by the next day, articles appeared in local newspapers all over the country about PBS's decision. Stations had little time to react.

## Press Coverage of the Cancellation

The press, fresh from the "Tongues Untied" controversy, was already up to speed on PBS and ready to jump on PBS's cancellation of "Stop the Church." Hundreds of articles about it appeared in newspapers all over the country— more than sixty within the first week of the announcement. Most reporters interpreted the PBS cancellation as an act of self-censorship, one chilling effect from the "Tongues Untied" case. That was the main angle.

Howard Rosenberg of the *Los Angeles Times* wrote, "PBS is once again teetering dangerously on the cutting edge of timidity. The medium envisioned as a beacon on the TV landscape is sinking deeper and deeper into the safe, cushy middle ground under the crushing weight of its own network of cautious stations."[17]

PBS's former ally Arthur Kropp, president of People for the American Way, broke ranks with PBS after standing firm with PBS and *P.O.V.* only a month earlier in defense of "Tongues Untied." Now he publicly condemned PBS's decision to cancel "Stop the Church." "This is the kind of censorship you can't fight—self-censorship," Kropp told the press. "It illustrates just what kind of environment we're working in. . . . There have been so many attacks and so many threats that people are going to begin to run scared."[18]

Robert Hilferty described PBS's decision as "outrageous" and "cowardly."[19] "It feels like self-censorship of a form, of a censorship in advance of what someone might say about the film," he said.[20] He denied that the film "ridiculed" the Catholic Church. "It's an attack on the Catholic Church's political role and the politics of this one man, O'Connor."[21] He was amazed that PBS decided the program ridiculed the church *in August* when *P.O.V.* had accepted it in February.

Although *P.O.V.* had not sent out preview copies of "Stop the Church" and most reporters had not seen it, several reporters, such as Julia Keller of the *Columbus Dispatch*, criticized PBS for "wimpish behavior" for canceling the program.[22]

Marvin Kitman at *Newsday* described PBS's decision as the "new heights or depths of self-censorship, the most insidious kind. . . . Now they are acting like commercial networks in program content."[23]

Editorials and press accounts covered the "Stop the Church" case in relation to "Tongues Untied." A *Washington Times* editorial, "PBS: Propaganda Broadcasting Service," argued, "This is not the first time 'P.O.V.' has stepped in the cheese dip because of its penchant for leftism and sexual oddity."[24]

Another editorial in the *Charleston Gazette* titled "PBS Surrenders" read, "PBS fearing a new public outcry, backed down. That's as wrong as the bigotry on both sides. PBS should stand fast and air the film."[25]

*P.O.V.* had its own problems with independent producers who were angry about the series's about-face on "Stop the Church." The *Independent Film and Video Monthly*, the publication of the Foundation for Independent Video and Film, attacked the series for backing away from its mission.[26] But Peter Adair, the gay independent producer of "Absolutely Positive," a film about people who are HIV-positive which led off the 1991 *P.O.V.* season, defended *P.O.V.* against its critics on the left who felt betrayed and who thought the series had "sold out."

"Broadcast television is a game of compromise," he told Howard Rosenberg. "*P.O.V.* doesn't exist without the cooperation of the station managers. Marc [Weiss] and Dave [Davis] felt the series was really threatened if they ran this piece. They could go down firing and say the hell with you all. But that would end any kind of voice for independents."[27]

While PBS appeared to bow to an anticipated negative reaction from the stations and viewers, the decentralized public television system provided other venues for the program to air. Despite PBS's cancellation on the national schedule, individual stations could still broadcast it. The station that led the way was KCET in Los Angeles.

## KCET's Broadcast and the Response from Press and Public

In Los Angeles, Barbara Goen, KCET vice president of public information, heard about the cancellation from PBS on Monday, August 12, and the next day, articles appeared in the *Hollywood Reporter*, the *New York Times*, the

*Washington Post*, and other newspapers about the controversial decision. The *Los Angeles Times* published two articles on August 14.[28]

Goen said the articles fueled "a great deal of fire" in the Los Angeles area because of its "very active gay and lesbian population." "We got calls from organizations that we have strong partnerships with, that we like and respect, that we've worked with on other projects: the AIDS Project Los Angeles, the Gay and Lesbian Anti-Defamation League, and other organizations," Goen told me. "They immediately started calling KCET asking, 'What are you gonna do?'"[29]

The first step was to call an internal meeting of key station executives and staff to build a "strategic communications team."[30] This team was made up of the KCET president, the executive vice president, vice presidents of public information and community relations, the station manager, and an outside communications consultant who was an expert in "crisis communications" as well as both political and community relations. The team met with the chairman of the KCET board and KCET's fund-raisers since the group believed the impact of a controversy on major underwriting could be "catastrophic."

In the first days after the news broke about the PBS cancellation, the group developed a plan. They identified which constituencies needed to be communicated with, established a consistent message about the station's ultimate decision (once it was decided), set a timetable and priority list of communications, and planned ways to follow up. They also prepared for possible demonstrations against the station. Their preparations were well timed.

Then on August 16, the *Los Angeles Times* reported three gay rights groups—Gay and Lesbian Alliance Against Discrimination (GLAAD), Queer Nation, and ACT-UP—were going to hold a "phone zap" on KCET during its thirteen-day pledge drive.[31] The threatened action would tie up the pledge phone lines unless the station agreed to air both "Stop the Church" and another gay film, "Son of Sam and Delilah," which PBS had also declined to broadcast.[32] GLAAD was planning other protests and demonstrations in New York, San Francisco, and Los Angeles.[33]

"They're not treating us as part of their public and they are censoring what little material there is," Richard Jennings, executive director of GLAAD/Los Angeles, told the *Los Angeles Daily News*.[34]

Barbara Goen of KCET told the *Los Angeles Times* the station was "extremely anxious to gather input from and talk to leaders in the gay and lesbian community."[35] As planned by the strategic communications team, Goen invited the gay leaders to discuss their grievances and consult with them at the station before deciding whether KCET would go ahead with a broadcast.[36]

The press report did not say she would consult with Catholic Church leaders for their opinion.[37]

Within a week of PBS's cancellation, KCET had decided to create a local production, of which 'Stop the Church' would be a part, according to Goen. This special "would treat the program as the news media were treating it. By that I mean we would look at the program in the context of its controversy."[38] The station began negotiating with Hilferty to clear the rights to broadcast the program.

The decision to broadcast "Stop the Church" was not made public right away—not until Wednesday, August 21.[39] In the intervening few days, word spread through news articles that KCET would consult with a gay group before deciding to air the program. The Reverend Gregory Coiro of the Los Angeles Catholic Archdiocese public affairs office called Goen on Monday, August 19, to express his concern that he would like the Church to be consulted before the station decided on the broadcast. According to his notes from their conversation, Goen had him speak to a person in KCET's community relations department, who told him the decision to air the program would be made by 7 p.m. that very evening. He was asked to send a fax about his concerns ASAP to William Kobin, KCET president.[40]

The next day, Coiro received a call from KCET informing him that the station had decided to broadcast the documentary in a special program that would include a discussion of the controversy around it. Coiro was invited to a screening of the documentary with Ted Mayer of the Catholic League and then to meet with KCET station manager Stephen Kulczycki.[41]

After viewing the program, Coiro was disgusted. "We felt this was a very bigoted piece, and that it was anti-Catholic and had no place on television," he told me. "Any other religious or ethnic group would not be treated that way, and we didn't feel it was right for the Catholic Church to be treated that way. And they said, 'Well, the decision's made.'"[42]

The film offended him particularly because ACT-UP disrupted a sacred ritual—the celebration of Mass—and "attacked Cardinal O'Connor for teaching what the Catholic Church teaches."[43] Coiro did not want anything to do with the program, and he didn't accept Kulczycki's argument that viewers "should be intelligent enough to watch this and make their own decisions," as the KCET station executive argued.[44]

Coiro turned down KCET's request for an interview and an offer to appear on a panel discussion when "Stop the Church" aired on Friday, September 6, at 10:30 p.m. Coiro said appearing on KCET would only legitimize KCET's decision to air "Catholic-bashing propaganda."[45]

Meanwhile, during the last two weeks in August and in early September, Cardinal Roger M. Mahony, archbishop of Los Angeles, had quiet, behind-the-scenes communication with KCET President William Kobin.[46] He sent letters to Kobin and members of the KCET board of directors urging them to kill the broadcast of "Stop the Church." He spoke on the telephone with the KCET president about his concerns.[47]

When word spread about the dispute between the archdiocese and KCET, groups and supporters called Coiro to weigh in on the matter. For three weeks, Coiro said his office phone rang "off the hook" from people expressing their views on "Stop the Church." "At first they were running fifty-fifty before the program aired, and then after the program aired, the calls were running about two to one in favor of the cardinal," Coiro told me.[48]

Several religious groups, including members of the Islamic and Jewish community, as well as some Protestant organizations, called to express support for the stand taken by the archdiocese. He also received phone calls and background literature on public television from the Committee for Media Integrity (COMINT), a politically conservative media-watch group founded by David Horowitz, a former *Ramparts* editor.

Although ACT-UP had stopped talking about a "phone zap," activists in the gay and lesbian community now were pressuring KCET to invite Robert Hilferty to appear on the panel, and according to Goen, they wanted to dictate who should and should not appear. As part of KCET's strategic communications plan, Goen was also meeting with or communicating with other constituents: the KCET board of directors, the Community Advisory Board, funders and donors at the corporate and foundation level, individual major donors, the three hundred members of the station staff, and 280,000 subscribers.[49]

The conflict between the Los Angeles Archdiocese and KCET escalated on September 5, the day before the scheduled broadcast, when Cardinal Mahony called a press conference that made the front page of the *Los Angeles Times* the next day. Mahony declared that KCET was "unworthy of public support" since it chose to broadcast "Stop the Church."[50] He publicly accused the station of caving in to "blackmail" by gay rights groups and of encouraging "hate crimes" against religious institutions by people "who would burn, loot and vandalize houses of worship or disrupt religious services in the name of one cause or another."[51]

Mahony said his private efforts to stop KCET from airing the program had proven futile, so he had decided to go public. Soon afterward, George Pla, a member of the KCET board of directors and owner of a corporation, resigned from the board to protest the station's decision. He also withdrew a $98,000 verbal pledge to KCET.[52]

Mahony also took out ads in the *Los Angeles Times* and the *Los Angeles Daily News* the day of the broadcast, putting his case directly before their readers. In "A Case of Bigotry?: An Open Letter to the People of Southern California," the cardinal listed the recent firebombing of a Jewish synagogue; stink bombs placed in a Christian bookstore, a religious television station, and a cathedral; and the desecration of several Catholic churches in the area—religious "hate crimes" which he saw as on the rise. He again condemned KCET for its decision to air "Stop the Church," which he said would "encourage the hate mongers in our midst" by glorifying and celebrating "anti-religious bigotry, specifically, Catholic-bashing," and alienate the area's four million Catholics.

Cardinal Mahony encouraged viewers to watch "this despicable film," and if they found the content to be "anti-Catholic," to let KCET know about it and to join the Los Angeles chapter of the Catholic League for Religious and Civil Rights (an 18,000-member organization based in Philadelphia). Mahony also provided phone numbers for KCET and the Catholic League. The cardinal stopped short of calling for a formal boycott, although he urged subscribers to "reexamine whether you believe KCET is worthy of your financial support." He told them he wasn't going to give any money to the station, and he stated his belief that KCET wasn't worthy of financial support from individuals or businesses.

A KCET crew videotaped Mahony's press conference, and later that afternoon, William Kobin, president of KCET, held a press conference of his own to answer Mahony's charges and to put forth the station's public position. That was taped by a KCET crew, too. "KCET believes strongly that its viewers deserved the same opportunity as Cardinal Mahony to view this film and make up their own minds regarding this controversy," Kobin told the cameras.

KCET succeeded in rounding up panelists from opposing sides, who were interviewed by host Jeffrey Kaye eight hours before the evening broadcast. Goen said the program producers were not sure how much of the program would be devoted to these discussions. "We didn't even know up until a few hours before we put it [the special] on the air whether this was going to be a sixty-minute show or a ninety-minute show," Goen said.[53] By the 10:30 p.m. broadcast of KCET's "Stop the Church: Issues and Outrage," station producers Martin Burns and Joseph Angier put together a wraparound with two panel discussions following the twenty-four-minute documentary.

The Gay and Lesbian Alliance Against Defamation (GLAAD) refused to participate in the panel discussions because KCET did not extend an invitation to the film's producer, Robert Hilferty, or any member of ACT-UP. No official from the Los Angeles Archdiocese was allowed to appear, on orders from Cardinal Mahony, but KCET producers were able to get three sets of guests. In the first panel discussion, they had Paul Freeze from the Catholic League and Father William Wood, S.J., a former lobbyist for the California Catholic Conference, to express the views of the Catholic Church. To represent gay perspectives, KCET invited Lee Klosinski from the AIDS Project Los Angeles and the Reverend Stephen Pieters of the Metropolitan Community Church, who mentioned in passing that he had AIDS. (Klosinski, a former Catholic priest, believed his former vocation influenced the station's decision to invite him to appear on the panel.)[54] In a final discussion to close the program, KCET hosted former CBS News president Van Gordon Sauter and Professor Tracy Weston from the University of Southern California Annenberg School of Communications.

The entire program, with the twenty-four-minute film, ran ninety minutes. Goen said it started out with a very high rating during the first fifteen minutes—a 4.5—which tapered off as the program progressed toward midnight.[55] That meant an estimated 292,500 people tuned in—more than four times the average number for the Friday night time-slot.[56] But only an estimated 104,000 viewers were still on hand by the end of the show.[57]

KCET president William Kobin opened and closed the special report by recounting how PBS had pulled "Stop the Church" for its "pervasive tone of ridicule," a decision he said some saw as an "unacceptable act of censorship," and defended KCET's decision to air "Stop the Church." A two-minute background segment about the relationship between the Catholic Church, AIDS, Cardinal O'Connor, and homosexuality followed the Kobin introduction, and the host, Jeffrey Kaye, introduced an excerpt from Cardinal Mahony's press conference, an excerpt of Kobin's KCET response, and then "Stop the Church" began.

After the documentary came the taped press conference, during which Cardinal Mahony read his statement condemning KCET's decision to air the program and took several questions from the press. He alleged that Kobin admitted caving in to pressure from gay groups, who were organizing a phone zap during the station's August pledge drive. He also said KCET owes Catholics in southern California "a public apology."

The host then engaged his two Catholic guests in a discussion about the film. Predictably, they did not like it, but Father Wood said he felt hurt and saddened by the anger expressed toward the Church in the video. Later, the two gay guests joined the conversation. One said it was not very "loving" for Cardinal O'Connor to have people arrested while he talked to his congregation about love and understanding.

From William Kobin's press conference, the KCET president read his statement and answered questions from the press about Mahony's allegation that he had simply succumbed to pressure from the gay groups, an allegation he denied. He said he had received "extreme pressure" from both sides. The station president also defended the film as worthy of broadcasting because the controversy raised important issues about television and censorship. He also mentioned that "Stop the Church" had won awards at film festivals.

Kaye returned for a final discussion with Van Gordon Sauter, former president of CBS News, who did not like "Stop the Church" or approve of its airing because it was "a trite, unimaginative, doctrinaire piece of cinéma vérité about a tantrum." Tracy Weston liked the film because it *wasn't* balanced, polished, and professional like most other documentaries on public television, and believed it was exactly the kind of program that lived up to public television's mission to provide diverse perspectives regardless of whether one agrees with them.

Kobin returned at the end of the program to reiterate how agonizing the decision had been but that it is part of the mandate of public television stations to address controversy.

KCET received 8,800 pieces of mail and 5,800 phone calls about "Stop the Church."[58] "More people were unhappy than happy," Goen recalled, with negative responses outweighing positive responses two to one.[59] However, "those who congratulated KCET and supported KCET sent extra donations and unsolicited checks."[60] She estimated in the June 1992 *Guide to Crisis Management* that she had received $85,000 in viewer pledges.

In the short term, however, these financial windfalls did not offset entirely the withdrawal of the $98,000 pledge from businessman and former KCET board member George Pla, nor the 365 canceled subscriptions worth about $21,900, a figure cited by the *Los Angeles Times*.[61]

The actual number of canceled subscriptions turned out to be much higher. Months later, the *Guide to Crisis Management* noted that "approximately 1,900 people canceled their [KCET] membership to protest the program, and 32 members requested refunds."

These cancellations—at $60 a subscription—amounted to a loss of more than $115,000 for KCET alone. Combined with the withdrawal of the verbal pledge for $98,000, the figure for lost revenue rises to $213,000. Based on available figures, if the station received $85,000 in pledges of support *for* airing "Stop the Church," KCET still paid a steep financial price for going ahead with the program: $128,000. (How much the station might have lost in revenue had it refused to broadcast the program in any form remains, of course, a matter of speculation.)

KCET handled the cancellations through carefully written letters. Goen helped prepare two kinds of letters signed by Bill Kobin and mailed to about 7,000 viewers upset over the decision to air "Stop the Church."[62] One was for people who were canceling their subscriptions, and the other was for those who were simply angry about the decision to air the show. In the letters, Kobin expressed "sincere regret" for "the hurt and distress which many viewers have expressed," called the controversy "the most wrenching experience of my nearly four-decade career," and said the station experienced "intense pressure from both sides of the issue." Both letters repeated KCET's rationale for airing the program: "One of our central mandates as a public television station is to explore significant issues of controversy and to present a wide diversity of opinion and programming, including opinions which may not be generally popular and material which may not be to everyone's taste."[63]

But when these letters were received, Coiro said the Right to Life League of southern California took those words to heart and asked the station to broadcast the antiabortion film "Eclipse of Reason." If the station were truly interested in presenting "a wide diversity of opinion," including unpopular views, then broadcasting this antiabortion film would certainly meet that criterion. Coiro said the station did not respond to the Right to Life League's request; he felt KCET was "yankin' our chains" since it had taken only a week for the station to decide to put on "Stop the Church" but it did not do anything about "Eclipse of Reason."[64] Goen recalled a different set of circumstances. She said the station had several discussions about the antiabortion film and turned it down "because we felt that it required a context of other opinions." She maintained a formal letter of explanation had been sent to the producers.[65]

The diverse sources of funds for public television stations—a mix of money from local, state, and federal government, corporate and foundation donors, as well as major individual donors and subscribers—insulate stations like KCET from all but the biggest, most inclusive financial boycotts. But the outcome of this controversy extended beyond matters of money to the rationale for public television's existence.

A month after the event, Goen and Kobin felt KCET had made "the right decision" to air "Stop the Church" because the program raised important issues, even though the process had been painful. Three years later, Goen still felt the same way. "If the circumstances were identical [today], we'd be forced to make the same decision," she said. "Public television is mandated to serve a huge variety of constituents, and by its very nature it is going to antagonize people on different sides of an issue. If we aren't doing that, we're not doing our jobs. It can't be safe television. . . . With that mandate it is inevitable that there will be programs of controversy."[66]

Gregory Coiro told the *Los Angeles Times* he still wanted an apology from KCET but that the controversy was a wake-up call alerting Catholics in southern California to the reality of "anti-Catholicism." He also hoped the Church's stand in the controversy would deter others from attacking the Catholic Church, and he defended Cardinal Mahony's position, even if it might have backfired when Mahony tried to intervene with KCET's programming decisions by generating more publicity about the program.

Other news reports quoted local Catholics who gave Mahony mixed marks for feuding with KCET. Some parishioners were glad the cardinal said something about "Catholic bashing," but others felt he had given KCET too much free publicity by responding as he did, and one resented his suggestion that Catholics withhold subscriptions from the station.[67] Tom Mayer, executive director of the Catholic League for Religious and Civil Rights in Los Angeles, said he received "hundreds of calls" from people who had seen "Stop the Church" and wanted to find out about joining his organization.[68]

The archdiocese's concerns about "Catholic bashing" also received some attention through a *Los Angeles Times* article published three days after the broadcast. Especially in the Los Angeles area, anti-Catholic "hate crimes" seemed on the rise, along with a general, national anti-Catholic sentiment as indicated by the "hate mail" journalist Cokie Roberts received after she mentioned on television that she is a Catholic.[69]

The *Los Angeles Times* coverage consisted of one article on September 9, a feature on anti-Catholic sentiment which included these findings: between October 1989 and July 1990, the Los Angeles County Commission on Human Relations reported that nine churches had been vandalized "15 times with graffiti, smashed and decapitated statues and painted swastikas. Some of the incidents were related to the church's stand on homosexuality and abortion." At one Catholic church, an unexploded pipe bomb was also found, as well as Satanic graffiti spray-painted on statues.

On the national level, several Catholic conservatives, including former secretary of education William Bennett, founded a group called the Catholic Campaign for America and held a press conference on September 5 to let it be known it had "had enough of Catholic bashing." Michael Schwartz, then a fellow at the Free Congress Foundation, a conservative think tank, went on the offensive, charging that Church officials themselves were "extremely mistaken" in letting attacks on Catholics go unanswered. (Interestingly, none of the articles in the mainstream press mentioned rising incidents of "gay bashing.")

Local newspaper reaction to the special was mixed. An editorial in the *Los Angeles Daily News* said KCET owes *all* its viewers an apology for providing "a crude showcase for religious intolerance." The special did not shed light on the conflict between the Church and some AIDS activists "by allowing a few extremists to commandeer its air time and give vent to their hatred."[70]

*Los Angeles Times* media critic Howard Rosenberg called the evening special "rather interesting" because everyone "acted correctly." He concluded the whole "Stop the Church" episode dramatizes "how vulnerable PBS and its stations are without permanent long-range funding. When your existence depends on contributions, foundation grants and periodic government stipends—and this lifeblood can be clotted by a decision to air or not air a controversial program—the instinct to survive by being inoffensive is overwhelming."[71]

Later, Rosenberg allowed himself to be drawn into the fray by responding to loads of letters he received accusing him of being a "fence-sitter and biased against Catholicism." Some wondered if he would be as open-minded about a hypothetical program that portrayed the disruption of a Jewish service, say, a show like "Stop the Yids," about a gang of neo-Nazis painting swastikas on the walls of a Jewish temple. Rosenberg said he would air that, too, because the anti-Nazi message of such a hypothetical film would bury its hate message. The main value of "Stop the Church," according to Rosenberg, is that it "captures the frustrations that feed radicalism and militancy on the part of some AIDS activists."[72]

Now that KCET had produced a ninety-minute special around "Stop the Church," other stations had a packaged product that was neutralized and suitable for broadcast. However, not all stations felt the need for packaging: KQED/San Francisco broadcast the program with a brief statement to viewers about the controversy at 11:30 p.m. Friday, August 30 before *P.O.V.*'s "Short Notice" program.[73] WGBH/Boston aired it at 12:30 a.m. Tuesday, September 3.[74] North Carolina Public Television showed it at 11 p.m. also on September 3.[75] Wisconsin Public Television planned to air it in October with its own wraparound.[76] Like many other stations, KCTS/Seattle refused to broadcast the program in any form.[77] WNET/New York aired the KCET special, but in a different media environment and context.

## WNET's Broadcast and the Press Response

Harry Chancey, Jr., executive vice president and director of programming at WNET/New York, who had received "a considerable number" of telephone calls protesting PBS's decision to cancel the program, told *New York Newsday*, "Things are in the works. . . . Ultimately, we're looking to do what's best for the audience, which is to allow for them to see and decide for themselves."[78]

In September, the *New York Times* featured articles exploring different aspects of the controversy. The first article, by television critic Walter Goodman, appeared on September 1. In "Prime Time vs. the Art of Ridicule," Goodman noted that "television executives are nervous about ridicule, except when it is directed at permissible targets like George Bush or John Sununu." Ridicule, he wrote, is an invitation to trouble, especially if it's directed against any of the nation's protected species: most religions, all races and ethnic groups. He observed "television treats its audience like adolescents who have to be protected from adult entertainment," and the "cancellation of the film offers a glimpse of one of the many forms that ridicule may not take. . . . So the medium can be expected to tread carefully, avoid offense and so make its contribution to public order and even to good feelings. The gain is by no means negligible, but the price is a humorless leveling of political discourse."[79]

Goodman also suggested that the "prevailing timidity" has certain social benefits. Television provides a communal experience with the capacity to bring together people of different faiths, races, politics, and economic classes around its hearth; it is a kind of "multicultural assimilator." But ridicule undermines this unifying function, he argues. While programs can air differences on divisive issues, open wounds "must not be left to fester."[80]

Hilferty took an active role in defending his program in the press. He was quoted in news articles in the mainstream press, and wrote an opinion piece in the September 4 issue of *New York Newsday*. With the title "Why Is PBS Afraid of AIDS?" the film maker charged PBS with "censorship" for canceling his program for an "anticipated reaction." He also denied his film "ridicules" the church. "It *criticizes*, intelligently and passionately, and at times quite harshly—the church's *political* role without denigrating religion," he wrote. He also placed the attacks on his film in the same vein as the conservatives' campaign against Robert Mapplethorpe's photos and "Tongues Untied," the main difference being that his program did not show any sexual acts.

WNET's Harry Chancey, the programming director, appeared to be sitting on the fence about whether or not to broadcast "Stop the Church"; according to the film maker, Chancey decided in its favor after he heard that Hilferty planned to show his film on September 12 across the street from WNET in a vacant lot. Hilferty had invited the media and interested New Yorkers to attend the event to see what WNET wouldn't air.

The day of Hilferty's outdoor showing, while the film maker was running around making the arrangements for the evening's event, Chancey called and left messages on the film maker's answering machine informing him that the station had decided to broadcast the KCET "Stop the Church: Issues and Outrage" special on September 13 at 11:30 p.m.[81] WNET announced the decision

to the press the same afternoon.[82] The announcement was carried on four radio stations: public radio, WABC, WINS, and WCBS.[83] Chancey told the
press he wanted to capitalize on the public interest in the subject.[84]

Whether Chancey genuinely wanted to take advantage of current interest in the film (as he told the *New York Times*), or whether he intentionally
tried to get the program on the air with little notice "to sabotage" Hilferty's
media event (as the film maker believes) or to "sneak it on quickly" with little
fanfare (as Joseph Zwilling, director of communications at the Catholic Archdiocese of New York, suspected), the WNET broadcast of the KCET program
ended the broadcast battle over "Stop the Church" in New York.[85] It also provided an opportunity for a kind of postmortem discussion, played out in the
pages of the *New York Times*.

In his "Beliefs" column, religion columnist Peter Steinfels expressed the
views of many Catholics, including the official spokespeople I interviewed:
Gregory Coiro of the Los Angeles Archdiocese and Joseph Zwilling of the New
York Archdiocese. Steinfels imagined how a hypothetical film about Planned
Parenthood would be treated by public television if it used the same structural and aesthetic grammar as "Stop the Church," only with a different institution. Suppose Planned Parenthood were described by people as "an
organization that kills babies" or "ruins young lives by promoting sexual pro-
miscuity, or as a "a group of eugenically minded rich folks who have always
disguised their real aim of reducing the number of blacks and poor people."
Imagine the film's producers presenting the closing of an abortion clinic
in the most favorable light, with all the clinicians shown to be cruel or
ignorant.[86]

Steinfels praised Van Gordon Sauter as "the one pungent voice on the
intellectually feeble panels" for pointing out that the mere fact something is
controversial "doesn't justify its necessarily being on television." He asked:
"What are the rules, the limits of acceptability? And are they really the same
for all the players? WNET and KCET seem to think that televising a medio-
cre discussion about responsibility is a sufficient way to exercise it."[87]

Both Hilferty and Harry Chancey responded to Steinfels's article. Hilferty
asserted his film ought to be shown "for being valid, not for being 'controversial.'" He stressed that PBS and *P.O.V.* broke the contract. Chancey defended
WNET's decision to air it, reiterating that the special "allowed a full and fair
discussion of the issues."[88]

## Analysis of the Controversy

The "Stop the Church" case shows how powerful a short, $4,000 video from the gay rights movement can be, as a result of the timing of the controversy inside the public television world, the PBS cancellation which made the news, and the presence of groups and a producer willing to make an issue of it. The controversy also unfolded when the press was already up to speed on PBS, P.O.V., and groups like People for the American Way that were prepared to frame the rejection of "Stop the Church" as a censorship issue. PBS's decision actually resulted from a judgment about the political climate and the institutional trauma stemming from the "Tongues Untied" controversy, but the cancellation vaulted the program and PBS into the newspapers.

The video did find two places in the public television system—in San Francisco and North Carolina—where it aired at night unpackaged. KCET and WNET, two of the system's largest stations, did not allow it to air on its own without an hour of disclaimers, and they added context that reiterated the controversy around the film and repeated the allegation that the film was "anti-Catholic."

### KCET'S SAFE FORMAT

Consistent with the controversies around "Dark Circle" and "Days of Rage," KCET's panel discussions of "Stop the Church" dealt more with how the Church and O'Connor were portrayed than with the fact-claims raised by the protesters. Gay rights groups saw the controversy over "Stop the Church" as a matter of "censorship," while the Los Angeles Archdiocese saw it as a matter of KCET's complicity in "anti-Catholicism." The panelists charged that the film was "unfair," "unprofessional," and about "a tantrum." The Catholic Church guests did acknowledge the ACT-UP activists' emotions—that they were angry—but the reasons for that anger were not taken seriously or fully explored.

As in the "Days of Rage" case, the panel discussions tilted in favor of the program's critics, for example, in the mismatch between the bellicose Van Gordon Sauter and the mild-mannered academic Tracy Weston. They didn't deal head-on with the rights or wrongs of Cardinal O'Connor's positions on abortion and sex education, or with the question of whether the Catholic Church was a political institution. In them, the messenger—that is, the film and the film maker—became the focus rather than the fact-claims in the films.

Rather than letting the program stand on its own, or in the point-of-view context of the P.O.V. series, KCET broadcast "Stop the Church" in a format that made it safer for viewers and the station. The station could broadcast it and not be accused of being "a censor" or of caving in to Catholic pressure, and at the same time, KCET's packaging with panel discussions made the documentary acceptable by its *own* standards.

THE CONSERVATIVE INFLUENCE OF AFFILIATE STATIONS
PBS's decision to cancel "Stop the Church" originated not with corporations or the government, but with an affiliate station that called to express concern. A station can sometimes use its influence to change the programming that PBS makes available to other affiliate stations. This way, stations can exert a conservative influence and check on PBS and *P.O.V.*, tightening the leash while avoiding anticipated public relations hassles and controversy.

One need not look very far to understand why the stations have this power. PBS was set up as a service organization to provide high-quality programming for the stations. The series *P.O.V.* needs the stations for revenue and carriage, and it already had a reputation, in Weiss's words, as "the bad boys and girls in public television."[89]

The conservative influence of the stations stems from several factors, but a major one is the economic configuration of the system resulting from two government policies. The first was the 1967 Public Broadcasting Act itself, which failed to set up a secure and politically insulated source of funding for the public television system. The second was President Richard Nixon's vetoes of federal funding for the system, which threw local stations into the arms of subscribers, local businesses, foundations, and corporations. Rocked by the station revolt over "Tongues Untied" and its anticipated negative viewer reaction amplified and orchestrated in part by the American Family Association, PBS did not want to risk further upsetting the fragile economics of the system.

Thus the economic structure of public television, the timing of the "Stop the Church" case, and the desire of PBS and *P.O.V.* executives to have the only series devoted to independently produced films remain on the air, made it possible for an unnamed station manager from the Midwest to start the ball rolling that killed the national broadcast.

## Postscript

A few months after the broadcast, Robert Hilferty felt proud his video had made an impact. "My film is a videotape film, and it looks like it was made for $4,000, but this $4,000 pebble has managed to unrock a multimillion-dollar, 2,000-year-old boulder," he said.[90]

Three years later, he was still pleased that "a lot of stuffed shirts were getting hot under the collar," but the film maker was more reticent about the film's impact on his career. "I thought I'd be getting funding for other projects, but I haven't," Hilferty said.[91] Although "Stop the Church" has become part of the gay cultural canon and is still being shown, it has not opened financial doors to other projects.

Hilferty has distanced himself from ACT-UP. He left the organization in 1992, he said, more out of boredom and for his own personal development than because he was abandoning the cause of AIDS. "I don't want to be part of a group. I had trouble saying I was a member of ACT-UP even then," he recalled. "I'm not really a group identifier. It's not who I am. If you want to be an artist, you can't really be too closely associated with a political organization because in the politics of this kind, you have to think in terms of black and white and I'm really not that way. Things are really much more complex." The film maker wanted to move on.

"I've been developing my aesthetic concerns that preceded my activist political work," he told me. He has returned to earlier interests in the relationship between music and film structure, music and sexuality, and a more subtle form of "aesthetic activism." Hilferty is currently working on a documentary about the composer Milton Babbitt and writing about gay issues in film.

About a year after the flap with KCET, Cardinal Mahony received word that KCET gave some public assurances that it would try to exhibit more sensitivity toward religious and ethnic groups in its programming decisions. While the station did not exactly offer an "apology" to Catholics in southern California, as the cardinal requested during the "Stop the Church" episode, Mahony felt reassured that KCET was sincere in its intentions.[92] The cardinal publicly renewed his membership to KCET and encouraged others to do so as well, an act reported in the *Los Angeles Times*.[93] Coiro described the relations between the archdiocese and KCET since then as "amicable."[94]

# "Roger & Me" and "The Heartbeat of America"

## Chapter 7

> We have to protect ourselves from companies like GM
> and others who create factory closings purely in the name
> of greed. Where does it say in the Constitution that we
> live in a society of, by, and for the shareholders? It says,
> "of, by, and for the people."
>
> —Michael Moore, film maker

The independently made films discussed in earlier chapters sought to challenge viewers' images of homosexuality, their tacit faith in our government's nuclear weapons programs and Mideast policy. Each reflected volatile issues and transitory movements for social or political change, but none addressed directly the relatively unchanging structure of the U.S. economic system.

In 1992 and 1993, General Motors was the subject of two ninety-minute documentaries. "Roger & Me" first gained fame outside public television, and indeed, the rough edit of the program had been turned down by PBS and P.O.V. before its runaway success in the theatrical market. The other documentary, *Frontline*'s "The Heartbeat of America," was an investigative program probing the decisions behind GM's decline. Taken together, not only do these works underscore the different aesthetic and journalistic conventions of the theatrical, feature documentary and the traditional public television public affairs documentary, but more important, they illustrate who gets to say what on public television about a corporate giant, and in what style.

General Motors responded to the programs differently. Initially, it ignored "Roger & Me"—much as its chairman of the board, Roger Smith, had ignored the documentary's producer—a media strategy it could not maintain when the program became a theatrical sensation prior to its broadcast on PBS. Yet in the wake of "The Heartbeat of America," GM engaged in the familiar saber

12. Michael Moore. *Photo: Courtesy Dog Eat Dog Films.*

rattling of corporate underwriters who threaten to withhold funding from public television programs if they feel they are not getting good press.

## *"Roger & Me"*

### PROGRAM DESCRIPTION

"Roger & Me" is a first-person account of film maker Michael Moore's effort to interview Roger Smith, GM's board chairman who presided over the largest auto corporation in the world from 1980 until his retirement in 1990. Moore, a burly guy in his midthirties in jeans, sneakers, and a baseball cap, narrates the film, which he also wrote and directed. Moore wants Smith to visit the film maker's hometown to see the havoc GM's decisions have wrought on his community. The prosperous Flint, Michigan, of Moore's childhood has dissolved into a decaying, run-down city.

"Roger & Me" opens with home movies of Moore's family and archival footage of Flint when it was home to the largest concentration of GM workers in the world. When he was a young child, Moore says, he thought only three people worked for GM: Pat Boone, Dinah Shore, and his dad. "Every day was a great day" is how Moore remembers that time. Uplifting music and clips from a GM-sponsored film convey the dazzling optimism of the United States in the 1950s when white, middle-class families "saw the U.S.A. in their Chevrolet." Moore looked up to famous people born in his hometown, including Bob Eubanks of *The Newlywed Game*. He figured if Bob Eubanks could get out of Flint, so could he.

Parade footage with marching bands, floats with the sword-swinging television hero Zorro, and the governor and mayor waving at crowds evoke memories of a wholesome time before small Japanese cars and the oil embargo profoundly impacted the U.S. auto industry. Music artfully binds together scenes showing the gulf between the rich and the poor, the past and the present, the comic drama of Moore's search for Roger Smith. Not wedded to the aesthetic conventions of *Frontline's* public affairs programs, Moore and his editors soared to new heights in documentary film making; they were making *a movie*, after all, not an extended news story where music is generally absent.

Intercut with local television news stories, Moore narrates his own story about leaving Flint for California to become the editor of the muckraking magazine *Mother Jones*. But the job did not last—he was fired—and he returned home to Flint.

In February 1988, soon after his return to the birthplace of General Motors and the UAW, Flint was brought to its knees. GM closed the eleven auto plants there—despite soaring profits, according to the film maker. Moore recounts GM's strategy: "Close plants in Flint and open new ones in Mexico where the company pays workers seventy cents an hour. Tell the UAW you're broke so the union gives back to the company billions of dollars in wage cuts ostensibly to save jobs. But instead of saving the jobs, GM eliminates them, takes the money saved, and invests in weapons companies like Hughes Air."

The economic devastation created a city with the highest murder rate in the country and widespread poverty. Moore strings together scenes that bring this situation to life. For example, when *Money* magazine named Flint "the worst place to live in America," Ted Koppel came to town to do a live hookup with the city for *Nightline*, only to have the program go off the air a few minutes into the broadcast. An unemployed worker apparently stole the TV truck. When the UAW called for a massive protest against the closing of the historic Fisher #1 plant, the site of the 1937 Sit-Down Strike that gave rise to the UAW, Moore said only four people and his film crew showed up.

Moore asks GM lobbyist Tom Kay about the effect of the layoffs; Kay paints a promising picture of new industry in the area, such as Flint's lint-roller manufacturing plant. Laid-off workers, some frustrated and distraught over the loss of their jobs and their dismal prospects for the future, turn to crime or move away seeking a better future. Postal workers forward their mail. Truck rental agencies run out of vehicles. These scenes and others present Flint as a place *not* to live.

An unemployed auto worker Moore has known for years recalls walking off his job in a bout of depression.[1] When riding home, he remembers hearing the Beach Boys singing "Wouldn't It Be Nice" on the radio. The music that accompanied his depression extends over another one: scenes of boarded-up houses, burned-out buildings, and graffiti-covered storefronts long since abandoned.

As factories close and more Flint residents descend into poverty, and rats outstrip the city's human population by 50,000, Moore recounts harebrained efforts by civic boosters to save the city from further decline by trying to turn Flint into a tourist destination. Thirteen million dollars were spent to build a new Hyatt Regency downtown, and "Auto World," pitched as "the world's largest indoor theme park," cost $100 million. Moore says both went bankrupt within months. "I guess it was like expecting a million people a year to go to New Jersey to visit Chemical World or a million people going to Alaska to Exxon World," Moore comments. "Some people just don't like to celebrate human tragedy while vacationing."

With residents sliding further into despair, the city pays evangelist Robert Schuller $20,000 to address a "good times" rally to boost public morale. The preacher tells Flint residents, "Tough times don't last, but tough people do" and to "turn your hurt into a halo." Anita Bryant sings some of her old songs and urges the unemployed "to be thankful for the sunshine." Pat Boone suggests unemployed workers start new careers as Amway representatives, and Ronald Reagan takes a dozen former autoworkers out for pizza in a restaurant where someone apparently stole the cash register from under the nose of the Secret Service. Television reporters capture the people's reactions to Reagan: one woman feels honored that he listened to them; another is dubious about his suggestion that unemployed autoworkers find jobs in Texas or other places in the South.

Staying fed and sheltered is a daily struggle for some residents portrayed in "Roger & Me." Some line up to sell blood at the local plasma center. A woman on Social Security makes an extra $10 to $15 a week selling live rabbits as pets or butchered ones as meat. After the bunny lady cuddles and coos to a large, furry brown rabbit, she clubs it to death, hangs it by its rear legs, skins and guts it. This scene serves as a stinging metaphor for what GM did to its former workers once they were no longer needed.

Moore follows the activities of one man who never seems to lack for work: Fred Ross, a deputy sheriff in charge of evicting people. Viewers see Ross evicting families, watching as they move their possessions onto the parking strip. "It's my job," he says. "I treat people the way I'd like to be treated." He explains it is hard for some to pay their rent because of the plant closures.

The wealthy appear to do their part by hiring people to work as human statues wearing period costumes at the annual "Great Gatsby" garden party. Women in sequined dresses and feather boas, and men in tuxes and suits, tell Moore Flint is "a nice place to live."

Local society people party all night at a $100-a-couple "Jailhouse Rock" benefit inside the new jail. Trying on riot gear and dressed in inmates' garb, they spend the night in the new building before it is open for its intended use.

Later, Moore interviews a former GM worker with a new job as a guard who now jails other former autoworkers who weren't as fortunate as he. The guard makes a great deal less than when he worked at the company but is glad to have a job.

Fuming at the injustice of GM's lack of accountability, Moore searches for Roger Smith. With the *William Tell* overture playing, he drives through wealthy neighborhoods, pays visits to the exclusive Grosse Pointe Yacht Club, the Detroit Athletic Club, and GM's world headquarters in Detroit, where Moore is met by security guards and public relations flacks who escort him off the premises, a scene repeated in different settings throughout the movie.

Despite the army of GM publicists that shield Smith from the film maker, Moore slips into an annual stockholders' meeting posing as a stockholder.

When he stands at a microphone ready to ask Smith a question, the meeting is abruptly adjourned. Toward the end of the film, Moore is ejected from a GM Christmas Eve bash where choirboys sing "Santa Claus Is Coming to Town" and Roger Smith piously quotes from "A Christmas Carol" while the camera cuts to the local deputy sheriff evicting a mother and her kids, tossing out the family's Christmas tree, tinsel and all, onto the cold, wet parking strip. Before Moore leaves, he finally manages to invite Roger Smith to Flint to see the impact of his company's decisions on his hometown. Smith declines.

While Pat Boone sings "I'm Proud to Be an American," a slate appears with the days the Flint Plasma Center is open and the toll-free number for the Flint Tourist Office. As the credits roll by, two slates appear: first, "This film cannot be shown in Flint," and then, "The movie theater has closed."

## THE PRODUCER AND THE PRODUCTION

Michael Moore hadn't been to film school and hadn't made a film before "Roger & Me," but he did have extensive experience as a muckraking journalist and had experienced film makers working with him.

"I made 'Roger & Me' as my personal statement against an economic system that I believe is unfair, unjust and undemocratic," Moore explained. "I chose to create a satirical documentary about what happened to my hometown in the 1980s as a result of the decisions made by GM (and the Reagan administration). I sought to stimulate a discussion regarding the direction the country was heading."[2]

"My politics were shaped by living in the shadow of General Motors, not some left-wing community," he told me. "This is a country that's supposed to be 'for and by the people,' not 'by and for the shareholders.'"[3]

Michael Moore is a homegrown populist from a city that once had a socialist mayor. The future film maker came to media out of a strong commitment to change the world as he knows it.

Moore's father worked on GM's AC Spark Plug assembly line for thirty-three years, and his uncle took part in the 1937 Sit-Down Strike that led to the recognition of the UAW at the company. Moore himself nearly became a GM worker; he was hired out of high school but panicked at the prospect of living a life like his father's. The first day he was to report to work, he crawled back into bed instead of showing up at the GM plant.

The future film maker attended a Catholic seminary and considered becoming a priest, but he left with a calling to the secular political arena.[4] At eighteen, Moore became the youngest person in Michigan history to be elected to the local school board. The same year he was voted the high school clown. He later launched the *Flint Voice*, which became the *Michigan Voice*, an

alternative newspaper that he edited for ten years. *Mother Jones* in San Francisco hired him as an editor in 1986, but he fell out of favor with the magazine's
publisher after five months and was fired.[5] Moore sued for breach of contract
and won a $58,000 out-of-court settlement, money that he put into his film.

Moore did not grow up watching PBS—Flint didn't have its own PBS
station until 1980—and he had no idea his film would become a theatrical
movie or a runaway success when he first started it. He figured it would be a
local film about what he saw going on in his hometown, told from his own
perspective. Moore thought he would show it in union halls and church base-
ments around Flint, but he did not think he would sell it to anybody.[6]

"I wanted to make a movie about the real America at the end of the
Reagan decade," Moore told a reviewer. "I didn't want to make another 'Dying Steeltown' documentary with all the clichés about how horrible it is to
be unemployed. I think everyone knows it's rough not to have money. So I
decided that this film would not have a single shot of an unemployment line.
I wanted the images you don't see on the 6 o'clock news. I wanted the ugly
underpinnings of our economic system exposed. And I wanted to tell a somewhat offbeat, funny story about what the richest company in the world has
done to its hometown."[7]

"The larger issue is that we have an economic system in this country that
is not very fair," he told the *Christian Science Monitor*, a theme he has reiterated in his work. "We say we live in a democracy. . . . But if we have [democ-
racy] in our government, why don't we have it in the workplace, in our
economy?"[8]

Moore produced the film with $160,000 in cash.[9] He sold his house in
downtown Flint, most of his furniture and other belongings, and held weekly
Tuesday night bingo games to finance it. He also received grants from the J.
Roderick MacArthur Foundation; the Michigan Council for the Arts; the
Edelman Family Fund; Ralph Nader's organization, Essential Information; the
Center for New Television; the Greater Flint Arts Council; actor Ed Asner;
and about two dozen other individual donors.

Moore made "Roger & Me" with an agenda for change. "Who wants to
sit in a dark theater and watch people collect free federal surplus cheese?" he
said, criticizing the standard documentaries filled with wrenching images of
the downtrodden, and which leave viewers sadly wringing their hands and
shaking their heads. "How's that going to change anything?"[10]

In Flint, he called together some of his film-making friends from the East
and San Francisco and started filming plant closures. On his crew were experienced documentarians Judy Irving, Chris Beaver, and Kevin Rafferty. Wendey
Stanzler and Jennifer Beman edited the movie. Moore never dreamed his film

would become a theatrical success nor that it would bring him so many opportunities.

### THE REVIEWS AND DISTRIBUTION

The initial reviews of "Roger & Me" were glowing. When the film debuted on September 1 at the 1989 Telluride Film Festival in Colorado, film critic Roger Ebert heralded it as "an angry yet hilarious film that cuts through the statistics and the PR language to show an American city being destroyed by a giant corporation that cares more for profits than for its own employees."[11] In a subsequent review, Ebert applauded the film as "the right film at the right time—a movie that deflates the balloon of the selfish 1980s, and urinates on the bonfire of the vanities."[12] His headline—"'Roger & Me' Strikes Out at the Greed That Fuels General Motors"—captured sentiments shared by many other reviewers and viewers, that finally a major corporation had gotten its comeuppance. Ebert's reviews were syndicated in more than one hundred newspapers.

The film set an all-time attendance record, selling out six screenings at the Telluride festival. It won the top film award at the Toronto Festival, and when it premiered at the New York Film Festival on September 27, it received a seven-minute standing ovation.[13] *New York Times* film critic Vincent Canby anointed Michael Moore as a modern-day Mark Twain, "an irrepressible new humorist," and "as sharp and sophisticated a documentary film maker as has come on the scene in years." Canby acknowledged Moore "makes no attempt to be fair. Playing fair is for college football. In social criticism, anything goes." He praised "Roger and Me" as a triumph.[14]

Four major film distribution companies competed to sign the film. In late October, Moore announced that Warner Brothers had won.[15] The media giant would pay him $3 million for the worldwide distribution rights and spend an additional $3 million for promotion and publicity.[16] Moore chose Warner Brothers because the company agreed to a list of conditions that included giving the four families evicted in the film a total of $25,000 to be divided among themselves, promising one free seat for Roger Smith at every screening should he ever want to attend, and insisting that Warner Brothers promise it wouldn't allow the show to be aired on PBS without the director's consent. Warner Brothers agreed to cover the cost of errors and omissions insurance, and to bear the responsibility and cost of any legal defense that might arise out of the film.[17]

A master at finding locations to underscore the themes in his show, Moore announced the Warner Brothers deal at a news conference in front of the county jail because, he said, it represents Flint's "new growth industry."

## THE FRAMING OF THE CONTROVERSY

The key players in the "Roger & Me" controversy were prominent national critics who gave the film rave reviews, the handful who panned it, a local reporter in Flint, GM's public relations staff, and Michael Moore. Viewers and readers could decide for themselves who was trying to pull the wool over their eyes.

GM's public position was to remain mostly mum about "Roger & Me." The company arrived at this media strategy on the recommendation of a staff member who had seen and assessed the film at the Telluride Film Festival. "Our guy went out and took a look at it," John Mueller, GM's director of corporate media relations, told me. "The advice we got was that we ought not to react strongly because the feeling was that it would probably give credibility and strengthen the film rather than make it go away. There was this discussion of the big corporation and the little guy with the freedom of the press, and if we started clobbering him or taking a major offensive, it might seem like the giant General Motors Corporation overwhelming some little guy with the freedom of speech and all that. We decided it would be better not to be heavy-handed with it."[18] Meetings were held with GM's public relations staff in Flint and Detroit, after which GM adopted a strategy of ignoring the film. GM just wanted the matter to blow over and to maintain a low profile until it did.

But when Siskel and Ebert gave the film two "thumbs up" on their television show, and other positive reviews began to appear, GM started fielding calls from reporters nationwide. It was difficult to keep that low profile, but the company maintained a cautious approach. GM public relations staff refused journalists' requests for interviews with Smith and provided instead a spokesperson who explained that GM "has had to reduce its work force to become competitive."[19] The staff also released a statement by Roger Smith charging the film with doing "a great disservice to the community of Flint and thousands of GM employees." The statement read: "How I personally feel is unimportant. It is unfortunate that people who have pride in their community and the products they build are subjected to public embarrassment at a time when they are producing some of the finest products in America."[20]

Journalists, however, did Michael Moore's work for him by cornering Roger Smith at a press conference called to tout GM's new electric car. Smith said he had not seen the film and added, "I'm not much for sick humor, and I don't like things that take advantage of poor people's problems." He denied intentionally trying to duck Moore or refusing an interview. "I don't know that he ever asked anybody for an appointment," he said.[21]

Moore's critics did not have to wait long before negative stories about the film maker and his film began to appear in the local and then the national press. On October 1, 1989, the first article taking Moore to task for alleged distortions of the chronology appeared in the *Flint Journal*.

The *Flint Journal* had been described by Michael Moore as "the GM Gazette" for its long history of siding with the corporation, beginning with the 1937 Sit-Down Strike, and he wasn't surprised that the paper published a story that criticized his film.[22] Moore had repeatedly criticized the paper for toeing the GM line when he edited the *Flint Voice* and the *Michigan Voice*, and the paper had fired a longtime friend of his a few days earlier, accusing him of leaking an editorial to Moore.[23]

In September, the *Flint Journal* sent reporter John Foren to the New York Film Festival premiere of "Roger & Me" at Lincoln Center. After Foren returned to Flint, "some of the early reviews started coming out with the facts in them, and some of the people around here would say 'wait a minute, this isn't how it is,'" Foren told me. "So I went back and saw the movie again, taking a more careful look at it."[24]

Although he was new to the area, having moved to Flint in 1985, the layoff numbers did not seem right to him, and he remembered reading the Vincent Canby review that mentioned 40,000 people had been laid off in Flint. Foren believed the number wasn't that high, and if it were, the layoffs would have been spread over a decade. The film reviewers wouldn't have known this by watching the film.

When Foren checked out other details, other apparent discrepancies in sequencing caught his attention as a news reporter: The cash register that was supposedly stolen during Ronald Reagan's visit to the Italian restaurant actually was stolen a few days earlier. Reagan took workers out for pizza in 1980 when he was a candidate, not while he was the president, but a viewer watching the film would not know the event took place before Moore even decided to make the film. (Moore acquired the footage from a local TV station.) The Reverend Robert Schuller came to Flint in 1982, *before* the GM layoffs in 1986.

Foren solicited local reactions to the film. He quoted GM public relations spokesman John Mueller, who said Moore never submitted a "formal interview request," and Frank Joyce, a UAW spokesman, who chided the film for lacking perspective on the job losses. The mayor of Flint, Matthew Collier, defended GM as having done "a heck of a lot" for the city.

After his story appeared in the *Flint Journal*, Foren received a call from film critic Harlan Jacobson, who was preparing to interview Moore for *Film Comment*, a publication he edited for the Film Society of Lincoln Center in New York. Jacobson first saw "Roger & Me" at the Toronto Film Festival, drawn by the buzz surrounding the movie. He wanted to interview Moore in time for the New York Film Festival, but the film maker was not available for an extended interview, and Jacobson did not want to do a short, quick one. The interview date kept being postponed, and when they finally did arrange to meet in New York, Jacobson wanted a private meeting but Moore brought along his mother and his film crew, too. Jacobson refused to conduct the interview under those circumstances, but they did have lunch.[25]

While Moore was busy promoting his program, negotiating the terms of distribution, and holding press conferences, Jacobson was finding out more about the film maker. "I didn't go out looking for bear," he told me. "I was really trying to be prepared."[26]

Jacobson called up a congressional representative, who led him to sources in Flint who mentioned Foren's article. Jacobson contacted a local political pollster, Douglas Weiland, and spoke several times with Foren. At first, Jacobson thought Foren's listing of the discrepancies was picky and not particularly relevant, but during one of those conversations, it occurred to him that the discrepancies in chronology Foren had identified went beyond questions of quibbling to questions of factual truth, the film's structure, and the director's credibility as a truth teller. Foren, a daily news reporter, had not seen what the film critic had: that these factors together undermined the central premise of Moore's film—that GM was responsible for the demise of Flint.

"I couldn't understand why Foren missed the forest for the trees," Jacobson told me. "I looked at the structure of the film, and it began to fall apart. I asked larger questions. If John Foren had made a big deal about this stuff, I wouldn't have done much because it would have seemed that I copied his work. But I also had a national audience.

"Moore was using the real world but misrepresenting it. He didn't have to distort the history to do it, but he did."[27]

When Jacobson finally interviewed Moore, the film maker acknowledged some of the events in the film were out of time sequence. Auto World, the Hyatt Regency, and another retail pavilion opened and closed *before* the 1986 GM layoffs. Finally, GM laid off only 10,000 workers that year, not 30,000 as an uninformed viewer—or reviewer—might think.

Jacobson acknowledged Moore was "glitteringly smart in his analysis and arrestingly right in essence," but he felt the sequencing questions were "disquieting." He also felt on guard since he said Moore had been combative and defensive during their interview when Jacobson brought up the sequencing issue. Moore simply dismissed it as "a nonissue," arguing he was making a "movie" rather than a news documentary. He said presenting scenes in chronological order would have destroyed the coherency of the story. Besides, Moore defended himself by arguing all films are embellished in some ways to make the stories more presentable.[28] He explained he chose not to use dates in the film so as not to get trapped by chronology. He said his show is about the *decade* and the overall *trend*, not individual years. Moore regarded the criticism of the chronology and sequencing as quibbling.[29] So did his defenders.

But when his defenders rose to his defense, the framing of the debate had shifted from the content of the film to its integrity. Jacobson's article gave legs to Foren's initial story and placed it in the national arena of film critics. He shifted the discussion away from the broad theme of the realities depicted by Moore's representation of the Reagan era to allegations of inaccuracy, and Moore's personality, and his journalistic credibility. In this escalation, prominent critics came to Moore's defense, while others probed Moore's use of acquired footage and his alleged exploitation of other people's misery for his own benefit. Moore's sudden celebrity status, fueled by the critics and his visibility, made him a target.

Vincent Canby argued that the sequencing issue was not relevant because Moore had artistic license to tell his own story, and all films express a point of view anyway. Roger Ebert said the sequencing criticisms were "cheap shots," and they did not stop him from joining the film critics who put "Roger & Me" on more than one hundred "ten best" lists, or the National Society of Film Critics and the National Board of Review from giving the film its top awards.[30] Siskel and Ebert placed it alongside *Do the Right Thing* as a film that future historians would cite as emblematic of the Reagan period.

Other critics and reporters began scrutinizing Moore and his film. A major boost in this effort was Pauline Kael's review in the *New Yorker* (January 8, 1990), which took Jacobson's concerns a step farther. She panned "Roger & Me" as "a piece of gonzo demagoguery that made me feel cheap for laughing." Kael, the influential film critic whose opinions make news and set the agenda for other reviewers, described the film as "shallow, facetious and manipulative." "I had stopped believing what Moore was saying very early; he was just too glib," she wrote. Kael also criticized Moore for making unsuspecting people targets of the audience's laughter.[31] Reviews in *Newsweek* echoed her criticisms.[32] So did those in *Time* magazine, whose parent corporation, Time, Inc., had recently merged with Warner to create Time Warner, Inc.[33]

As the film critics debated the film and its director, some of Moore's former colleagues joined in the fray, putting their personal gripes in the public forum and providing more for reporters to write about. On January 19, the *New York Times* published an article filed from Detroit with the headline "Maker of Documentary that Attacks G.M. Alienates His Allies." It was the first national story containing criticism of Moore by his associates and former associates on the left. Ralph Nader told the reporter he wanted Moore to repay him $30,000 for previous support he had given the film maker through Essential Information, a nonprofit foundation. The article brought the bad blood between Nader and Moore into the public sphere. Nader's attorney said Moore "hijacked" Nader's approach by focusing on Smith, as was done in Nader's book *The Big Boys*, and did not credit him or others for ideas that were used in the film. Moore's former boss at *Mother Jones*, Don Hazen, told the *Washington Times* the film maker was "impossible" to work with.[34]

Meanwhile, Moore was becoming a celebrity as he and his entourage traveled around the country on a 110-city tour, showing the film in movie theaters and union halls, and giving out free Helmac lint rollers from Flint at special events, a symbolic reminder of GM lobbyist Tom Kay, who praised the manufacture of lint rollers as one of Flint's promising new industries. Wearing his trademark "Roger & Me" baseball cap, jeans, and sneakers, Moore continued to stress the main point of the film—the injustice of our economic system—and he became a hot guest on the talk show circuit. General Motors was not pleased by the attention.

GM's media strategy to keep a low profile could not work when Moore was in the media spotlight. By January 1990, the company had activated another media strategy: tell the media "the facts" about Flint, Michigan, point out Moore's alleged errors in the film, and criticize his "appalling lack of objectivity." GM put together an information packet for the press and even sent it out to schools that requested details regarding GM's reaction to "Roger & Me." "We weren't proactive," Mueller said. "We waited for people to ask about it." [35] The "truth packet" listed GM's accomplishments in Flint, such as how the company had invested more than $200 million in the city for various projects. It also included "talking points" and "points to make" about the film, which reiterated GM's position that the film is "one-sided and misrepresents the facts about GM plant closings and layoffs," and that it "is not a documentary but represents the filmmaker's personal viewpoint about the free enterprise economic system."[36]

When Moore appeared on national talk shows to promote the national launch of his movie, GM made sure the program producers were aware of its perspective on the film. GM provided the producers of *Entertainment Tonight*, *The Late Show with David Letterman*, *The Tonight Show*, and *Donahue* with the "truth packets" containing the critical reviews by Pauline Kael and Harlan Jacobson, its press statement outlining GM's perspective, talking points, and a formal statement from Roger Smith. Mueller told me the packet sometimes included other clippings, such as John Foren's article and excerpts from Michael Moore's own writings.[37]

"I was sitting in the dressing room and ten minutes before going on the air, Jay Leno [then the guest host of *The Tonight Show*] walks in with this manila envelope and tells me this PR guy from GM in southern California delivered this packet to him and wanted to talk to him about why I shouldn't be on the show tonight, and that Jay should nail me with this stuff," Moore remembered.[38]

Moore said the packet contained articles he had written ten years earlier, and anything that sounded vaguely "socialistic" was highlighted in yellow marker. "There were photos of me from 1972 with long hair halfway down my back, like that was supposed to mean something, like I had no credibility because I had long hair." Moore interpreted the packet as a GM effort to red-bait him as a communist.[39] GM spokesperson John Mueller confirmed the sending out of "truth packets" with the reviews to media producers and reporters, but he denied GM tried to red-bait Moore as a communist. "We knew we couldn't win with that because it wasn't the right way to go," he told me when I asked about this specifically. "We needed to argue about this based on the facts."[40]

GM also instructed its ad agencies to pull its TV and radio commercials scheduled for programs where Moore was to appear.[41] "It's very customary not to put your ads in a bad environment," John W. McNulty, GM vice president of public affairs, told the *Wall Street Journal*. He admitted telling GM's advertising agencies "to act accordingly," but he denied ordering them directly to pull ads.[42]

By early February 1990, GM's actions with the ad agencies became a story in its own right. The *New York Times* and the *Wall Street Journal* reported GM asked its ad agencies not to place GM commercials within or adjacent to television programs that featured Michael Moore.[43]

Despite GM's backdoor efforts to keep Moore off TV and radio, he made use of his forum to blast GM, corporate greed, and engage in a dialogue about the direction of the country. Some hosts joined in, fueled by GM's own attempt to influence the content of their programs. GM's strategy to discredit Moore and his documentary seemed to backfire momentarily.

"A lot of people called and wanted comment, and we made sure they saw the things that had been written about, that pointed out the inaccuracies," Mueller said. "Different press reacted differently. Some simply didn't want to know the facts. A woman in Florida—all she wanted to know about was 'Doesn't this film point out that corporations have a social responsibility?' Some took off in that direction; some took off examining 'What is a documentary?' 'Is a documentary supposed to be factual reporting about something, or is it a documentary if the facts aren't all correct?'"[44]

When he fielded calls from reporters like the one from Florida who asked about GM's social responsibility, Mueller listed GM's philanthropic contributions to its employees. "Nobody else has done as well in the auto industry," he told me. "No matter what I said to that reporter—she was very strident— the questions were like 'When did I stop beating my wife?'"[45]

Reporters framed their coverage from a handful of available newsworthy angles echoing those of the rival film critics. Many were basically positive profiles of Michael Moore as a blue-collar celebrity and a new Mark Twain who gave corporate America, and Roger Smith, a good kick in the pants. Another angle was Michael Moore, the shambling, working-class rabble-rouser who played loose with "the facts" but told an entertaining story. Most contained elements of both. As for Moore himself, he kept explaining to the press that he was making a movie, not a news documentary, and he continued trying to focus the coverage on the film's message: that the economic system is unjust and undemocratic.

### THE OSCARS

The buzz about "Roger & Me" between September 1989 and January 1990 pivoted on an anticipated Oscar nomination. From the first few months since its film festival premieres, film critics and reporters hinted that "Roger & Me" would be at least a nominee, if not a sure win, for an Academy Award in the "Feature Documentary" category, and some even suggested it might take "Best Picture." This was a common news hook, but they were wrong. The academy did not even nominate "Roger & Me." Although the nomination process is secret, the sequencing concerns raised in the national press by Harlan Jacobson and Pauline Kael, whose review appeared two weeks before the Oscar nominations, were among the reasons cited for the decision.[46]

The decision ignited a protest by forty film makers, some of whom were former Oscar nominees and winners. In an open letter to the academy, the film makers said the questions about the sequencing "could be raised about many of our documentary films."[47]

Allegations of conflict of interest swirled around the nomination process, especially around Mitchell Block, who sat on the nominating committee and distributed several of the documentaries under consideration. In the end, three of the five documentaries nominated, including the year's winner, were distributed by his company, Direct Cinema.

Block disqualified himself from nominations involving his company's films, but his presence on the committee suggests its preference for the more educational, traditional, humanist genre in documentary film making rather than new styles in nonfiction film that pushed the boundaries of the documentary form in the 1980s, such as "Roger & Me."

Despite the disappointment at being left out of the running for the Oscar, Moore felt he was in good company: the academy also failed to nominate Spike Lee's *Do the Right Thing* in the "Feature Film" category.

Warner Brothers had hoped for an Oscar nomination when it bought the film for $3 million, but even without it, "Roger & Me" was the feature-documentary success of the year. By the end of 1992, Warner Brothers had grossed an estimated $12 million through theatrical, home video, nontheatrical distribution, foreign sales, and other rights.[48] Excluding concert films, it remains the largest-grossing feature documentary in U.S. history. The loss of the nomination, however, prompted Warner Brothers to scale back its advertising budget and lower its financial expectations.[49]

### P.O.V.'S BROADCAST

While theatrical success was sweet, Moore wanted his movie to reach a mass audience on commercial television. But the commercial networks weren't interested in broadcasting the film, perhaps because it made fun of one of their most prominent advertisers. Eventually, Marc Weiss at *P.O.V.* persuaded Moore to allow Warner Brothers to let his series air "Roger & Me." Warner Brothers was paid $50,000 for these rights.[50]

This was not the first contact between Moore and Weiss.

Film making is expensive. Moore had run out of money when he was trying to pull the show into a coherent story in the editing room in 1988. That winter, he called PBS and eventually reached Weiss at *P.O.V.* to see if the new series would be interested in his "comedy documentary." Weiss, who didn't know much about Moore except that he had worked at *Mother Jones*, explained that *P.O.V.* accepted only completed films but he would be happy to take a look at a rough edit. Weiss hoped he might find a way to help Moore finish the program in return for the rights to broadcast the documentary on *P.O.V.*[51]

Weiss was disappointed by what he saw. "I called him [Moore] up and said, 'I don't know how to tell you this, but your comedy documentary is not funny,'" Weiss told me. "The magic and genius of 'Roger & Me' is the way Michael positions himself and his relationship to Flint and GM, but he hadn't written that part yet." Weiss told Moore he'd like to see the program when it was further developed. It was hard for him to say this since he knew that Moore needed money to complete the film.[52]

When Weiss watched the finished "Roger & Me" at the New York Film Festival, he sauntered up to the film maker and admitted he had "blown it." Now Weiss wanted the film for *P.O.V.*, but Warner Brothers had sold the film to HBO. When those broadcast rights expired, Weiss moved to pick them up for *P.O.V.*

Besides liking "Roger & Me," Weiss had another motive for broadcasting it: it was an opportunity to get back into the good graces of the public television stations who were still fuming from the "Tongues Untied" controversy and the fiasco over "Stop the Church."

When "Roger & Me" aired as a *P.O.V.* special on September 28, 1992, an estimated three million viewers tuned in. The Michael Moore package helped heal the rift between *P.O.V.*, PBS, and the stations, and there wasn't a peep from General Motors.

Because "Roger & Me" was already three years old, Weiss took the unprecedented step of commissioning a half-hour follow-up documentary for $55,000 to accompany it. It was called "Pets or Meat: The Return to Flint." Those who had seen "Roger & Me" could find out what had happened to some of the characters in the film, such as Deputy Fred Ross and Rhonda Britton, "the bunny lady."

DESCRIPTION OF THE *P.O.V.* SPECIAL. This special follows the format of other *P.O.V.* offerings, except director Michael Moore does not introduce his film while being interviewed in a dramatically lit studio. Instead he delivers his introduction on the street in Flint, Michigan, beneath a huge sign reading "Buick City Welcomes You." Moore welcomes *P.O.V.* viewers to Flint, the "hometown of the world's richest corporation and the birthplace of the depression we and you and the rest of the country are now experiencing." Then he introduces the evening's lineup, the showing of "Roger & Me" followed by a new documentary, "Pets or Meat."

Each documentary has its own "viewer discretion" advisory, and Moore uses the one for "Pets or Meat" to poke fun at public television: a man with a British accent warns viewers the program "contains scenes of explicit corporate behavior which may be offensive to young children, vegetarians and General Motors shareholders. Viewer discretion is advised."

Moore goes on to spoof Ken Burns, trying to imitate the successful independent film maker's writing and visual style. Moore tells a crew member this approach just "isn't me." Then Moore tries something more "upbeat": President Bush boasting about how well the economy is doing. That false start doesn't work either. Finally, Moore tells the story about what has happened in Flint since the release of "Roger & Me" and begins with clips from his television appearances on *Donahue*, where locals express their reaction to the film—both praise and outrage. On *The Late Show with David Letterman*, he tells the host, "To most people, the American dream is just a dream." He has a good laugh with Jay Leno and gets into a tussle with Pat Buchanan on CNN when he tries to hold the conservative's feet to the fire of the unemployed.

Moore visits with Deputy Fred Ross, who has expanded his business to include the repossessing of cars and other goods, and with a color consultant, who shows Moore how downtown Flint's image has been improved by colored flags. Rhonda Britton, also known as "the bunny lady," has had a baby, but she has continued to have a rough time financially. After landing a temporary, part-time job at the local K-Mart, she is still deeply in debt. She has expanded her cottage business to include rats, and she has found a new market for her live animals: as pet food. The documentary ends with a tale of survival where one of her big, cuddly brown rabbits is eaten alive by a huge pet snake, a vivid metaphor of a carnivorous capitalism.

WFUM'S AIRING OF THE SPECIAL IN FLINT. While most stations carrying *P.O.V.* broadcast the special, the station manager in Flint felt some pressure not to air it. Jim Gaver, station manager at PBS affiliate WFUM/Flint, said several community leaders, some of whom were members of the station's community advisory committee, told him they were "disappointed" when he made the decision to carry the program.[53]

Gaver had his own misgivings about the film and about Michael Moore that predated the broadcast. He said Moore misrepresented himself to get access to events such as the "Great Gatsby" party by allegedly claiming he was producing a documentary for WFUM. Gaver said concerned community leaders then contacted him wanting to know what WFUM was up to working with Michael Moore.

In a town long divided by economic class, "Roger & Me" became a lightning rod for a deep-rooted class mistrust that pitted blue-collar workers and white-collar management types against each other. Gaver observed that community leaders and those sympathetic to GM mirrored Roger Smith's response by taking pride in *not* having seen the program while people who saw their lives sympathetically portrayed in the special defended it. Since GM had already largely eliminated its corporate underwriting to the Flint and Detroit affiliate stations, it had nothing to withdraw in retaliation for the broadcast.

### THE LEGAL ARENA

A handful of Flint citizens who appeared in the film expressed their discomfort by filing lawsuits. Sheriff Deputy Fred Ross, who appeared on camera evicting families, sued Michael Moore and Dog Eat Dog Films, arguing that Moore had not told him he would be a "full-fledged 'co-star.'"[54] The case was dismissed on April 22, 1991, after an out-of-court settlement which stipulated that the parties not discuss the case, including the amount of the settlement. Others sued PBS for broadcasting "Roger & Me" on *P.O.V.* in 1992, and Warner Brothers for distributing it.

13. Michael Moore with Rhonda Britton—the bunny lady—in "Pets or Meat." *Photo: Daymon Hartley, courtesy Dog Eat Dog Films.*

The fuse for the only lawsuit that went to trial was lit at the Flint premiere of the show. Two personal injury lawyers sat in the audience; one was Glen N. Lenhoff, who represented three clients in suits related to "Roger & Me," and the other was Larry Stecco, who saw himself on the screen at the "Great Gatsby" event dressed in a tuxedo and saying Flint was "a great place to live."

Stecco, a prominent member of the local Democratic Party, felt he came off as a "racist," and Lenhoff argued to the jury's satisfaction that the film put Stecco "in a false light." The plaintiff received $6,250 in the settlement, the same amount as had the evicted tenants in the film, a paltry sum compared to the $200,000 an arbitration board had recommended. Despite the small monetary award, Lenhoff claimed victory and vowed to continue protecting his clients. "If there's another mass showing," Lenhoff told me, "we'll sue again."[55]

The Stecco case raised the professional profile of Lenhoff because the case was covered by the local and some of the national trade press. It also showed the extent to which an injured party would go to redress a perceived wrong and secure compensation. Warner Brothers and PBS maintained a posture of "no comment" on the case, but Lenhoff took the opposite strategy—and acquired three more clients.

One of the three was Karen Martin, a housewife married to a GM manager and active in the local Republican Party, who appeared in a scene speaking favorably about Ronald Reagan. She testified on Stecco's behalf and soon became one of Lenhoff's new clients. Lenhoff argued that Martin's comments were taken out of context and were actually taped at a local Republican convention during the primaries, and that Moore acquired the footage from a local news station.[56] He said the way Moore edited the scene gave the impression that Martin was an unemployed autoworker and had just had pizza with the president. Martin filed suit against PBS and Warner Brothers, alleging the film slandered her by depicting her "in blatantly false light" as "a silly fool."[57] Martin settled out of court for "a nominal amount," according to a source close to the case.

Lenhoff also represented two part-time models hired to pose as human statues during the "Great Gatsby" party. The models filed their suit five years after the film's release and after others had settled their cases out of court. They charged they were depicted "in a false light" and felt singled out by Moore because they were black. Lenhoff argued Moore's commentary implied his clients were "unemployed," but one worked as a fireman, and the other was "unemployed" from her job as a flight attendant. He said they felt demeaned, and besides, they were "private persons" not public figures.

14. Michael Moore with Deputy Fred. *Photo: Daymon Hartley, courtesy Dog Eat Dog Films.*

While Moore did not use the word "unemployment" in his narration over the images of the human statues, Lenhoff based his case in part on a photo caption written by a staff writer at *Film Comment*. The magazine's caption writer described one of the models in the photo as an "unemployed Flint inhabitant." The case was settled out of court for an undisclosed amount.[58]

While no evidence links GM to the plaintiffs' lawsuits, the lawsuits ultimately reinforced GM's public posture: that Moore made his film at the expense of "exploiting little people," that he distorted reality to score unjustified political points, and that he did this in a self-serving manner.[59] The motivations of GM may have been different from the motivations of the plaintiffs' lawyers and other critics, but the intended outcome was the same: to cast doubt on the truthfulness of the film and the honesty of the film maker.

The allegations of inaccuracies can be traced back from Harlan Jacobson's *Film Comment* article directly to John Foren's report in the *Flint Journal*. The paper had a long-standing editorial tradition of defending GM, and Moore had pilloried the paper when he edited the *Flint Voice* and the *Michigan Voice*. In the 1980s, some observers noted a climate of animosity existed between them, which Moore has argued continues to this day.[60] It is also true that Moore had a contentious, high-profile presence in his hometown as a local gadfly. But he also had a loyal following; he was a breath of fresh air for the downtrodden of Flint, who finally had their perspective expressed in his work.

### ANALYSIS OF THE CONTROVERSY

In contemporary America, unlike in Britain, there is little room for scathing satire from an economic class perspective, and an underdeveloped tradition of pillorying the powerful outside the political arena. While established cultural authorities, such as Bill Moyers and producers associated with the *Frontline* series, have challenged the moral politics of their day, Moore was an outsider, a modern-day muckraker and gadfly from the working class. A previously unheard voice, Moore found a receptive audience among millions of Americans seeking explanations for their economic despair. Moore addressed the taboos of economic class inequality.

A NEW KIND OF POLITICAL FILM. While the other documentaries examined in this book were also critical of the Reagan era, "Roger & Me" was unique in several respects: It broke with the conventions of most American political documentaries because it was funny and entertaining instead of downbeat and depressing. It reached a mainstream audience through movie theaters, television, and video stores. It was more successful at putting a human face on corporate greed, business decisions, and unemployment than any other documentary produced during the 1980s, and it did this with laughter. And finally, it was a film about economic class and economic power, a political film that used humor as a weapon in the class struggle—without using the term "class struggle." By pillorying the powerful, "Roger & Me" gave voice to a popular backlash against corporate and government leaders, arguing they were responsible for the decisions that left millions unemployed. "Roger & Me" captured the discontent of the nation.

LOSING SIGHT OF THE FILM'S MESSAGE. As in the other controversies, the discussion about the film upstaged the film's message in the press. A local press reporter broke a story that was then amplified in the elite national press. Harlan Jacobson's interview and the panning of the film by Pauline Kael set in motion the sinking of the Oscar nomination. Prominent film makers took sides, the academy defended itself, and the battle kept the film in the news.

The debate around the film showed the power of film critics and journalists to successfully frame an interpretation of the film away from the film maker's intention, and contain the discussion within ideologically safe boundaries. They were looking for the newsworthy angles and offering rival contexts for interpreting the film. Their framing relegated the main subject matter of the film into the background when the film maker became the story, not the realities he sought to represent. They were doing their job by steering the discussion about the film away from the injustice of the economic system to a safer discussion about personality and journalistic practice.

General Motors, of course, had its own agenda. When Moore suggested that what's good for corporate America is not necessarily good for working and unemployed Americans, GM used the reporting of journalists and film critics to attempt to discredit Moore and his portrayal of the company. The company's effort was not nearly as successful as the film maker in reaching an audience of millions, but the chronology of events indicates a close connection between the appearance of critical stories, the failure of the Academy of Motion Picture Arts and Sciences to nominate "Roger & Me" for an Oscar, and the merger of Time with Warner Brothers.

Unwittingly, a handful of journalists strengthened GM's campaign to discredit the film, indicating the power of reviewers to reinforce the dominant economic values of corporate America. But reviewers also have the power to voice a counterperspective, which most of them exercised when they praised the film.

TWO CONFLICTING PERSPECTIVES AMONG FILM CRITICS. The "Roger & Me" controversy cut to the heart of two critical traditions: The first, espoused by

Vincent Canby, grants broad artistic license to the film maker as a storyteller, with no requirement for "fairness" when telling a larger truth. The second, embraced by Harlan Jacobson and Pauline Kael, applies the journalist's standards of accuracy and trust to the film criticism of documentary.

This distinction has its roots in the documentary tradition. Canby's enthusiastic support and defense of "Roger & Me" underscore a view of the documentary producer as an activist, an essayist, and a revolutionary, who is an active participant in the telling of the story and turns a satirical eye on the realities of the day. By focusing on the accuracy of details in the story rather than the purpose of telling it, Jacobson and Kael presupposed a view of the documentary film maker as an extension of the journalistic observer and a chronicler of modern life, more akin to Mitchell Block's perspective on the Oscar nominating committee.

The conflicting perspectives pivoted on what counts as a documentary, the never-ending debate about "truth" in documentary, differing views on a film maker's license to use real people to tell a story from his or her point of view, and Michael Moore's personality. The economic devastation of the 1980s was largely jettisoned in the film critics' debate, with the exception of Roger Ebert.

MICHAEL MOORE'S SPIN ON THE CONTROVERSY. "Roger & Me" vaulted Michael Moore into the mainstream of American media as a media personality, a comedian, an author, and a populist critic. "I've been able to do a TV show on two different networks, make a new film, and now I have two pilots," he told me. "I have more work than I can do.

"I have not been stopped, and it's not because the corporations love me— it's simply because they think they can make money off me."[61]

For Moore, the lawsuits, the film critics' criticism, the rejection of the Oscar, the repeating of the inaccuracies in sequencing are all sideshows to the main event. He says the real story of "Roger & Me" is whose voices are allowed to be heard in the media forum, and how efforts to contain voices critical of a major corporation have fared.

"Every time someone stops me on the street and says to me, 'I'm so sorry you didn't get the Oscar,' I say for once, I'd like someone to say, 'I'm so sorry about what happened to Flint, Michigan.' I didn't make the film to make an Oscar.

"Our voices, the voices of people who come from Flint, Gary, Indiana, or Pittsburgh—we don't get heard. We don't get on national TV. We don't get to make movies. We don't get distributed by Warner Brothers. It's so rare what has happened to us. I didn't come from the accepted loop of the left, from the academic world or legitimate activist world, like Ralph Nader or Jesse Jackson. Mine was just a voice from somebody who barely got a high school education and made this movie. That's why the public took to the film. They could relate to it because they were experiencing it themselves, or knew someone who was."

"There are no inaccuracies in the film. This is the big lie the *Flint Journal* started," Moore said, seven years after the film premiered. "It's very frustrating that it gets repeated."

"Why is it that the visible attacks against the film didn't come from conservatives or corporate America, but from liberals and the left, like Ralph Nader, the *New Yorker*, and *Film Comment?*" Moore asked. "Here was a film on its way to becoming the largest-grossing documentary in all time . . . distributed by a Hollywood studio and placed in shopping mall theaters instead of art houses only to be seen by the choir. You'd think we'd be throwing a party that our philosophical bent would be out there to a wider audience, but instead, they circled the wagons and got out the knives and wanted to chop it up."

Moore believes the efforts to contain his work have not succeeded because "the viewer doesn't give a shit, doesn't buy it, and considers the source." He contends viewers didn't listen to the handful of critics who criticized his film over sequencing. "The only thing factually wrong in the film is that the restaurant owner told me the stealing of the cash register took place during the Reagan lunch when it had actually happened the day before."

THE RHETORIC OF MOTIVES AND OF FACTS. Michael Moore ascribed motives to the different players—especially to the journalists—and this was one way he responded to their attacks, just as other players ascribed political motives to Moore. From a distance, this ascribing of motives seems reasonable and understandable, but a closer look reveals a more insidious process and a different, less personal set of motivations.

It is true that the *Flint Journal's* editorial policy had supported GM over decades. But Harlan Jacobson and John Foren aren't dupes, and neither is Pauline Kael. As reporters and critics, they were doing what they are trained to do, which is to scrutinize a new celebrity and his work; they were not out "to get Michael Moore." Yet they did not have control over how their writings would be used. GM did employ their work effectively in a low-key media strategy that sought to undermine Michael Moore's film. And lawyers, such as Glen Lenhoff, cited their writings for legal purposes (as when the caption written in Harlan Jacobson's article became evidence supporting allegations that the human statues were portrayed "in a false light").

Michael Moore responded to his critics by trying to divert discussion away from the "sideshow" of criticism about the "inaccuracies in sequencing." He was understandably frustrated when journalists would want to harp on them.

In our conversations, Foren and Jacobson both described Moore as "very defensive," which, in their view, did not help his case. "If he just would have come out and said, 'Hey, I took a little artistic license here,' it would have been fine," Foren told me. "Instead he got red in the face and accused the *Journal* of being a mouthpiece for GM."[62]

Moore's perception that the *Flint Journal* was a microphone for GM had less to do with the journalistic practices of John Foren than with the newspaper's work culture, where supporting GM and criticizing the film maker had been acceptable.

Foren was doing his job as a reporter. "It was a good story. Should I have not reported it because it would play into Michael Moore's hands that GM was out to get him?" The ascription of personal motives by the various players shifted the discussion away from the arena of politics to a personality dispute.

GM objected to its portrayal in "Roger & Me" and employed the rhetoric of "facts" to frame the issue so as to minimize the negative impact on GM and tarnish Michael Moore in the process. "The facts" became a rhetorical device used effectively by GM to put a lid on Michael Moore's depiction of the United States in an era of downsizing. Even GM's John Mueller kept repeating the words "the facts" when I asked him about the case, and he would reinforce this in conversation to criticize other journalists who "weren't interested in the facts" of the case, that is, who refused to accept his playing field for discussion.[63]

Mueller ascribed different motives to Moore, which justified the corporation's stance. "Moore wasn't interested in having a cup of coffee with Roger to have Roger explain the facts of life to him. He had a political viewpoint," Mueller told me.[64]

The "Roger & Me" case raises a thicket of questions about the price of success, the making of a celebrity, and most important, who gets to say what to whom about a corporate giant. It also illuminates the roles of critics and reporters, whose job it is to contextualize films and their makers to the best of their abilities within the confines of their genres.

"Roger & Me" was produced by an independent producer and aired in the context of *P.O.V.* The following year, another program about GM became controversial. It stands as a useful counterpoint to Michael Moore's film because it was a work of investigative journalism presented under the auspices of the *Frontline* series.

## "The Heartbeat of America"

In October and November 1992, a flurry of articles appeared in the *New York Times* and other influential mainstream newspapers about the decline of General Motors, which was again in financial trouble. This prompted *Frontline's* senior producer, Martin Smith, to place a phone call to the Center for Investigative Reporting (CIR). *Frontline* had produced several investigative documentaries with the assistance of the CIR over the years, and now Smith suggested the same CIR team that had worked on an award-winning program about political campaign financing earlier in 1992 be reassembled to examine General Motors. Steve Talbot would produce and direct the program, and Robert Krulwich would be the on-camera reporter.

Normally, *Frontline* provides half the funding to get its coproduced documentaries rolling, but in a program that addressed the economic decline of a major corporation, funding from major corporate underwriters or foundations seemed unlikely.[65] So *Frontline's* executive producer, David Fanning, decided the series would cover the entire cost of research, production, and postproduction.

Talbot had previously worked as a public affairs documentary producer at San Francisco's KQED and had developed a good working relationship with *Frontline* on an earlier program, "The Best Campaign Money Can Buy" (1992).[66] Not only was *Frontline* a national forum, but the topic of corporate power appealed to him. He and a team of researchers zeroed in on a reluctant General Motors.

### RESISTANCE FROM GM

GM was more media shy than usual after the humiliation of its former chairman in Michael Moore's "Roger & Me." The company was also still stinging from a recent NBC *Dateline* debacle. Just eight months before the *Frontline* broadcast, General Motors had forced an apology from *Dateline* after company investigators discovered that the network and outside consultants had rigged fiery crash tests on full-size GM pickups to support their contention that a side-mounted gasoline tank made the trucks more vulnerable to fires in side-impact collisions. *Dateline* producers were trying to simulate a crash like the one that killed Shawn Mosely, a seventeen-year-old teenager who burned to death when the gas tank in his GM truck exploded in a crash. The Mosely family sued GM and won. A Georgia jury awarded $105 million to the parents of Shawn Mosely, but an appeals judge overturned the decision.[67] The court fined the company $1.4 million in punitive damages, but GM's subsequent attack on *Dateline* overshadowed the verdict, deflecting public atten-

15. President Bill Clinton with GM president Jack Smith. *Photo: Copyright © the White House*

tion away from GM's apparent design flaw to the ethics of media reenactments.[68]

Even though General Motors won the battle with *Dateline*, public relations managers, like William O'Neill, were wary of investigative broadcast journalists who could do the company image more harm than good. Why run the risk of having another story explode in their lap?

Talbot and his associate producer, Eve Pell, knew that anything *Frontline* produced would have to be carefully researched, with all details substantiated. GM had shown it could fight back effectively if any significant violations of accepted journalistic practice came to light.[69]

In the early stages, General Motors refused to cooperate with the *Frontline*-CIR team by requesting information about the documentary as well as questions in writing before considering whether anyone from the company would be available for an interview. Talbot and Pell sent information on the program, but Bruce MacDonald, vice president of corporate communications, felt the proposed program was "vague and unfocused." He, in consultation with his staff, decided GM had little to gain by cooperating with the *Frontline* producers.

"We were straightforward with them in the beginning that the proposal they were bringing to us had a focus rearward, and we admitted we had made mistakes in our organization but we were not going to spend time or effort dwelling on them," GM spokesman William O'Neill told me. "They couldn't provide us—in our opinion—with a credible look at GM today and where we are trying to go, so we decided not to participate."[70]

GM spokesman Ed Lechtzin said the company offered *Frontline* "more cooperation than any other media during that period," a time right after "the whole management" of GM had changed. "Their requests were too onerous," he said. "They wanted to hang out at the Saturn plant for a week when it was trying to add another shift. It would have been totally disruptive." He said the *Frontline* crew initially wanted to follow GM president Jack Smith around for "two or three days," and he wasn't going to let that happen. "You can't conduct your business with a camera around."[71]

The *Frontline* producers tell a different story. They said GM strung them along for ten months, politely declining interview requests, then giving them some hope of access to the GM leadership after an article appeared in the local newspaper about their difficulty in getting GM's cooperation.[72]

The *Frontline* producers said they first wrote GM's Bruce MacDonald on December 10, 1992, requesting interviews with top GM management and permission to film in company plants. They hoped GM would cooperate with them and were encouraged by remarks made by GM executive vice president William Hoglund, who said the company would be more open and less arrogant than it had in the past.[73] Public appearances aside, GM successfully stonewalled the producers until it was too late for them to incorporate interviews with GM top management even if GM changed its mind. For his part, MacDonald used time to his advantage by waiting weeks or months to reply to *Frontline* requests. He responded with a combination of polite letters declining requests for interviews, but he also dispatched a GM representative to CIR "to check out" Talbot and the organization.[74] In March, the producers wrote another letter to MacDonald and stepped up their efforts to get access to GM by contacting current and former members of the GM board of directors. On May 21, 1993, at GM's annual shareholders' meeting, MacDonald deviated from the polite tone of his letters. He reportedly told Talbot, "I don't like your Center for Investigative Reporting. . . . I know what kind of show *Frontline* wants you to do. . . . This is a fist fight with our car competitors, and we're not going to give anything away!"[75]

On August 3, Talbot's difficulties in gaining access to GM became public in a *Detroit Free Press* article, "PBS Documentary Takes Aim at General Motors, Which Plays Hard to Get." Talbot said GM's refusal to cooperate made it hard for him to "tell positive things about General Motors." About a week later, MacDonald wrote the producers saying he would try to make a top executive available for an interview. By this time, the program was nearly finished and running close to its October broadcast deadline. On September 13, MacDonald wrote the producers a final letter declining an interview with a GM executive because he felt the program was "already done" and the producers were "only looking for sound bites to fill in your preconceived viewpoint on General Motors. Our senior leadership unfortunately is not available for that type of interview."[76]

PROGRAM DESCRIPTION

"The Heartbeat of America" asks whether General Motors, the largest auto company in the world, can be revitalized. The company came close to financial collapse in 1992 after decades of poor business decisions, missed opportunities, and unsuccessful investments. General Motors symbolizes the economic decline of the United States through the story of the grand corporation that once defined American life, culture, and prosperity but now flounders, falling farther behind its competitors.

Unlike "Roger & Me," "The Heartbeat of America" is structured in the dominant *Frontline* news documentary style.[77] An on-camera reporter, Robert Krulwich, narrates the story. He interviews experts and key figures: Ross Perot, formerly the largest individual stockholder, criticizes GM's top management for poor judgment, arrogance, and complacency. Ralph Nader, author of *Unsafe at Any Speed*, about GM's ill-fated Corvair, criticizes GM's safety record. Financial analyst and author Maryann Keller explains specific instances where GM missed opportunities to save itself. Brad Snell recounts GM's management history. The Car Guys, Tom and Ray Magliozzi from National Public Radio's popular *Car Talk* call-in program, talk straight about GM's promise and liabilities, cracking jokes usually at GM's expense.

Viewers see footage from New York's International Auto Show, where attendees watch a fire-eater devour flames to promote GM trucks, a surreal twist given the recent litigation. They see GM's management at stockholder meetings, automobile conventions, and a meeting with President Bill Clinton, but missing in the documentary is an interview with GM's current president, Jack Smith, or anyone from GM's top management responding to the barrage of critical comments made by the others in the program.

GM's refusal to participate in the program becomes part of the story when reporter Krulwich stands outside GM headquarters and tells viewers the company refused to let *Frontline* interview Jack Smith or others in the company. He even cites the rejection letter from Bruce MacDonald, vice president of corporate communications, which arrived well past the documentary's production deadline. The *Frontline* team then turns to David Cole, director of the University of Michigan's Office for the Study of Automotive Transportation, for an explanation of GM's decision not to participate. Cole, whose father was once president of GM, says the company is "media shy," and that its refusal to give an interview is also indicative of GM's arrogance.

Despite GM's decision, the documentary is not entirely unfavorable to the company. It features a segment on GM's new Saturn, a car built with the "team concept," the result of a GM experiment in a management style imitative of Japanese car manufacturers'. The new approach projects a customer-friendly sales style where the "customer" becomes a "client." Rather than simply filling out the papers and being handed the keys to their new car, buyers "join the Saturn family" and count down for the "Saturn launch," a ritual of applause and words of goodwill from the Saturn sales "team." Customers seem pleased by this new approach, and Saturn appears to be a promising development within the company, a beacon of hope for beleaguered GM. Saturn's management seems much more open and accessible. The vice president of the Saturn plant tells reporter Krulwich he would be happy to make himself available for an interview if the main office would give him the okay. Krulwich explains to the somewhat baffled Saturn executive that permission was denied by GM headquarters.

In "The Heartbeat of America," Talbot and Krulwich appear reasonable and fair; GM seems unreasonable, suspicious, and arrogant, an observation echoed in many of the program's reviews.

## PRESS COVERAGE

Nearly three million households tuned in to "The Heartbeat of America" when it opened *Frontline*'s fall season on October 12, 1993.[78] The program received more press coverage than any of producer Steve Talbot's previous documentaries. Predictably, the reviews compared "The Heartbeat of America" with Michael Moore's "Roger & Me." "Heartbeat" was judged to be more serious but just as damning of the corporation's business practices and arrogance.

Most of the reviews were favorable and criticized GM for refusing to participate in the program. Walter Goodman in the *New York Times* described the show as a "scathing account of the breakdown of General Motors."[79] Ben Kubasik at *Newsday* wrote, "'The Heartbeat of America' (WNET/13, 9 pm) unmasks as never before the maddening arrogance of GM's chief executives, especially former CEO Roger Smith, who betrayed their customers, workers and dealers' trust, and seemed for years to learn nothing from foreign auto inroads. . . . Do yourself a favor tonight. See how far wrong things can go with insular leaders unwilling either to listen to good ideas or to grasp the truths in what they consider bad news."[80] Phil Kloer of the *Atlanta Journal/Constitution* wrote that "The Heartbeat of America" is "a somber, more credible version of Michael Moore's documentary 'Roger and Me.'"[81]

A few reviewers criticized the program's tone. The *Washington Post's* Warren Brown suggested that the program "be recalled," and that "both the program and the company share the same problem—arrogance."[82] David Zurawik of the *Baltimore Sun* observed that the program's style was "glib" and points were scored through "wisecracks" rather than facts.[83] Greg Gardner of the *Detroit Free Press* wrote that the *Frontline* program was a "video history" and "essentially a remake of 'Roger & Me' for the business school set."[84]

THE VERBAL SKIRMISH BETWEEN GM AND PBS

GM had requested a preview copy of the documentary to prepare its response, but *Frontline* refused to give the company a copy before the broadcast. GM staff and management saw the program for the first time with millions of other viewers.

The next morning, the saber rattling between GM and *Frontline* began when Bruce MacDonald, GM's vice president of corporate communications, denounced the documentary as "yellow journalism" and fired off a fax to Talbot, the press, and his GM employees. This fax was widely excerpted in follow-up articles in the *Detroit Free Press*, the *Wall Street Journal*, *New York Newsday*, and the *Hollywood Reporter*. "While we've made and admitted our mistakes, we've learned from the past and today have a new management team in position solidly focused on building a strong, competitive future, factors either ignored or unfairly distorted by the program," wrote MacDonald. "We will be re-evaluating our corporate involvement and financial underwriting of PBS shows, if programs such as *Frontline* reflect a value shift on the part of PBS."[85]

After talking with his senior producer, Martin Smith, Talbot faxed back a response that charged MacDonald with doing a disservice to his company by refusing to cooperate with *Frontline* and that denied he was out to do a "hit piece on GM." He cited the *New York Times* reviewer who even complained that the documentary was "a commercial for Saturn," the new GM car. Finally, Talbot responded to MacDonald's final volley at PBS: "Your not-so-veiled threat to cut off GM's funding of public television reminds me of the worst of the bad-old-days of GM arrogance."[86]

GM seemed to back away from MacDonald's statement when GM spokesman Ed Lechtzin told the *Hollywood Reporter* that GM had no plans to cut PBS funding and admitted the *Frontline* program was "as balanced as it could be."[87] But Lechtzin later denied GM was "backing off" because there was no funding to back off from, except Ken Burns's projects. Lechtzin told me there was "no chance" GM would stop working with Burns.[88] (Burns's relationship with GM is examined in the next section.) Another GM spokesman, William O'Neill, was not as charitable. He emphasized that if PBS is a "hostile environment," GM would "think twice" about contributing to it.[89]

PBS prepared a vaguely worded fax for the press regarding the GM incident, explaining its belief that businesses value their association with public television because the programs are "highly acclaimed" and have "editorial integrity." Without providing any specific financial data, this fax acknowledged GM as "a significant and loyal supporter of public television for many years" and expressed hope "it will continue to be our partners in bringing to the nation high-quality public TV programming."[90]

In addition, Robert Ottenhoff, PBS executive vice president and chief operating officer, sent a letter to GM's Bruce MacDonald, hoping to smooth any ruffled feathers left by the "Heartbeat" incident. The letter sought to reassure GM that neither public television nor PBS was a hostile environment and that no value shift had occurred. Ottenhoff stressed how PBS and public television appreciated GM's support.[91]

## Ken Burns, GM, and PBS

At the 1994 PBS Annual Convention in Orlando, Florida, 1,100 awestruck public broadcasters rose to their feet in a dimly lit hall, hands over hearts, staring at two gigantic video monitors projecting the logo for Ken Burns's new series, *Baseball: The American Epic*, as the National Anthem played. They were honoring their country, PBS, baseball, Ken Burns—and General Motors.

Ken Burns, a slender, bearded man wearing a tie with a pattern of huge baseballs, took the podium to introduce that fall season's premiere of *Base-*

*ball*, a nine-part homage to the "national tonic." The film maker recalled standing before a similar audience four years earlier to introduce *The Civil War*, the blockbuster PBS series also generously underwritten by General Motors.[92]

"I have to take one moment again to thank General Motors," he told the raptured audience, some of whom wore *Baseball* caps. "In fact, they are spending nearly double what they spent underwriting the film to promote and to produce educational components." (Audience applause drowned out the end of this sentence.) Burns went on to list the pledge items and merchandise to promote the series: CDs, leather jackets, mugs, books, T-shirts, and even polo shirts with a little GM logo printed discreetly beneath the series's title.

Ken Burns has shown public broadcasters and corporate underwriters that his historical programs can make money and enhance corporate images for $5 million or less. His successful marriage of GM's money with public television serves as a model to attract corporate underwriting back to the system, pleasing public television executives by the revenue brought in from pledge drives and increased visibility.

Many see his work as the ideal of public television realized, bringing history alive in eloquent films filled with anecdotes that humanize history and probe the seemingly unchanging yet evolving character of Americans. This is one reason over a thousand public broadcasters stopped eating their dessert and spontaneously rose to their feet. At that messianic moment, Burns had become a momentary messiah.

But not all public broadcasters felt at ease with the fanfare about the Burns series despite the standing ovations, merchandise, and free souvenirs given out at WETA's evening *Baseball* party where public broadcasters lined up for thirty minutes stretching from the WETA suite down the hotel hallway. While many scrambled for autographed baseballs, posed for a photo with Burns, and praised the film maker and the series effusively, others worried about what they saw as "a conservative direction" for the system, away from provocative programs that challenged viewers to reexamine their worlds. "Ken Burns is the poster boy for PBS. They've gotten conservative since 'Tongues Untied,'" one told me. "Who's going to argue about *Baseball?*"

The spectacle surrounding Burns, which has been repeated at subsequent gatherings, reveals much about what now constitutes success in the public television world. General Motors has agreed to serve as the sole corporate underwriter of Ken Burns's program through the year 2000. The company contributed $4 million toward the production of the *Baseball* series, invested $6 million to promote it, and spent a similar amount to promote *The West* (1996).

GM spokesman Ed Lechtzin believes GM gets its money's worth by supporting programs produced by Ken Burns. "We work with him because he produces excellent stuff," he said. "Being associated with nice things, people have
good feelings about it. That's what advertising is all about—leave everybody
with a warm fuzzy. They'll think nice of you."

The millions GM has contributed to each of Burns's projects amounts to
a small portion of its overall advertising budget.[93] GM's association with "quality" television products and producers, like Burns and, in previous years, Bill
Moyers, enhances the corporation's image to the public television viewing
audience. With its reputation for cars that don't hold up as well as Toyotas or
Hondas, many Americans don't immediately associate GM with quality products. GM's promotion of Ken Burns's programs makes this connection for them.

The merging of Ken Burns's film making with General Motors's money
to air on PBS is a happy union, in which each of the parties gets what it wants.
Ken Burns gets to create his series without scrambling for funding.[94] Burns's
good press enhances GM's public image by associating the corporation with
"quality." PBS gets a model to hold up to other public broadcasters (programmers, producers, and fund-raisers) of a series likely to bring more members and
donations into the system, and the model also sends a message to major corporate underwriters that public television is corporate friendly, a cost-effective
place for corporations to put their money if they want to be associated with
high-quality television.

## The Ultimate Triumph of General Motors

"Roger & Me" and "The Heartbeat of America" were broadcast on PBS, and
both were shown in the context of PBS series. Both portray the leadership of
General Motors as arrogant and often inept. Both programs and their series
coexist on the same PBS that presents Ken Burns's documentaries to the viewing public. PBS serves as a venue for all three portrayals of General Motors: a
socially callous destroyer of communities, as in "Roger & Me"; an arrogant
company in decline through poor management, as in "The Heartbeat of
America"; and a generous patron that made possible the highest-rated documentary series in PBS history.

The programs' different places on the PBS schedule reveal how national
and local gatekeepers regard them. The differences correlate with the respective status of the programs' producers, the status of the series, and the funding that made all three of them possible. GM also reacted differently to each
one.

After its theatrical success, "Roger & Me" aired as a *P.O.V.* special in

September 1992. The documentary was produced by an independent producer who paid for his film with foundation grants and his own resources. "Roger & Me" launched Michael Moore's national television career as a political jester.

"The Heartbeat of America" was business as usual for the *Frontline* series, which is scheduled and carried by most public television stations in prime time during the main broadcast season. The flak from GM over the broadcast lasted just a few days in the newspaper. The company rattled its saber, *Frontline* defended the program, and that was the end of it.[95]

Since *Frontline* receives most of its revenue from PBS and CPB with the support of stations, it is not dependent on corporate underwriters or foundations for its financial support. *Frontline* has a special status in the public television world. The only ongoing public affairs documentary series on PBS, *Frontline* is where "controversial" topics are addressed. Because the series's funding comes from public television sources, executive producer David Fanning said he does not feel compromised journalistically by this funding, as he might if the series were underwritten by an insurance company, for example. Fanning said he feels free to pursue any story he likes so long as he can find the right people to do it.[96]

Ken Burns doesn't need an umbrella series to present his work; his work is treated as a series in itself. The funding for Burns's series is distinct from *Frontline*'s and Michael Moore's. While Burns mixes grants from public and private foundations, and has a major corporate underwriter, it is the corporate underwriter who receives the greatest visibility. In effect, public and foundation funds underwrite GM's image enhancement as a generous corporate patron.

GM associates itself with high-quality film making by supporting Ken Burns's works, such as *The Civil War*, *Baseball*, and *The West*. The success of these series suggests that what's good for GM is good for PBS. GM gets more positive public relations mileage out of Ken Burns than the few days of negative press from "The Heartbeat of America" and the comic barbs from "Roger & Me." Indeed, soon after the broadcast, "Heartbeat" faded from public consciousness, and while "Roger & Me" has remained a presence in the public arena through home video outlets and movie rentals, it hasn't been adopted as widely as Burns's programs in the educational market, a place where young consumers—schoolchildren—are presented with GM's logo and slogan, the "Mark of Excellence."

Burns's major projects are in no danger of "fading away" because they make television history. Both *The Civil War* and *Baseball* have become icons of the "best" PBS has to offer. They have received among the largest viewing audiences in public television history and have been rebroadcast several times by stations during pledge drives.

Hence GM's relationship with independent film maker Ken Burns over-shadowed any perceived damage to its image caused by "The Heartbeat of America" and "Roger & Me." While these shows were critical of the major U.S. corporation, Burns's series epitomize an ideal arrangement between a cor-porate underwriter, PBS, and a prestigious independent producer whose work suits GM's public relations goals.

# Conclusion:
## A Hostile Home

Public television was a hostile home for the independent producers whose work has been discussed here, but it was a home nonetheless. For it to be a home at all required programmers who believed in the value of their voices, funders who recognized merit in their projects, and producers who continued producing despite the obstacles in their way.

All of these producers had important stories to tell, stories set against the backdrop of a larger story about the relationship between the arts, the political and economic order, the organizational structure of public broadcasting, and the struggle for a vital public sphere. All of the documentaries and the controversies were vectors of social movements and reflected changing attitudes in U.S. society between 1985 and 1993. They indicated a lack of consensus not only about what was appropriate for public television but also about whose views of reality were worthy of a place in the public forum. The independent producers of these programs brought uncommon views to the airwaves, yet when their voices became audible, a complex collective response from programmers, interest groups, and reviewers rose to contain them.

### The Making of a Controversy

There were three distinct steps in the making of these controversies. The first was the documentary producer's selection of the story to tell. The second was the acceptance of the final product by PBS either directly or through a series, such as *P.O.V.* or *Frontline*. The third step was the way the documentaries were framed in the media environment—both in the context of the broadcast and in the press. All along the way, the participants made a number of decisions that were part of a complex agenda-setting process in which various parties sought to tell the public what to think about, and how to think about it.

THE FIRST STEP: THE FILM MAKER'S SELECTION OF THE STORY

All the film makers chose topics that dealt with divisive social or political issues, and they were often linked to grassroots concerns of the 1980s and 1990s: the peace movement, the gay liberation movement, the Palestinian-Israeli conflict, or Reagan's economic policies.

All the programs violated the beliefs or perspectives held by vocal or powerful organizations. In "Days of Rage: The Young Palestinians," Jo Franklin-Trout put a human face on Palestinian youth while organized groups sought to demonize them. The "Dark Circle" producers publicized decades of nuclear mismanagement and environmental damage by the federal government, a hidden cost of the Cold War, while the Reagan administration called for a stronger nuclear defense. They also questioned the long-standing belief that major corporations, such as General Electric, and the federal government were protecting the health and safety of American citizens. In "Tongues Untied," Marlon Riggs depicted a black, gay man's experience at a time when organized interest groups sought to keep gays in the closet and off the airwaves, and others sought to limit the dissemination of gay sexual imagery and provocative language. Robert Hilferty's "Stop the Church" criticized the Catholic Church's official stand on AIDS and sex education. Michael Moore's "Roger & Me" and Steve Talbot's "The Heartbeat of America" dispelled the belief that what was good for General Motors was also good for working Americans and the U.S. economy.

These film makers lived up to their description as "poets, prophets and pamphleteers" because they used their talents to draw attention to realities that exist in the society but that had been ignored, marginalized, or poorly represented by the mainstream media or on public television. They were answering the call to use documentary to broaden the range of views available on public television and to create a more inclusive media culture.

THE SECOND STEP: THE GATEKEEPERS' ACCEPTANCE OF THE PROGRAM

PBS programmers, local station programmers, and the P.O.V. series gatekeepers were key players in these controversies because they determined whether the program—and therefore its subject matter—would find a place on the national or local schedule.

At the national programming level, six factors entered into the PBS gatekeepers' routine decision making. First, PBS programmers considered the nature and timing of the documentary's topic. They needed to believe the program was newsworthy, timely, and not redundant. This editorial judgment determined whether the subject matter would be deemed worthy of public attention. The second factor was the PBS programmers' perception of the producer. Was he or she an "advocate" or a "journalist"? If the gatekeepers didn't trust the producer or questioned the producer's journalistic standards, they rejected the program unless it came to them as "commentary"—usually from a highly regarded cultural authority, such as Bill Moyers—or was part of an ongoing series, like *Frontline*. Third and fourth factors were the aesthetic style of the documentary's presentation (did it follow or deviate from the more traditional style of public affairs documentaries?) and whether the program conformed to journalistic conventions and norms as understood by the PBS gatekeepers. A fifth factor was whether there was room on the national schedule, and the sixth was the national programmers' judgment about whether the stations were likely to carry it.

Within the context of these factors, PBS programmers struggled with ways to present programs by nonelite cultural authorities on highly contested social or political issues. They felt programs such as "Days of Rage" and "Dark Circle" didn't fit easily into the PBS lineup as freestanding programs, so they sought to "wrap" them with supplemental video or discussions.

When the *P.O.V.* series was established, it was a welcome addition to the PBS cosmology because it served to showcase works by independent producers with strong or uncommon points of view while containing them to a ten-week summer series. *P.O.V.* series editors sought programs that they believed represented some of the best work in the independent documentary community. They made a commitment to enhancing viewers' understanding of the world by scheduling and broadcasting programs that reflected some of the diversity of American society. PBS programmers went along with their decisions, with the exception of "Stop the Church."

Local station programmers sometimes chose to hinder *P.O.V.*'s effort to bring these works to the viewing public by refusing to broadcast the programs, even late at night and in the summer. These local programmers were in a position to help realize or hinder the promise of public television as a genuine public forum for the expression of views outside the established consensus. Many chose to hinder it.

When the national PBS programmers and the local programmers made their decisions, they had to take their respective audiences into consideration. For PBS programmers, this audience was the stations. For station programmers, the audience was their viewers and subscribers. Nevertheless, programmers like Gail Christian at PBS and others at local stations sometimes sought to use their positions to "push the envelope" on social issues rather than succumb to complacency by avoiding potentially controversial programming.

These programmers and gatekeepers made judgments about who does and who does not have the privilege to speak on the contested issues of the day. If a potentially controversial program came from an established cultural authority, such as Bill Moyers or David Fanning at *Frontline*, PBS programmers said they were more likely to trust it as a work of journalism. Independent producers generally did not command this degree of trust, nor did they have this ongoing relationship and track record, but they did find support at *P.O.V.*, a small outlet for nonelite cultural authorities.

Even if independent producers had journalistic credentials inside the public television world, as Jo Franklin-Trout did as a former senior producer for *The MacNeil/Lehrer NewsHour*, PBS programmers regarded them with suspicion when they took on hot topics. They perceived them as likely advocates for particular points of view, despite the soundness and evidence of facts, and in Franklin-Trout's case, her track record as a producer of previous series. Even though the international press and the *New York Times* had covered the story and background of the Intifada, Trout was dismissed by critics inside and outside of public television as "biased." Verification of her truth-claims in the press weren't sufficient to counter her organized critics' allegation that she was "pro-Palestinian."[1] Pro-Israeli, anti-Palestinian interest groups tried to stop the broadcast and succeeded in launching national and local campaigns against public television. This was a political war waged in the media. The press echoed the pro-Israeli groups' concerns and those of public television insiders like Chloe Aaron, and amplified them for the reading public.

The producers of "Dark Circle" were dismissed by their public television critics as propagandists and advocates due to the way they told the story. Barry Chase felt the documentary was manipulative and that the film makers could not be trusted to know or present the truth. He criticized the links the film makers drew between the nuclear weapons industry, major corporations, and the U.S. government, as well as the film's aesthetic style. Unlike Franklin-Trout, the "Dark Circle" producers did not have a previous "relationship of trust" with PBS or insider journalistic credentials. PBS programmers and their colleagues at KQED evoked journalistic conventions and norms to undermine the initial PBS broadcast.

The other independently produced documentaries presented here—with the exception of "Stop the Church"—did find a niche on the national schedule, but that didn't insulate them, or the series, from groups and individuals intent on creating controversy.

The decisions of programmers to schedule or not schedule the documentaries set the stage for the controversies to unfold in the public arena.

### THE THIRD STEP: FRAMING OF THE CONTROVERSY
### IN THE MEDIA ENVIRONMENT

The press provided a platform for critics and supporters of the program to express their views within the framework set up by the reporters. The controversies' participants, including the press, sought to spin the story to their own advantage. If critics couldn't "kill the message," they would at least try to shape it or sometimes to discredit the producer—to "kill the messenger."

The controversies resulted from complex interactions between individuals, organized groups and institutions, and the media. Once the program was finished and the overture to public television was made, each party behaved in predictable ways and seemed to know how to get the attention of the press. First, initiators chose to make an issue about a particular program. Sometimes the initiators were station managers, as Chloe Aaron was in the "Days of Rage" controversy. Sometimes they were the producers, as in the case of Judy Irving and Chris Beaver and "Dark Circle," or else they were members of the press or interest groups, such as Paul Lomartire at the *Palm Beach Post* and Donald Wildmon of the American Family Association in the "Tongues Untied" case and John Foren at the *Flint Journal* in the case of "Roger & Me." Regardless of the person who took the first step, the controversies became a public event once initiators found a hearing in the press. This escalated the conflict from a private disagreement to a public controversy as organized advocacy and special interest groups mobilized, and more members of the public television community entered the fray.

The broadcast and print media covered the disputes by quoting or referring to various interest groups or their viewpoints in their stories. Organized interest groups, such as pro-Israeli organizations like CAMERA ("Days of Rage") and the Catholic Church ("Stop the Church"), mobilized their national and local supporters and used the credibility granted them by the news media to pressure public television to cancel the broadcasts or to create wraparound discussions within which their perspectives would be respectfully incorporated into the broadcast. This gave the programs' critics the opportunity to influence how viewers perceived the program both in the actual broadcast and in the print coverage. Was "Days of Rage" "propaganda" or "journalism?" Was "Dark Circle" "journalism" or "advocacy?" Was "Tongues Untied" "indecent pornography" or "a work of art?" Was "Roger and Me" factually inaccurate or a perceptive representation of greed in corporate America?

The coverage of the controversies in the press was significant because it meant that viewers were tipped off that the programs in question were aberrations. The packaging of the program on screen reinforced this view. It also illustrated an important agenda-setting function: how powerful, organized groups, in association with the press and broadcasters, sought to shape the context in which viewers would watch the program.

## Controversy and the Struggle for Democracy

While all the documentaries eventually gained access to the airwaves—all but one over PBS—the controversies surrounding them were part of the struggle to bring uncommon perspectives to a common table. The documentaries presented views of reality and aesthetic styles marginalized in the mainstream public television media. They spoke to complex truths that need to be heard not because they fit some particular political line but because they help us, as citizens, to understand our lives and to make informed political decisions.

The Rocky Flats Nuclear Weapons Facility emitted radioactive substances during several accidents that have been linked by studies to rising rates of cancer, birth defects, and environmental pollution in the surrounding community. This is not a radical statement but an accurate description of what occurred. These facts in the film had even been documented in government and scientific studies, and in legal cases. While "Dark Circle" was held off the air as KQED and PBS argued about logos and whether the work was "propaganda" or "journalism," the government continued to allow the nuclear weapons industry to pollute the environment and endanger the health of people living and working at Rocky Flats and at similar facilities. "Dark Circle" cast a human light on the policy decisions when the Reagan administration sought to expand nuclear weapons production. The delay and containment of the information presented in the film bore directly on the ability of millions of citizens to be informed about their world and to participate in the political debate.

The economic tragedy Michael Moore portrayed in Flint, Michigan, was not a liberal or radical fantasy. Moore saw close-up the effects of economic policies and corporate decisions that occurred when U.S. factories closed and relocated abroad where labor costs were lower. He captured the results of an overall, growing disparity of wealth during the 1980s when changes in the tax law contributed significantly to the growing gap between the rich and the poor. (The 1986 Tax Reform Act eased the tax burden on wealthy Americans making between $500,000 and $1 million per year, dropping their taxes from 70 percent to 31 percent of their income.)[2] The disparity in wealth was evident in the astronomical rises in the salaries of the CEOs of major corporations.[3] Michael Moore didn't create these disparities, but his film sought to illuminate some of their effects on working-class people. The criticism of the film for deviating from a tight chronology detracted from its message: that corporate America is insensitive to the lives of its workers, and that our economic system allows corporate executives to routinely put profit and shareholder interests before the good of the local community.

The lives portrayed in "Tongues Untied" and "Stop the Church" fit less neatly into demographic or economic categories; they were voices from the gay and lesbian social movement. These works dealt with human journeys and the truths of specific lives, not with whether homosexuality is morally right or wrong. Having an opportunity to hear those stories is not a liberal or conservative act, but an act of common respect and understanding, from one citizen to another.

With some exceptions (such as when they had an advocate inside PBS programming), independent producers were on a collision course with PBS programmers, who sought to maintain their journalistic standards and saw themselves as accountable to affiliate stations. While the programmers were also obligated to realize public television's mandate to provide a forum for voices outside the mainstream, they made their decisions to accept or reject the programs with the knowledge that some stations and audiences did not want to hear what the film makers had to say or did not want to hear it in the form it was presented. They felt a responsibility to the stations who paid their bills.

The controversies marked the bumps along the road of social change. It was often not an easy ride, especially for an independent producer who wasn't backed up by a powerful station, a series, or—when push came to shove—PBS. Challenges to the producers' integrity by programmers or critics, and producer's charges that PBS was unfair or irresponsible, were all part of the pattern. For participants, it was like traveling in a Jeep without seat belts, riding fast on an unpaved road riddled with curves and potholes. Some passengers got thrown from the vehicle, such as the programmers who resigned or the producers who felt so frustrated that they gave up making films with strong points of view or in even trying to get their work on public television. When powerful people or organizations exerted pressure on the system, the ride was very rocky until they had been heard, gotten their way, or the broadcast was over. The conflicting viewpoints expressed in the controversies weren't fully reconciled in any definitive way; they just faded into the background until another opportunity arose to make controversy.

As a communication event, the controversies brought conflicting values and perspectives on the issues of the day to the public forum. For this to happen, all the participants in the controversy had to choose to engage in the dispute. All of the participants had their own constituents and agendas that they sought to advance. The "Tongues Untied" case serves as a good example here. Marlon Riggs wanted to start a dialogue on the black, gay experience. The American Family Association (AFA) condemned the PBS broadcast of this program because it disapproved of the "homosexual lifestyle" it represented. It was also up to speed in the culture wars being waged by Senators Jesse Helms and Bob Dole from the Senate floor against public funding of the arts. The AFA had a track record with the National Endowment for the Arts over the Mapplethorpe controversy—the same funder that contributed a small grant to Marlon Riggs—and was ready to take on public television.

The National Endowment for the Arts sent out press statements defending itself against the AFA and making the case that funding "Tongues Untied" was appropriate. PBS and *P.O.V.* did their parts by defending the documentary as a rare glimpse into the gay, black experience, even though there was strong dissent inside the public television affiliate community. Journalists recorded the battles in local markets, telling the story from the same general leads: the revolt within the ranks of affiliate stations and where the local station stood, linking the story to the NEA and attacks on it by the AFA.

Hence each participant played a specific role and interacted with the others. Together they made controversy like an orchestra makes music, with every section playing its part.

The programs that became controversial were the fortunate ones: at least they were produced, and after struggles for access to the airwaves, eventually they were broadcast. It is difficult to document the producers who ran out of funds, gave up before completing their projects, or were able to complete their programs but were unable to secure an airdate on public television. Not being able to hear the voices of talented independent film makers limits the public discussion of certain issues and the inclusion of certain viewpoints. This is at odds with the democratic principles on which the United States was founded.

Censorship is perhaps too strong a word to describe the complex, collective communication process that has kept provocative works by nonelite cultural authorities marginalized or off the public television airwaves. While all the documentaries presented here eventually aired, some were wrapped with lengthy supplemental discussions or ghettoized in the only series outlet for their innovative work, *P.O.V.*, and all were framed in the media coverage in terms of the controversy around them.

Public television is structured to preclude controversies like the ones described because programmers usually reject outright independently produced programs they fear will trigger major disputes with the stations. The works examined here sought to push the boundaries of the acceptable on PBS and to widen viewers' exposure to unfamiliar realities—to challenge public broadcasting to fulfill its promise as a vehicle for democratic culture.

Public television could be a more vital forum for a democracy of expression with the creation of additional series like *P.O.V.* Certainly, *P.O.V.* could be expanded beyond its ten-week summer schedule. The issue is not simply that the views of minority and marginalized groups are worthy of public attention, but that the quality of our political life depends on all of us knowing more about the life experience of each of us, especially those whose lives are underrepresented in the mass media. The struggle for representation and access to the public television airwaves is a political struggle for legitimacy in the public forum.

But as we have seen, the financial and organizational structure of public television, along with its rigid conventions of journalism, work to keep the programming cautious.[4] So long as the system is vulnerable to the withdrawal of federal funding, and dependent on a mix of private funds from corporations, foundations, and private donors, public television's promise as a vital forum in our democracy will remain unrealized.[5]

The independently produced documentaries examined here held public television to that promise. Although the immediate result was controversy, the airing of the programs before a national PBS audience offered a glimmer of hope. The independent producers not only communicated stories and perspectives that the mainstream media were not ready or willing to address, but also helped further the cause of various movements for social and political change. Finally, they forced PBS programmers, and the public television system overall, to address the challenges of a democratic society.

# Epilogue

At the 1995 PBS annual meeting in the Chicago Hilton, the same building that housed the raucous 1968 Democratic Party Convention, about a thousand attendees gathered to take stock of the political effort to eliminate federal funding for public broadcasting.

The conference, like the previous ones I attended, had sessions dedicated to marketing and financial planning for stations, fund-raising workshops, and showcases for high-profile stations and independent productions. Producers, programmers, and marketers mingled. Conflicts seemed to be handled with civility—with occasional bravado in the general sessions.

At one general meeting, I listened to a station programmer, saddened by the forthcoming season's plethora of nature and music shows, challenge PBS programmers to schedule more works like Marlon Riggs's "Black Is . . . Black Ain't" (1995) in the national feed. As in previous years, the comments took on a ritual quality: an acknowledgment that public television had become too safe, and that programming had drifted too far from its original mission to provide programming that addresses the needs of unserved and underserved audiences. This older, inclusive vision collided with the hard scheduling priorities and the ratings-driven reality that more public television viewers prefer "educational" as opposed to "alternative" programming, and highbrow entertainment over provocative, challenging work by independents, such as Marlon Riggs. "It's the old conflict between the mission and the market," a station executive told me.

Later, at a table sprinkled with gold confetti dollar signs, and foil wrapped, chocolate dollar coins to commemorate the twenty-fifth anniversary of *Wall Street Week with Louis Rukeyser*, I dined beneath huge chandeliers in the hotel's grand ballroom where the afternoon meeting had taken place. The chandeliers glittered and the confetti sparkled. The tuxedo-clad host of the financial program held forth from the stage, reminiscing about his long career. For a moment, I felt as if I were on the *Titanic* just before it went down, momentarily immersed in a community in denial that was unaware of the forces leading to its own demise.

The number of financial programs addressing the interests of stockholders and upper-income Americans far exceeds the few, single documentaries about the travails of working people that appear occasionally on public television, usually around Labor Day or on *The American Experience*. *Wall Street Week* is just one of several business talk shows underwritten by major corporations. Prudential-Bache, FGIC, and the Travelers underwrite *Wall Street Week*; Digital Equipment Corporation, A. G. Edwards, and the Franklin Group sponsor *The Nightly Business Report*; Metropolitan Life funds *Adam Smith's Money World*.[1] While major corporations support several national talk shows that offer viewers a business or a conservative perspective, the lone public affairs program from a liberal-left perspective, *The Kwitny Report*, was canceled after it failed to attract adequate funding. *Rights and Wrongs*, a series on human rights hosted by Charlayne Hunter-Gault of *The MacNeil/Lehrer NewsHour*, had funding but was rejected by PBS because "human rights is not a sufficient organizing principle for a television series."[2] In addition, PBS underwriting guidelines prohibit labor unions from underwriting programs or series with a decidedly labor focus.

The unstable public and private funding of public television reinforces this unequal balance of programs, where business interests outweigh those with another point of view. This trend signals an increasingly commercialized future with programs benefiting those who pay for them at both ends: the underwriters of programs and the upper tier of subscribers. Lower-income Americans, the unemployed, the marginalized, blue- and pink-collar workers— what does public television offer them? Where were *these* publics in public television? Their realities certainly weren't evident amid the confetti dollar signs.

The creeping commercialism of the system was evident throughout the conference. Bruce Christensen, PBS president from 1983 to 1993, said without government funding, public television would be commercial by the year 2000.[3] His successor, Ervin Duggan, told broadcasters, "It may be time to stop talking about entitlements and to start talking about enterprise zones."[4] Under Duggan's leadership, PBS loosened its program underwriting guidelines to make the service more attractive to corporate funders, and enhanced off-air, "value added" benefits where funders receive additional publicity in conjunction with the broadcast and postbroadcast distribution to schools. PBS also developed its own "co-branding" strategy to link public television's local and national "brand" identity through a slick advertising campaign with the slogan "If PBS doesn't do it, who will?"

At the 1995 PBS conference, John Grant, then senior vice president of PBS national programming, told broadcasters not to expect PBS to push "fringe programs."[5] He also acknowledged the dilemma facing the service when a major underwriter funds a program with the understanding that this program, which may take years to produce, will be scheduled during prime time on PBS, but the program isn't one the stations or PBS still want in that time-slot. He advised station fund-raising staff to contact him if a major corporate underwriter for a proposed PBS series was "at risk" unless it was guaranteed a national prime-time broadcast. He reassured his audience that the series would probably be broadcast on PBS but not necessarily in prime time.

Each annual PBS conference showcases the fall season's coming attractions. Each year, public television executives understandably extend their gratitude to corporate underwriters. During the 1995 session, Judy Crichton, the outgoing executive producer of *The American Experience*, gratefully announced that American Express had just signed on as corporate sponsor. Other series executives thanked their sponsors as they introduced previews of the programs that would not have been made without them: Texaco provided underwriting to a series, *Rock-and-Roll*; Sears underwrote *The Puzzle Place*, a children's program of "high quality family entertainment"; an insurance company underwrote *The American Promise*, a series filled with images of risk-taking individuals revitalizing their communities.[6] David Fanning, whose *Frontline* series is the only one without a major corporate underwriter, introduced a crowd-pleasing tape of fire and brimstone in Waco, Texas, and the new *Frontline* website. Overall, the lineup seemed to be the standard PBS fare, punctuated by a few high-profile independent productions, such as the special "Hoop Dreams" and *Wishbone*, a new daily, literary series for children starring a Jack Russell terrier with big ideas.[7]

In work sessions, peers advised peers at other stations about how to mobilize support to save public broadcasting from federal funding cuts, and to advocate for the formation of the Public Broadcasting Trust. (This fund would be established with private contributions and public funding, and the government appropriations would be gradually phased out as the trust reached a sufficient level of solvency.)[8] Some of the suggestions were directed at making the most of upcoming Independence Day celebrations by asking public television supporters to participate in parades with banners such as "Save Public Broadcasting," "Speak Out for Public TV," "Save Public TV—An American Tradition." Some asked congressional officials to march with stations and their supporters. Others suggested supporters ride bicycles decorated with pictures of their favorite PBS shows and personalities, create parade floats, set up booths or tables at community events, sell T-shirts, buttons, bumper stickers, Frisbees, refrigerator magnets, water bottles, and baseball caps—all promoting public television. Organizers urged station staff to utilize their volunteers in the effort and to build on local partnerships with local underwriters.

This grassroots campaign opened up public television to its communities in summer 1995, but the door opened only so far: public television staff seemed interested in involving "the public" just to preserve the system as it was, not to challenge or change it.

During the 1995 PBS conference, a local Chicago media activist came to the hotel to distribute bright orange brochures asking "Why is there public broadcasting?" He belonged to a local community group, the Coalition for Democracy in Public Broadcasting, that sought more community involvement in the decisions made at Chicago's public station, WTTW. The man was escorted from the premises by three Chicago Hilton security guards on orders of "an executive from the planning of the conference," a fact I verified with hotel security and PBS.[9] As he left the premises, his situation seemed emblematic of PBS as a closed system where citizens, independent producers, and even some station staff are treated as intruders.

My encounter with a PBS public relations official reinforced this demarcation between insiders and outsiders in the PBS world. When I asked why "Closed to the Press" signs suddenly started appearing at workshops to which I and other reporters had been invited, my question was treated as an affront.

"I didn't have to let you come here," the PBS public relations official snapped. His discomfort at my presence and question was palpable. When I reached for my tape recorder to have a record of our interaction, one of his colleagues pulled him aside. "Don't you dare!" were his final words to me.

I felt I was once again an unwelcome guest in the PBS world. By excluding the press, and a lone community activist, PBS was excluding representatives of the public from its domain. It was treating us as arrogantly as General Motors had treated Steve Talbot and Michael Moore.

This exclusion from the PBS realm did not, however, extend uniformly to the station level. When PBS staff stonewalled, several station staff welcomed us to their meetings and told us they were annoyed by PBS's efforts to limit our access; they saw us as their links to a larger, public audience if we could be enlisted to help them publicize their campaign or write about it thoughtfully.

Local stations have been supportive of independent film makers on occasion and served as their points of entry to PBS or other national distributors. I know this from personal experience. As I lead the dual life of scholar and independent film maker, my documentary work has found a home at KCTS/Seattle.[10] Local stations, such as KCTS, that have cultivated their relationships with local film makers can serve as a model for integrating independents into the public television system as production partners. Working with independents, stations can enable work to be made and seen that would not otherwise be produced. Of course, this is a path of compromise. For independents, the editorial content and aesthetic style must meet the station's criteria. For stations, building working relationships with independents may require station executive producers to serve as mentors as well as "product" managers. And the issue of funding is critical: generally, if no funding can be found, the film will not be made. Market censorship permeates both the independent and public television worlds. So do aesthetic constraints. And then, once a program is completed, the struggle for a decent place in the broadcast schedule is yet another challenge.

Even when independent producers with award-winning documentaries present their work to a station, they cannot count on getting it broadcast. This is because most stations have prime-time schedules that are largely taken up with strand programming—such as *Masterpiece Theater* and *The Lawrence Welk Show*—and most do not have regular venues to showcase local independently produced programs.

If stations do find room for the programs, it is often outside of prime time. My program on Earl Robinson was initially scheduled on a Saturday afternoon, and it took the divine intervention of a new station programmer who had a fresh eye and an appreciation of Robinson's music to schedule the show on a Wednesday might at 7 p.m.

Understandably, many independents resent a system that broadcasts their programs but that doesn't pay much, if anything, in return. There are exceptions, however. KTEH in San Jose recently provided postproduction facilities for film makers Beth Sanders and Randy Baker to finish a provocative documentary about censorship in the news media, "Fear and Favor in the Newsroom" (1997), the latest of several projects brought to the station by independent film makers. KQED is coproducing a series, *Livelihoods*, with the California Working Group, which also produced *We Do the Work*, the only program on public television dedicated to working people's lives. My former coproducer, John de Graaf, has coproduced several documentaries in conjunction with KCTS and Oregon Public Broadcasting, including "Running Out of Time" (1994), about the "time famine," and "Affluenza" (1997), about the cost of high living, the "disease" of affluence. These works realize public television's mission, but the film makers had to do their own fund-raising and cover most of their expenses.

As this book goes to press, I have two video projects in progress. One is a half-hour special about the birthplace of the city of Seattle told from the perspective of the Duwamish tribe and the early white settlers. This is a coproduction with KCTS/Seattle, which is providing in-kind postproduction services. The other is a profile of lyricist Yip Harburg ("Over the Rainbow," "Brother, Can You Spare a Dime?" "Paper Moon"). As an experimental, animated work, it will fall outside the arena of public television. I am also working on another book, and I teach college full-time.

My Seattle project fits within the constraints of public television, and the local station remains an appropriate outlet for this work. I have made the pragmatic choice and become a pragmatist activist, striking a wager with public television to have a relationship of manageable compromise.

My fifteen years as an independent producer have been difficult and challenging. My first program idea was on the human cost of unemployment, "They're Called Exhaustees," and it never made it beyond the proposal stage for lack of funding. Neither did a program on midwifery and the significance of the birth experience for parents. Both programs, and several others, remain with me like stillborn children. Most independent producers have similar stories.

Given the aesthetic, editorial, and economic constraints, most independents have turned their backs on public television and sought venues for their work in cable, public access, and film festivals. Even James Yee, executive director of the publicly funded Independent Television Service (ITVS), has hedged his bets with public television by entering into broadcast agreements with cable. "We felt too many of our films were being underutilized, despite the obvious demand for them in other markets such as foreign television and domestic cable," Yee said in a news release announcing that the Sundance Channel recently bought the exclusive rights to air five films funded by ITVS for one year. "This deal represents our continued commitment to help indie producers get their work to as broad an audience as possible."[11] Among the ITVS-funded films acquired by the Sundance Channel were the late Marlon Riggs's "Black Is . . . Black Ain't" (1995), about African-American identities within that community; "Coming Out under Fire" (1995), about gays in the military; "Jane: An Abortion Service" (1996), about abortion before it was legal; and "Struggles in Steel" (1996), about African-Americans in the labor movement. The first three films premiered on public television, but the latter two will have their premiere on the Sundance Channel.

ITVS was established by Congress to increase the diversity of programming available to public television and to promote the development of programming that involves creative risks and that addresses the needs of unserved and underserved audiences. The motivating vision behind ITVS is the same mythic vision of promise that marked the birth of public broadcasting.

Many in public television appear to have forgotten this original mission. Others invoke it as a rhetorical device during pledge drives or while lobbying the public and politicians, or to justify programming decisions when facing vocal critics. Nevertheless, there are still people in the system, such as Marc Weiss and others unnamed, who push for programming that is not safe or bland, and independent documentary producers, mostly working outside the system, who create it.

Independent film makers and enlightened public television programmers hold the promise of the system in their hands. The battle over the documentaries examined in this book boils down to questions of power, as Gail Christian put it, "who's powerful, who's weak, and who cares."[12] It is also about politics: the politics of funding, the politics of social change, and, ultimately, the politics of public television.

# Notes

## Preface

1. I did my research in San Francisco in the early 1990s.
2. Carol Cohn, "Sex and Death in the Rational World of Defense Intellectuals," *Signs* 2 (summer 1987), 687–718.
3. PBS rejected the only ongoing series on public television devoted to people's working lives and culture, *We Do the Work* (1990), produced by the California Working Group. The series is distributed to public television stations through the Central Education Network, a regional distributor. The programs have irregular carriage and scheduling, but about a hundred affiliate stations have broadcast the series. (Telephone interview with Patrice O'Neill, executive producer of *We Do the Work*, March 27, 1997.)

    Labor organizations and independent film makers have complained for years that PBS programmers have rejected programs with a labor-oriented focus. Marshaling the funds for such programs is no easy task, especially since PBS has interpreted its underwriting guidelines so that unions in general cannot fund programs with a labor focus, citing "conflict of interest" concerns.
4. Interview with Ervin Duggan, Orlando, Fla., June 6, 1994.
5. Telephone interview with Mary Jane McKinven, November 22, 1994.
6. Many of these films addressed U.S. foreign policy and were connected to grassroots, domestic political organizing.

    Barbara Trent's "The Panama Deception" (1992), about the U.S. overthrow of General Manuel Noriega and the subsequent occupation of the country, was rejected by PBS and the *P.O.V.* series. When the producer won an Academy Award for the documentary in 1993, she lambasted PBS before millions of television viewers, charging censorship. Unfortunately, I was unable to interview Trent. I also suspected this case would duplicate similar themes about journalism, propaganda, and trust contained in the "Dark Circle" case, though it might have shed new light on them, too.

    "Maria's Story" (1991), about a Salvadoran grandmother guerrilla leader, eventually aired on *P.O.V.* and was cited, with "Tongues Untied," by political conservatives to discredit public television during a congressional funding review.

The independent film makers who shot the film under life-threatening conditions were part of a grassroots effort in the United States to counter official statements about the civil war in El Salvador. The film makers were activists, part of the long-standing documentary tradition intent on using media as an instrument for change.

"When the Mountains Tremble" (1983) was about the future Guatemalan Nobel laureate Rigoberta Menchu. PBS initially rejected the program but broadcast it in 1985, creating such a stir at the station level that one headline writer dubbed the affair "When the Stations Tremble." This story was not included here because the director, Pam Yates, was unavailable for an interview. Yates simply did not have the time (or seemingly the desire) to dig into her old files from ten years earlier to reconstruct the series of events and conversations with PBS programming. Without this documentation and an interview, it would have been impossible to recreate the case with reasonable accuracy.

These factors also led me to jettison a case study about the documentary work of Bill Moyers and, with one exception, the programs produced for the *Frontline* series. Moyers's documentaries, notably "God and Politics" (1987), "The Secret Government: The Constitution in Crisis" (1987), and his *Frontline* special "High Crimes and Misdemeanors" (1990) drew criticism from conservative groups, who cited them as examples of PBS's "liberal bias." While I would have liked to investigate at least one of these controversies in depth, relevant sources were reluctant to open their files, and Moyers declined several interview requests. With regret, I decided not to include these case studies in this book.

Several documentaries produced for the *Frontline* series also became controversial, among them "Journey to the Occupied Lands" (1993) and "The Betrayal of Democracy" (1992), in addition to "High Crimes and Misdemeanors." *Frontline*, the only PBS public affairs documentary series, sets the journalistic standard against which other public affairs documentaries are measured.

7. Telephone interview with Owen Comora, October 4, 1996.
8. Telephone interview with Marlon Riggs, May 12, 1989.

## Introduction

1. Lyndon B. Johnson's State of the Union address delivered before a joint session of Congress, January 10, 1967, and quoted in *Public Papers of the Presidents of the United States, Lyndon B. Johnson*, contained in *The Weekly Compilation of Presidential Documents* (January 10, 1967), p. 30. See also *Public Broadcasting Act of 1967*, U.S. *Code*, Title 47, sec. 390 et seq., November 7, 1967, P.L. 90–129 #81 STAT 365. The law was signed by President Johnson on November 7, 1967.
2. "Legislative History of the Public Broadcasting Act of 1967," U.S. *Congressional Administrative News* (St. Paul: West Publishing, 1967), vol. 1, pp. 1777–1778.
3. *Report of the Special Committee on Program Policies and Procedures to the PBS Board of Directors*, PBS, April 15, 1987, p. 48.
4. Public broadcasting was originally supposed to be insulated from direct political or commercial interests by a stable funding structure. See *Public Broadcasting Act of 1967*, section 396 (g) (1) (D), which reads that the Corporation for Public Broadcasting is authorized to "carry out its purposes and functions and engage in its activities in ways that will most effectively assure the maximum freedom of the noncommercial educational television or radio broadcast systems and local stations from interference with or control of program content or other activities." See also "Legislative History of the Public Broadcasting Act of 1967,"

p. 1805, and *Report of the Special Committee on Program Policies and Procedures*, pp. 34–35.

5. Jo Franklin-Trout now uses the name Jo Franklin.

6. Patricia Aufderheide has followed the controversies and changes in the public television world longer and in more depth than any other academic scholar and media critic. Her work has appeared in *In These Times*, the *Progressive*, in specialized mass-media publications such as the *Independent Film and Video Monthly* and the *Columbia Journalism Review* as well as in academic journals such as *Critical Studies in Mass Communications*, the *Journal of Communications*, and *Journalism Quarterly*. (Especially insightful are "Public Television and the Public Sphere," *Critical Studies in Mass Communications* 8 [spring 1991], 168–183, and "Controversy and the Newspaper's Public: The Case of 'Tongues Untied,'" *Journalism Quarterly* 71 [autumn 1994], 499–508.) Aufderheide has focused much of her analysis on the commercial influences in public television and has consistently raised the question of who constitutes "the public" in "public television." See also William Hoynes's excellent book *Public Television for Sale: Media, the Market, and the Public Sphere* (Boulder: Westview Press, 1994).

7. Hoynes, *Public Television*, p. 94.

8. On "goal ambiguity," see ibid., especially pp. 151–155. Hoynes's book is the most comprehensive study to date of how the public television system has coped with the incursion of market forces in public television and the system's conflicting obligations. A sociologist who has worked with the media watchdog group Fairness and Accuracy in Reporting (FAIR), Hoynes sets today's public television system in its political, historical, and economic context and analyzes it in terms of its potential to serve and sustain democracy.

   I share much common ground with Hoynes. He even discusses controversial programming in passing, analyzing it from the perspective of public television producers who feel they can't take risks. However, Hoynes doesn't explore the role of independent producers in relation to controversy, nor does he examine controversy or public television from the independent producers' perspectives. Independent producers are virtually invisible in his book. This is not a shortcoming; it is simply a difference between his study's focus and mine.

9. See Ralph Engelman, *Public Radio and Television in America: A Political History* (Thousand Oaks, Calif.: Sage Publications, 1996).

10. For an overview of this research, see Maxwell E. McCombs and Donald L. Shaw, "The Evolution of Agenda-Setting Research: Twenty-five Years in the Marketplace of Ideas," *Journal of Communications* 43 (spring 1993), 58–67.

11. David Manning White, "The 'Gate Keeper': A Case Study in the Selection of News," *Journalism Quarterly* 27 (fall 1950), 383–390; D. Charles Whitney and Lee B. Becker, "'Keeping the Gates' for Gatekeepers: The Effects of Wire News," *Journalism Quarterly* 59 (spring 1982), 60–65; Herbert Gans, *Deciding What's News: A Study of CBS Evening News, NBC Nightly News, Newsweek, and* Time (New York: Vintage Books, 1980); Gaye Tuchman, *Making News* (New York: Free Press, 1978).

12. Todd Gitlin, *The Whole World Is Watching* (Berkeley: University of California Press, 1980); W. Lance Bennett, *Public Opinion in American Politics* (New York: Harcourt Brace Jovanovich, 1980).

13. Fay Lomax Cook, Tom R. Tyler, Edward G. Goetz, Margaret T. Gordon, David Protess, Donna R. Leff, and Harvey L. Molotch, "Media and Agenda Setting: Effects on the Public, Interest Group Leaders, Policy Makers, and Policy," *Public Opinion Quarterly* 47 (1983), 16–35.

14. Katheryn C. Montgomery, *Target: Prime Time: Advocacy Groups and the Struggle over Entertainment Television* (New York: Oxford University Press, 1989).

15. Bennett, *Public Opinion in American Politics.*

16. See Tuchman, *Making News*; Erving Goffman, *Frame Analysis: An Essay on the Organization of Experience* (New York: Harper and Row, 1974); and Gitlin, *Whole World.*

17. Gitlin, *Whole World*, p. 7.

18. Stuart Hall, "Which Public, Whose Service?" *All Our Futures: The Changing Role and Purpose of the BBC*, ed. Wilf Stevenson (London: British Film Institute 1993), pp. 23–38; James W. Carey, *Communication as Culture: Essays on Media and Society* (Boston: Unwin Hyman, 1989); John Fiske, *Television Culture* (London: Methuen, 1987); and Gitlin, *Whole World.*

19. See Jürgen Habermas, *The Theory of Communicative Action,* vol. 2, *Lifeworld and System: A Critique of Functionalist Reason* (Boston: Beacon Press, 1987), and *The Structural Transformation of the Public Sphere* (Cambridge: MIT Press, 1989); Steven Seidman, ed., *Jürgen Habermas on Society and Politics: A Reader* (Boston: Beacon Press, 1989); Carey, *Communication as Culture*; Ben Bagdikian, *The Media Monopoly,* 2d ed. (Boston: Beacon Press, 1987); Herbert Schiller, *Culture, Inc.* (New York: Oxford University Press, 1989).

20. Seidman, *Jürgen Habermas*, p. 232.

21. William Greider, *Who Will Tell the People? The Betrayal of American Democracy* (New York: Simon and Schuster, 1992), p. 12. Greider argues that the press doesn't work reliably as a "connective tissue" between the people and the government. As the ties have waned between ordinary citizens, on the one hand, and political parties and other mediating institutions, on the other, more people turn to the media to communicate with the nation's leaders.

22. See "Controversy" in *The Oxford English Dictionary*, 2d ed.: "1. The action of disputing or contending one with another. . . . 1.b. Disputation on a matter of opinion; the contending of opponents one with another on a subject of dispute; discussion in which opposite views are advanced and maintained by opponents. . . . 2.b. A debate or dispute on a matter of opinion; a discussion of contrary opinions."

23. My research on controversy is influenced by the work of two qualitative sociologists, Diane Vaughan and Howard S. Becker. Vaughan discovered patterns in what, at first glance, appear to be the chaotic breakup of intimate relationships. In her book *Uncoupling: How Relationships Come Apart* (New York: Vintage Books, 1987), she traces how a series of seemingly minor decisions led her informants down the path to separation or divorce. This approach toward her subject—retracing the steps in the interaction—has guided mine in unfolding controversies. Like Vaughan, I focus on the *how*, not the *why*, of the process.

   Howard S. Becker's research on "art worlds" has been useful in understanding the worlds of independent producers and PBS programmers. He defines an art world as "the network of people whose cooperative activity, organized via their joint knowledge of the conventional means of doing things, produces the kind of art works that the art world is noted for." (*Art Worlds* [Berkeley: University of California Press, 1982].) Becker suggests we can understand much of what goes on in those worlds by understanding the constraints under which members operate. Members of art worlds decide what's art and what's not, who's in and who's out. In public television, this means that members of the public television world decide who gets to speak in the public broadcasting forum to the viewing public, and who does not.

24. Journalists must judge the conflict worthy of coverage insofar as it meets the cri-

teria of timeliness and newsworthiness in order to convince their editors that the story has merit and deserves space in the paper.

### Chapter 1   *Producers and Programmers*

1. Following the definition put forth by the Independent Television Service (ITVS), I define an independent producer as a video or film maker who is "not regularly employed as a staff producer by a public or commercial broadcast entity or film studio." This definition is taken, verbatim, from the applications and guidelines of the Independent Television Service.

2. Telephone interview with Patricia Thomson, editor of the *Independent Film and Video Monthly* (the magazine of the Association of Independent Video and Film-makers), September 7, 1994.
   ITVS is a service established by Congress in 1988 to fund projects by independent producers with the stated purpose of increasing diversity of programming on public television and promoting programming that addresses the needs of unserved and underserved audiences.

3. These film makers are similar to the "mavericks" Howard Becker describes in *Art Worlds* (Berkeley: University of California Press, 1982) on p. 233.

4. *The Public Broadcasting Service: An Overview*, PBS background document, February 1994.

5. During PBS's budget for fiscal year 1994 (July 1, 1993, to June 30, 1994), 73.3 percent ($161,108 million) of its resources came from member stations. The Corporation for Public Broadcasting contributed 14.1 percent, and educational institutions, interest income, and other sources made up 12.6 percent. PBS does not produce programs, but 84.3 percent of its budget goes to program production, acquisitions, promotion, and distribution. See *Facts about PBS*, "Public Television Funding: How Is the Public Broadcasting Service Funded?" background document, February 1994, pp. 11–12.

6. The Pacific Mountain Network shut down in June 1997.

7. *Facts about PBS*, p. 12.

8. In fiscal year 1993, federal agencies excluding CPB contributed 9 percent of the National Programming Service's budget, foundations gave 8.1 percent, and others, including producers, individuals, associations, community groups, and so on, made up the remaining 17.1 percent. *Facts about PBS*, p. 12.

9. See *Report of the Special Committee on Program Policies and Procedures to the PBS Board of Directors*, PBS, April 15, 1987, p. vi.

10. Interview with Mary Jane McKinven, Alexandria, Va., April 14, 1993.

11. These criteria are listed in the *Report of the Special Committee on Program Policies and Procedures to the PBS Board of Directors*, p. 5.

12. Interview with McKinven, April 14, 1993.

13. Ibid.

14. For discussion of the Reagan administration's effort to eliminate federal funding for public television, see Patricia Aufderheide, "Public Television and the Public Sphere," *Critical Studies in Mass Communication* 8 (spring 1991), 181. Aufderheide quotes a conclusion from *The FY 1982 Budget Revisions: Corporation for Public Broadcasting*, statement by the U.S. Office of Management and Budget, April 1, 1981, p. 344: "Thus, there is no overriding national justification for the funding of CPB. Moreover, the audience of CPB-supported stations tend to be wealthier and more educated than the general populace; they certainly possess the personal resources to support such stations and they should do so, if they

want to enjoy the benefits of public broadcasting. Taxpayers as a whole should not be compelled to subsidize entertainment for a select few."

To keep a tighter rein on public broadcasting, President Reagan appointed Sheila Burke Tate to chair the board of the Corporation for Public Broadcasting (CPB). Tate was Nancy Reagan's press secretary, a former vice president of the public relations firm Hill and Knowlton, and president of her own public relations firm, Powell Tate. Tate was also the press secretary for the 1988 Bush campaign. (See "Who's Who on the CPB Board?" *Extra!* September–October 1993, p. 23.) Reagan also appointed other conservatives to the CPB board.

15. The Public Broadcasting Act of 1967 was a piece of President Johnson's "Great Society" puzzle. In his 1967 State of the Union address, Johnson told Congress and the American people, "We should develop educational television into a vital public resource to enrich our homes, educate our families, and to provide assistance in our classrooms. We should insist that the public interest be fully served through the nation's airwaves." He believed noncommercial broadcasting should "appeal to the minds and hearts" of the viewing public, providing cultural, informational programming in addition to offering public affairs coverage and analysis "which will lead to a better informed and enlightened public." ("Legislative History of the Public Broadcasting Act of 1967," *U.S. Congressional and Administrative News* (St. Paul: West Publishing, 1967), vol. 1, 1967, pp. 1777–1778.)

The 1967 act created the Corporation for Public Broadcasting with a mandate to facilitate the expansion and development of noncommercial television. CPB would provide grants for programming and production to national production centers, stations—and to independent producers.
16. "Legislative History of the Public Broadcasting Act of 1967," p. 1779.
17. Carnegie Commission on Educational Television, *Public Television: A Program for Action* (New York: Bantam Books, 1967), p. 68.
18. Erik Barnouw, *The Sponsor: Notes on a Modern Potentate* (New York: Oxford University Press, 1978), pp. 64–65.
19. Ibid.
20. Ibid.
21. Ibid. and interview with Al Perlmutter, Orlando, Fla., June 4, 1994.
22. Patricia Aufderheide, "Sapping Public TV's Political Power: Nixon's the One," *In These Times*, July 4–17, 1990.
23. George Gibson, *Public Broadcasting: The Role of the Federal Government, 1912–1976* (New York: Praeger Press, 1977), p. 185; John Witherspoon and Roselle Kovitz, *The History of Public Broadcasting* (Washington, D.C.: Corporation for Public Broadcasting, 1987), p. 45 (originally published in *Current*, the public telecommunications newspaper).
24. Aufderheide quotes the Nixon strategy from a 1972 memo by staff members Clay Whitehead and Charles Colson: "The president's basic objective [is] to get the left-wing commentators who are cutting us up off public television at once, indeed yesterday, if possible." (See Aufderheide, "Sapping Public TV's Political Power.")
25. See Gibson, *Public Broadcasting*, p. xviii; Barnouw, *The Sponsor*, pp. 65–66.
26. Aufderheide, "Sapping Public TV's Political Power."
27. Gibson, *Public Broadcasting*, p. 191.
28. Quoted in ibid. from an untitled article that appeared in the *New York Times*, May 28, 1973.
29. Gibson, *Public Broadcasting*, p. 192.
30. Interview with Barry Chase, New Orleans, June 21, 1993.
31. Telephone interview with Barry Chase, September 27, 1994.

32. Letter from Barry Chase to author dated June 28, 1993.
33. Peter Broderick, "Fair Market Values: 1985 Station Program Cooperative Convenes," *Independent Film and Video Monthly*, March 1986, p. 11.
34. Ibid., p. 12.
35. Interview with Chase, June 21, 1993.
36. See FAIR, "PBS Tilts toward Conservatives, Not the Left," *Extra!* June 1992, p. 15. PBS also broadcast "Television's Vietnam: The Real Story" (1984), produced by Accuracy in Media.
37. See Lawrence Daressa, "Independent Producers Propose New Program Service," *Current*, September 22, 1987. Daressa cites a decline in CPB program funding earmarked for independent producers through the "open solicitation" fund from 96 percent in 1982 to 40 percent in 1987. He also cites the 1978 congressional stipulation that "at least 50 percent" of CPB's national production budget go to independent producers (rather than stations) to ensure the production of diverse and innovative programming.
38. For a thorough background and detailed analysis of the creation of the Independent Television Service, see Susan C. Ivers, "Congress, the Corporation for Public Broadcasting, and Independent Producers: Agenda Setting and Policy Making in Public Television," paper presented at the Broadcasting Education Association Annual Convention, Las Vegas, Nev., April 1989.
39. Interview with Glenn Marcus, Alexandria, Va., April 14, 1993.
40. Ibid.

## Chapter 2    Frontline *and* P.O.V.

1. The series began with twenty-six programs a year but was scaled down through funding cuts and schedule pressures to twenty-two programs in 1994 and twenty in 1995.
2. This information is taken from a *Frontline* background document that cites the Nielsen National Television Index for the six-million-viewers figure.
3. This information and all quotes are taken from my interviews with David Fanning, Orlando, Fla., June 4, 1994, and New Orleans, June 20, 1993.
4. According to Fanning, Louis Wiley, Jr., previously wrote the proposal for *World* and had worked on the PBS television program *The Advocates*. (Interview with Fanning, June 4, 1994.)
5. "Innocence Lost" (120 minutes) aired on May 7, 1991. *Frontline* also aired a follow-up to the story, "Innocence Lost: The Verdict" (120 minutes), on July 21, 1993.
6. "Losing the War with Japan" (ninety minutes) was produced by Martin Koughan and broadcast on November 19, 1991.
7. The documentary "L.A. Is Burning: Five Reports from a Divided City," produced by Elena Mannes, aired on April 27, 1993.
8. McKinven confirmed that this was her response to KCET's concerns about "L.A. Is Burning" in our telephone conversation, November 22, 1994.
9. Interviews with Marc Weiss, Orlando, Fla., June 5, 1994, and with David Fanning, June 4, 1994.
    In the early 1970s, Weiss produced several programs for New York's National Educational Television and worked with Barbara Kopple on "Harlan County, U.S.A." (1976). Weiss is a founding board member of the Association of Independent Video and Filmmakers (AIVF), a national trade association of independent producers established in 1974. During the 1980s, he cofounded other organizations to address the needs of independent film makers, including Media

Network and ICAP, a nonprofit cooperative designed to sell programs to cable stations. In 1979, Weiss was the coordinating producer of WNET/New York's *Independent Focus,* a showcase for independent fiction and nonfiction films.
10. Interview with Weiss, June 5, 1994.
11. Interview with Mary Jane McKinven, Alexandria, Va., April 14, 1993.
12. "P.O.V.: An Overview," *P.O.V.* fact-sheet, 1994, p. 1.
13. Ibid.
14. Telephone interview with Marc Weiss, November 5, 1991.
15. Interview with Weiss, June 5, 1994. All quotes by Weiss in the following paragraphs are taken from this interview.
16. The introduction of "video letters" began on *P.O.V.* with the 1993 season. See Ellen Schneider, "Making Connections: 'P.O.V.' Viewers Welcome New Opportunities for Talking Back," *P.O.V.* Press Release, April 26, 1994.
17. "Pipeline '97," *Current,* September 30, 1996, p. 10.

## Chapter 3    *"Dark Circle"*

1. Prior to the creation of PBS, National Educational Television (NET) was the sole supplier of national educational and cultural programming to stations. In 1970, NET merged with WNDT/13 in New York, and they became WNET/13. (See James Day, *The Vanishing Vision: The Inside Story of Public Television* [Berkeley: University of California Press, 1995], pp. 72–73, 171, 191.)
2. Interview with Judy Irving, San Francisco, June 23, 1992.
3. Linda Harvey, "Colorado's Nuclear Contamination: What You're Not Told," *Denver Magazine,* March 1976, p. 37.
4. Interview with Irving, June 23, 1992.
5. See "High Rates of Cancer Found Near Nuclear Arms Plant," *New York Times,* April 10, 1979.
6. "10,000 Attend Protest Rally At Rocky Flats Atom Plant," *New York Times,* April 21, 1981.
7. "E.P.A. Asks A-Plant Test for Destruction of PCB" (Associated Press), *New York Times,* May 17, 1980; "U.S. to Build Security Zone at Colorado Weapons Plant" (Associated Press), *New York Times,* October 14, 1980; and "Nuclear Emergency Test Is Almost Taken for Real" (Associated Press), *New York Times,* October 15, 1981.
8. "Fire in Nuclear Plant Sowed Radioactivity Across Denver in '57" (Associated Press), *New York Times,* September 9, 1981.
9. Ibid.
10. "Suit Discloses '57 Fire Emitted Radioactive Material," *New York Times,* September 9, 1981. The case was brought by Marcus Church, a landowner whose property adjoined Rocky Flats. As part of an out-of-court settlement in 1984, Church received $9 million and the court sealed the case. The case's transcripts became public in 1990, and the *New York Times* published a news story on February 15, 1990, "Weapons Plant Is Pressed for Details of Toll on Health."
11. Tad Bartimus and Scott McCartney, *Trinity's Children: Living along America's Nuclear Highway* (New York: Harcourt Brace Jovanovich, 1991), pp. 187–188.
12. "Dark Circle" received major funding from the following sources, in addition to contributions from 250 individuals: the National Endowment for the Arts, the American Film Institute, the Film Fund, the Benton Foundation, the Columbia Foundation, the Lucien and Eva Eastman Fund, Friends of the Earth, Joint Foundation Support, the Albert Kunstadter Family Fund, the Nu Lambda Trust, the P.B.P. Foundation, William M. Roth, and the United Methodist Church.

13. Vincent Canby, "'Dark Circle,' Life Next to the Atom," *New York Times*, October 8, 1982.
14. "Revitalizing Nuclear Power," annual conference of the Atomic Industrial Forum, 1983.
15. These quotes attributed to Pam Porter are from notes taken by Irving or Beaver from conversations with her and from their recollections. Pam Porter is the only party whom I have as yet been unable to contact for an interview. I have cross-checked and confirmed her role in the "Dark Circle" case whenever possible in my interviews with Beverly Ornstein, Nat Katzman, Gail Christian, Barry Chase, Judy Irving, and Chris Beaver.
16. Telephone interview with Beverly Ornstein, February 21, 1994.
17. Ibid.
18. Telephone interview with Nat Katzman, February 11, 1993.
19. Ibid.
20. Telephone interview with Gail Christian, December 28, 1992.
21. Ibid.
22. In my telephone interview with Christian, she confirmed that she had made these comments to Beaver.
23. Telephone interview with Chris Beaver, January 7, 1993.
24. Telephone interview with Ornstein.
25. Interview with Irving, June 23, 1992.
26. Telephone interview with Katzman.
27. Ibid.
28. The *Independent Film and Video Monthly* is published by the Foundation for Independent Video and Film.
29. Telephone interview with Christian.
30. Telephone interview with Judy Irving, December 15, 1992.
31. Letter from Chase to Katzman, May 23, 1986, p. 1. (Chase gave me written permission to quote from his letter to Katzman, in a letter to me dated June 28, 1993.)
32. Ibid., p. 3.
33. Interview with Barry Chase, New Orleans, June 21, 1993. Chase's recollections in the following paragraphs are also from this interview.
34. Ibid.
35. Ibid.
36. Telephone interview with Ornstein.
37. Telephone interview with Chris Beaver, February 25, 1994.
38. See the chapter "The Nuclear Thunder," in Mark Hertsgaard, *On Bended Knee: The Press and the Reagan Presidency* (New York: Farrar Straus Giroux, 1988), especially pp. 281–282.
39. Ibid., p. 282.
40. Todd Gitlin, *The Whole World Is Watching* (Berkeley: University of California Press, 1980), p. 7.
41. Ibid., pp. 290–291.
42. The producers also sent cassettes to CBS, NBC, and ABC, but all three networks rejected the program, citing a general policy of not accepting documentaries from outside producers unless they are under contract to the network. (Telephone interview with Judy Irving, April 7, 1993.)
43. John Corry, "The Uses of Television and the Pitfalls of Politics," *New York Times*, December 7, 1986.
44. Tom Shales, "PBS's Atom Smasher," *Washington Post*, August 8, 1989.
45. Art Durbano, "This Week's Movies" column, *TV Guide*, August 5–11, 1989.

46. "Charges 'Insulting,' PBS Says," *USA Today*, August 8, 1989.
47. *AIM Report* (a biweekly publication of Accuracy in Media, Washington, D.C.), August-B 1989, p. 1.
48. Ibid.
49. Interview with Irving, June 23, 1992.
50. Telephone interview with Christian.

### Chapter 4    *"Days of Rage"*

1. It wasn't the first time the issue had been addressed. During PBS's experiment with "op-ed TV," the short-lived limited series *Flashpoint*, which paired films with opposing perspectives on the occupied territories, was canceled for poor carriage. (See chapter 1.) *Frontline* produced several documentaries on the Israeli-Palestinian issue and also came under fire from pro-Israeli media watchdog groups, but not to the extent that Jo Franklin-Trout did.
2. Before and during the Persian Gulf war, Franklin-Trout said the Defense Department, including U.S. Air Force, Marine Corps, and the Navy, requisitioned cassettes of her series *Saudi Arabia* and *The Oil Kingdoms*, and also "Days of Rage," to train personnel for work in that region and for the war. (Telephone interview with Jo Franklin-Trout, March 4, 1992.)
3. Telephone interview with Barry Chase, March 3, 1994. In May 1980, PBS broadcast "Death of a Princess," a dramatization of a real-life public execution of a Saudi princess and her lower-class lover for adultery. The docudrama by Anthony Thomas and David Fanning, the future *Frontline* executive producer, infuriated the Saudi Arabian government. Exxon took out ads in leading newspapers asking PBS to review its decision to broadcast the program. See Edward Said, *Covering Islam: How the Media and the Experts Determine How We See the Rest of the World* (New York: Pantheon Books, 1981), p. 66. Said also notes that when the program aired in the United Kingdom, the Saudis withdrew their ambassador from Britain, called for a boycott of Britain as a vacation spot, and threatened further sanctions (see p. 65).

    Arab-Americans criticized the program as hostile to the Saudis, perpetuating stereotypes of Muslims in the Middle East as barbarians, and giving a misleading impression of Islamic law. The Saudi Arabian government was especially wary of U.S. public television after the program aired. The docudrama, however, attracted one of the largest audiences in PBS history. For more information on "Death of a Princess," see Jack Sheheen, *The TV Arab* (Bowling Green: Popular Press, 1984.)
4. Telephone interview with Jo Franklin-Trout, March 2, 1994.
5. Ibid.
6. Telephone interview with Franklin-Trout, March 4, 1992.
7. The *Washington Post* reported each three-part series sold for $900 each, and several corporations and the Arab-American Cultural Foundation paid for their distribution to schools and universities around the country. The Arab-American Cultural Foundation paid $33,000 to cover this distribution, and these corporations paid the following amounts: Lockheed ($40,000), United Technologies ($36,000), the Frank E. Basil Corporation ($10,000), Garrett Corporation ($10,000), Esso ($9,900), the Boeing Company ($8,100), and Hughes Aircraft ($3,000). (See Phil McCombs, "The Producer & the 'Days of Rage' Quagmire," *Washington Post*, September 6, 1989.)
8. Telephone interview with Franklin-Trout, March 9, 1994.
9. Telephone interview with Franklin-Trout, March 4, 1992.

10. Interview with Sandy Heberer, Orlando, Fla., June 6, 1994.
11. Telephone interview with Franklin-Trout, March 2, 1994.
12. Ibid.
13. Interview with Heberer.
14. Interview with Steve Emerson, New York, September 21, 1995.
15. Telephone interview with Steve Emerson, July 9, 1996.
16. Telephone interview with Gail Christian, December 28, 1992.
17. Telephone interview with Chase, March 3, 1994.
18. Interviews with Mary Jane McKinven and Glenn Marcus, Alexandria, Va., April 14, 1993.
19. Stephen Singer, "N.Y. Station Ends 'Kwitny Report,'" *Current* (weekly), May 24, 1989. The presenting station gives credibility and support to independently produced programs. It also serves as a buffer between the producer, PBS, and other stations in the network.
20. Howard Rosenberg, "PBS Backs Away from Palestinian Documentary," *Los Angeles Times*, April 22, 1989.
21. Telephone interview with Christian.
22. Telephone interview with Franklin-Trout, March 4, 1992.
23. Stephen Singer, "N.Y. Station Ends 'Kwitny Report.'" *The Kwitny Report* ran for one season in 1988–1989 and produced twenty programs that were carried on about one hundred public television stations. The show presented a left-liberal perspective on a wide range of current affairs issues in a format similar to that for *The MacNeil/Lehrer NewsHour*, combining documentary feature stories with in-studio discussions with various experts and interested parties. The program was unable to secure adequate funding for a second season and was canceled by Chloe Aaron. (For more information, especially on how such ongoing, alternative programs are kept off the air by a shortage of sympathetic and wealthy funders, see William Hoynes, *Public Television for Sale: Media, the Market, and the Public Sphere* [Boulder: Westview Press, 1994], pp. 105–106. Hoynes described *The Kwitny Report* as "the flip side" of programs such as *McLaughlin Group* and *Firing Line* hosted by political conservatives.)
24. "Behind the Rage over 'Rage,' Film on Palestinians Sparks Furor," *Current*, May 10, 1989. The entire quote, on p. 19, reads, "'The business about confusion or misunderstanding is often used to hide a genuine disagreement,' Kwitny said. The documentary was to be a part of his series and 'senior producers at this station knew this.'"
25. Telephone interview with Christian. I have been unable to locate Chloe Aaron to verify Christian's recollection.
26. Telephone interview with Franklin-Trout, March 4, 1992. Rosenberg confirmed Franklin-Trout's recollection in my telephone interview with him on March 20, 1995.
27. Quoted by Jeremy Gerard, "PBS and Two of Its Affiliates Dispute Film on Palestinians," *New York Times*, May 2, 1989.
28. "Public TV Censorship under Fire," *Extra!* (a publication of Fairness and Accuracy in Media), May–June 1989, p. 1.
29. Anthony Lewis, "Fear of Freedom," *New York Times*, May 4, 1989.
30. Interview with Barry Chase, New Orleans, June 21, 1993.
31. Telephone interview with Christian.
32. Quoted by Walter Goodman, "Two Views of Mideast Conflict: A Delicate Balance for PBS," *New York Times*, May 29, 1989.
33. Telephone interview with Chase, March 3, 1994.
34. Goodman, "Two Views of Mideast Conflict."

35. Ibid.
36. Julius Liebb, "Channel 13 Fumbles on Palestinian Documentary," *Jewish Press* (New York, N.Y.), June 25, 1989.
37. In Seattle, the materials presented to local activists for use in dealing with local PBS affiliates were several newspaper articles and specially prepared analyses of "Days of Rage." (The article cited in the preceding note was among them.) The American Jewish Committee sent out the seven-page, single-spaced "An Analysis of Jo Franklin-Trout's TV Production, 'Days of Rage: The Young Palestinians,'" by George E. Gruen, Ph.D., director, Israel and Middle East Affairs. CAMERA mailed out a five-page critique, "Public Television Program on Israel Is Way Out of Bounds," by Bertram Korn, Jr., regional director of CAMERA. Neither of these documents is dated.
38. Korn, "Public Television Program on Israel Is Way Out of Bounds," p. 5.
39. Telephone interview with Rabbi Anson Laytner of Seattle's Jewish Federation Community Relations Council, February 16, 1990.
40. Liebb, "Channel 13 Fumbles."
41. Quoted in ibid.
42. Ibid.
43. "Storm Erupts over 'Days of Rage,'" *ADC Times*, May–June 1989, p. 5.
44. Jeremy Gerard, "PBS to Show Film on the Intifada Despite Protests," *New York Times*, July 20, 1989.
45. Ibid.
46. Telephone interview with Franklin-Trout, March 4, 1992.
47. Letter from Michael Posner to Jo Franklin-Trout dated August 15, 1989.
48. Ken Pellis, "Intifada Film to Air Amid Charges of Bias," *Palm Beach Post*, September 3, 1989.
49. Quoted by Marc Gunther, "PBS Gets an Angry Earful over 'Rage,'" *Detroit Free Press*, September 3, 1989.
50. Steve Emerson, "Film Flam," published in the September 18 and 25, 1989, combined issue of the *New Republic*. The issue of the magazine was published August 31, 1989.
51. See Jeremy Gerard, "PBS Investigating Financing of 'Days of Rage,'" *New York Times*, August 31, 1989.
52. Emerson, "Film Flam."
53. Telephone interview with Christian.
54. Ibid.
55. Alan L. Keyes is listed as an "advisor" to CAMERA on the organization's stationery, but he was not formally identified as having any link to the organization by the producers of the panel discussion. (See CAMERA stationery from national headquarters on correspondence dated July 1, 1989.)
56. Jeremy Gerard, "PBS Adds Disclaimer to Palestinian Program," *New York Times*, September 6, 1989.
57. Robert Goldberg, "Ms. Franklin-Trout Films the Intifada," *Wall Street Journal*, September 8, 1989.
58. Tom Shales, "On PBS, the Uprising through a Clouded Lens," *Washington Post*, September 6, 1989.
59. Scott Pendleton, "Long-Delayed View of Intifada," *Christian Science Monitor*, September 5, 1989.
60. John Voorhees, "'Days of Rage' Is Well-Rounded Look at Palestinian Uprising," *Seattle Times*, September 6, 1989.
61. Telephone interview with Chase, March 3, 1994.
62. Interview with Heberer.

63. Ibid.
64. "State Dept. Says Israel Still Violates Arab Rights," *New York Times*, February 12, 1990.
65. Ibid.
66. The internal review found that "Journey to the Occupied Lands" was not "fundamentally flawed," but that it included a few "factual errors," such as the failure to acknowledge that a small amount of citrus fruit from Gaza had been directly exported to Europe since 1988, the failure to identify a satellite photo as a composite image, and an allegedly oversimplified explanation for the construction of Palestinian homes outside village boundaries. David Fanning agreed to have the producers rerecord several lines of narration, and to broadcast a video "letter" to notify viewers about the investigation's conclusions. (See Karen Everhart Bedford, "WGBH Review Upholds Doc's Basic Premise," *Current*, May 1, 1995, p. 3.)
67. I confirmed that the film had been fact-checked by PBS in my interview with Heberer.
68. Telephone interview with Franklin-Trout, March 2, 1994.
69. Jeremy Gerard, "PBS Executive Resigns in 'Days of Rage' Dispute," *New York Times*, September 9, 1989.
70. Jeff Kayes, "Council Formation Raises Concern over PBS Documentaries," *Los Angeles Times*, September 9, 1989.
71. Jeremy Gerard, "PBS to Broadcast Israeli Side of West Bank Story," *New York Times*, November 30, 1989.
72. Ibid. See also Jeremy Gerard, "PBS Film on West Bank Had the Help of Israeli," *New York Times*, December 2, 1989.
73. Walter Goodman, "How PBS Handles Mideast Viewpoints in Two Documentaries," *New York Times*, December 5, 1989.
74. *The Wing of the Falcon* was published in July 1995 (Los Angeles: Atlantis Press).
75. Telephone interview with Jo Franklin, November 19, 1996.

## Chapter 5 *"Tongues Untied"*

1. Interview with Marc Weiss, Orlando, Fla., June 5, 1994.
2. E. B. White's often-quoted letter to the Carnegie Commission on Educational Television conveys the mission embraced by the report. White wrote, "Noncommercial television should address itself to the ideal of excellence, not the idea of acceptability—which is what keeps commercial television from climbing the staircase. I think public television should be the visual counterpart of the literary essay, should arouse our dreams, satisfy our hunger for beauty, take us on journeys, enable us to participate in events, present great drama and music, explore the sea and the sky and the woods and the hills. It should be our Lyceum, our Chautauqua, our Minsky's, and our Camelot. It should restate and clarify the social dilemma and the political pickle. Once in a while it does, and you get a quick glimpse of its potential." (Quoted in Carnegie Commission on Educational Television, *Public Television: A Program for Action* [New York, Bantam Books,1967], p. 13.)

   The Carnegie Commission sought to enlist "the great technology" of television in "the service of diversity" and "to serve more fully both the mass audience and the many separate audiences that constitute in their aggregate our American society." (Ibid., p. 14.)
3. Marlon Riggs died of AIDS before I could have a detailed face-to-face or telephone conversation with him about "Tongues Untied," although I interviewed

him on the telephone on May 12, 1989, about his earlier work. The quotes that appear in this chapter are taken from my interview with Riggs and other interviews or direct quotes that appeared in publications, press releases, and newspaper articles, and in recorded talks and lectures as cited.

4. On the expectations of Riggs's parents, see Craig Seligman, "Two Films Present a Culture Stifled by Silence," *San Francisco Examiner*, March 16, 1990.

5. "Ethnic Notions" is distributed by California Newsreel. For a detailed account of the resistance Riggs faced to create "Ethnic Notions," see my unpublished paper "Art Is a Hammer! Independent Producers' Challenge to American Public Broadcasting," May 1990.

6. Telephone interview with Riggs.

7. "Color Adjustment" also received the Distinguished Documentary Achievement Award from the International Documentary Association, the Erik Barnouw Award from the Organization of American Historians, and "Best of the Festival" at the National Educational Film and Video Festival.

8. Vivian Kleiman, "Passings: Marlon T. Riggs," *International Documentary* (Journal of the International Documentary Association) 13 (June 1994), 17.

9. Robert Anbian, "'Tongues Untied' Lets Loose Angry, Loving Words: An Interview with Marlon Riggs," *Release Print*, March 1990, p. 5.

10. Essex Hemphill and Joseph Beam, eds., *Brother to Brother: New Writings of Black Gay Men* (Boston: Alyson Publications, 1991), p. 197.

11. Anbian, "'Tongues Untied' Lets Loose Angry, Loving Words," p. 5.

12. Ibid.

13. For example, Riggs said then-California state assemblyman Willie Brown had agreed to host the premiere of "Ethnic Notions" in 1985, but after previewing the finished documentary, he backed out. When he asked what happened, Riggs said one of Brown's aides told him the film "serves no purpose for the black community, and that it supports racism." (Telephone interview with Riggs.) Riggs told me he believed this decision expressed the concerns of "a certain category of blacks who came of age during the civil rights movement who regard these images as so painful that they couldn't deal with them. Their only solution was to deny them."

14. Quoted by Anbian, "'Tongues Untied' Lets Loose Angry, Loving Words," p. 6.

15. Ibid., p. 16.

16. Telephone interview with Riggs.

17. "Many Stations Nix or Delay Gay Black Film," *Current*, June 24, 1991. The program aired without cuts April 23, 1990, on KQED, and twice on KCET/Los Angeles—June 22, 1990, and June 18, 1991—as part of "Gay Pride" programming. WNET broadcast the program during Gay Pride Week in June 1990 (see Hemphill and Beam, *Brother to Brother*, p. 189) and on February 5, 1991, as part of WNET's African-American Heritage programming.

18. Telephone interview with Marc Weiss, November 5, 1991.

19. Ibid.

20. Interview with Weiss, June 5, 1994.

21. Ibid.

22. Ibid.

23. Telephone interview with Mable Haddock, November 4, 1994. All quotes by Haddock are taken from this interview.

24. Haddock knew supporting "Tongues Untied" would make her job more difficult as she sought to get more programs by African-Americans on public television. In 1994, three years after the controversy, Haddock noted that many station programmers were shy of "multicultural programming" because they associated it with

"controversial programming" like "Tongues Untied." "They like performance programming because it's nonthreatening. Black people dancing and singing and entertaining," she said. "It's blatant racism, but it's very hard to convince people that they're being racist because they really don't think they are."

Looking back, she believed Marlon Riggs did the African-American community a "great service by bringing the issues to us" and noted, too, that he didn't have to worry about being ostracized or having to feed his family ten years in the future so he had nothing to lose. "Freedom gives you a clear eye," she said.

25. Telephone interview with Weiss, November 5, 1991.
26. PBS routinely sends out memos, which are referred to as "dacs," to stations on programs that contain strong language, nudity, or violence.
27. Telephone interview with Weiss, November 5, 1991.
28. Interview with Weiss, June 5, 1994.
29. Ibid. and telephone interview with Weiss, September 29, 1994.
30. Telephone interview with Haddock.
31. Paul Lomartire, "Explicit PBS Film on Black Gays Could Reignite NEA Controversy," *Palm Beach Post*, June 8, 1991.
32. Confirmed in telephone interview with Josh Dare, NEA public relations, June 2, 1994.
33. Interview with Paul Lomartire, Orlando, Fla., June 4, 1994.
34. Paul Lomartire, "Explicit PBS Film."
35. Ibid.
36. Interview with Lomartire.
37. Quoted by Lomartire, "Explicit PBS Film."
38. Riggs described Lomartire's article as "fair" in a handwritten note to Lomartire dated June 12, 1991.
39. Quoted by Lomartire, "Explicit PBS Film."
40. Ibid.
41. Interview with Lomartire.
42. Ibid.
43. Quoted by Gerry Yandel, "Atlanta's PBS Affiliates to Air Controversial Film," *Atlanta Constitution*, June 11, 1991.
44. Terry Ann Knopf, "PBS Stations Pull Program on Gay Blacks," *Patriot Ledger* (Quincy, Mass.), June 13, 1991.
45. Ibid.
46. Quoted by Ransdell Pierson, "Anti-Smut Rev Backs Gay Show So It'll 'Anger' U.S.," *New York Post*, June 22, 1991.

Donald Wildmon had not responded to requests for a telephone interview about "Tongues Untied" as of June 25, 1994, when I wrote this chapter. His comments here are taken from his AFA press release and direct quotes contained in news articles.

47. "AFA Head Wants People to Watch PBS Film Funded with NEA Dollars," American Family Press Release, June 20, 1991.
48. This was also quoted by John Carmody in "Now This," *Washington Post*, June 21, 1991.
49. This circulation figure was listed in "Attacks on Public Broadcasting: Who's Who on the Right," a report by People for the American Way Action Fund, April 14, 1992, p. 16.
50. Quoted by Pierson, "Anti-Smut Rev Backs Gay Show So It'll 'Anger' U.S."
51. "*People For* Responds to Wildmon Statement on New NEA Controversy," People for the American Way Press Release, June 20, 1991.
52. Quoted by John Carmody, "Now This."

53. Marlon Riggs, letter to supporters, June 20, 1991.
54. Quoted by Pierson, "Anti-Smut Rev Backs Gay Show."
55. Interview with Weiss, June 5, 1994.
56. Ellen Schneider quote appeared in *Communications Daily* (Washington, D.C.), June 21, 1991.
57. Terry Ann Knopf, "NEA Supports Controversial Documentary," *Patriot Ledger*, June 27, 1991.
58. Quoted by Joyce Price, "Most PBS Stations Pass on NEA-Aided Gay Film," *Washington Times*, June 28, 1991.
59. Ibid.
60. Patricia Aufderheide, "Controversy and the Newspaper's Public: The Case of 'Tongues Untied,'" *Journalism Quarterly* (autumn 1994), 504.
61. Quoted by Lisa de Moraes, "Wildmon Issues 'Tongues'-Lashing by Changing Tack," *Hollywood Reporter*, June 21, 1991.
62. "PBS Hurts Member Stations by Pushing 'Tongues Untied' Commentary," *Mail Tribune* (Medford, Ore.), July 16, 1991.
63. Quoted by Marc Gunther, "Gay Black Men Are Subject of Controversial PBS Film," *Detroit Free Press*, June 18, 1991.
64. Quoted by Sharon Bernstein, "PBS Stations Balk at 'Tongues Untied,'" *Los Angeles Times*, June 24, 1991.
65. Schneider quotes are from Mary Donoghue, "WNIT among Stations Not Airing Program about Gay Men," *South Bend Tribune* (South Bend, Ind.), June 29, 1991.
66. Michael Zahn, "WMVS Refuses to Air Documentary," *Milwaukee Journal*, June 23, 1991.
67. Janis Froelich, "WEDU Board Decides against Airing Film on Gay Black Men," *St. Petersburg Times* (St. Petersburg, Fla.), June 27, 1991.
68. "You Can't Say That on Television," *Maine Times* (weekly), July 19, 1991. (No author name given.)
69. Quoted in "Dialogue: Gatekeeper or Censor?" *Metro Times* (weekly; Detroit, Mich.), July 10–16, 1991.
70. Ibid.
71. John Engstrom, "Talking on 'Tongues,'" *Seattle Post-Intelligencer*, July 16, 1991.
72. Ibid.
73. Ibid.
74. Steve Bornfeld, "PBS Explicit 'Tongues Untied' Is Disturbing yet Enriching," *Times Union*, July 2, 1991.
75. David Zurawik, "P.O.V.: Real Civics Lesson," *Baltimore Sun*, July 2, 1991.
76. "More Filth on Your Tax Money," editorial, *Chattanooga News-Free Press*, July 3, 1991.
77. "Prim Public TV," editorial, *Charleston Gazette*, August 2, 1991.
78. Peggy McGlone, "Content Takes Back Seat to Controversy in PBS Film on Plight of Black Gay Men," *Star-Ledger* (New Jersey), July 16, 1991.
79. Quoted by John Martin, "A Tough Subject for Public TV," *Providence Journal-Bulletin*, July 16, 1991.
80. Matt Roush, "'Tongues Untied': PBS' Knotty Documentary," *USA Today*, July 16, 1991.
81. "Listen to What's Said in 'Tongues,'" *Atlanta Constitution*, July 18, 1991.
82. "Howard Rosenberg, "'Tongues Untied' Deserves to Be Seen and Heard," *Los Angeles Times*, July 15, 1991.
83. James Kilpatrick, "Porno Poets Must Be Stopped," *Rome News-Tribune*, July 8, 1991. The article was also syndicated in the *Chicago Sun-Times*, the *Mail Tri-*

*bune* (Medford, Ore.), the *Wichita Eagle*, the *Pantagraph* (Bloomington, Ill.), and at least five other papers.

84. Walter Goodman, "Growing Up Homosexual and Black," *New York Times*, July 15, 1991. The article was reprinted in several other newspapers through the *Times* wire service with different titles; for example, it appeared as "'Tongues Untied' Offers Powerful Message," in *South Bend Tribune* (South Bend, Ind.), July 16, 1991.

85. Valerie Helmbreck, "'Tongues Untied' PBS Gives Close-up of Different Lifestyle," *News Journal* (Wilmington, Del.), July 16, 1991. The article was reprinted in several other papers.

86. Jon Burlingame, "'P.O.V.' Study of Gay Black Men Is Aimed at Narrow Audience," *Sacramento Bee Final*, July 16, 1991. His article was reprinted in at least three other papers.

87. Debra A. Applegate, "WNIT to Offer Studio Screening of 'Tongues Untied' Documentary on Monday," *South Bend Tribune*, July 17, 1994.

88. M. Ferguson Tinsley, "Gay Film on PBS Unsettles Public," *Tribune Chronicle* (Warren, Ohio), July 17, 1991.

89. "Statement of the Georgia Public Telecommunications Commission Regarding the Program Entitled 'Tongues Untied,'" written in late September 1991, by the board of directors, GPTV.

90. Ed Bark, "Film on Gay Black Men Will Be Aired in Dallas," *Dallas Morning News*, June 29, 1991. The only other Texas public television station that planned not to preempt "Tongues Untied" was a small university station, Channel 46, in Killeen. The Killeen station scheduled the broadcast for 9 p.m. on July 16.

91. Ron Miller, "Local PBS Stations Don't Give in to 'P.O.V.' Panic," *San Jose Mercury News*, July 19, 1991.

92. Don Schanche, Jr., "Budget Writers Criticize Ga. Public TV Boss over Documentary on Gays," *Macon Telegraph*, October 18, 1991.

93. Quoted by Bill Shipp, "Programming Restrictions Asked for GPTV," *Douglas Neighbor*, September 11, 1991. This article was printed in three Georgia weekly newspapers.

94. "Screwed up" quote from "Metro Brief," *Atlanta Constitution*, October 18, 1991. "Poor judgment" quote from Schanche, "Budget Writers Criticize Ga. Public TV Boss."

95. "We have heard" quote from Ken Edelstein, "Legislators Rebuke GPTV for Airing Gay Documentary," *Columbus Ledger Enquirer*, October 18, 1991.

96. Quoted in Schanche, "Budget Writers Criticize Ga. Public TV Boss."

97. Ibid.

98. Ibid.

99. Telephone interview with Jeannie Bunton, CPB spokesperson, March 14, 1995.

100. "PBS Show Draws Indecency Complaints at FCC," *Broadcasting*, July 29, 1991.

101. For a detailed account of the conservative efforts to control public broadcasting, and the conflicting traditions inside public television and radio, see Ralph Engelman's excellent book, *Public Radio and Television in America: A Political History* (Thousand Oaks, Calif.: Sage Publications, 1996).

102. Sometimes staff inside the same station, as at WOSU/Columbus, were deeply divided on the question of airing or not airing "Tongues." Julia Keller, in "Debated Documentary Will Air Here," *Columbus Dispatch* (July 8, 1991), captured the essence of this split in a comment by WOSU general manager Dale K. Ouzts, who told her, "Almost every opinion you could have about running it, you can find around this station. Some say, 'If you run it, you're a pornographer.' Others say, 'If you don't run it, you're a censor.'"

103. Patricia Aufderheide, "Controversy at Issue: The Press and 'Tongues Untied,'" paper presented at the International Communications Association Annual Convention, May 1992, p. 2.

104. Hemphill and Beam, *Brother to Brother*, p. 193.

### Chapter 6    *"Stop the Church"*

1. This figure is cited by Joseph Cunneen in "'Stop the Church,' on ACT-UP Stoppage, Stopped by PBS," *National Catholic Reporter*, August 30, 1991.

2. Victor F. Zonana, "AIDS Activist Finds Creative Outlet in 'Church,'" *Los Angeles Times*, September 6, 1991.

3. All quotes by Hilferty in this section are taken from my interview with the film maker in New York on November 6, 1991.

4. The film maker also told me he took a few editing classes at New York University's Cinema Studies Department, but he was not in the school's film degree program.

5. Zonana, "AIDS Activist."

6. Telephone interview with Robert Hilferty, September 27, 1994.

7. Interview with Marc Weiss, Orlando, Fla., June 5, 1994, and telephone interview with Weiss on November 5, 1991.

8. Telephone interview with Glenn Dixon, November 6, 1995.

9. Quoted by Tom Sime, "Tongues Retied," *Dallas Observer*, August 29, 1991. The press statement was widely quoted and summarized by reporters.

10. These quotes appeared in numerous articles, including Lisa de Moraes, "PBS Changes Point of View, Pulls Film on Church Protest," *Hollywood Reporter*, August 13, 1991, and Sharon Bernstein and Robert Koehler, "PBS Network Hit by Charges of Censorship," *Los Angeles Times*, August 14, 1991.

11. According to Bernstein and Koehler in "PBS Network Hit by Charges of Censorship," the call came from "a local station," and an article published on August 21 in the *Los Angeles Times* said it came after "an *executive* at a local public television station complained" (my emphasis). The station executive and the station were not named. See "'Stop the Church' to Be Part of KCET Special," by Sharon Bernstein, *Los Angeles Times*, August 21, 1991.

12. Quoted by Bernstein and Koehler, "PBS Network Hit by Charges of Censorship."

13. Sharbutt, "PBS Yanks Film of Church Protest," *Houston Chronicle* (Associated Press), August 14, 1991.

14. Quoted by Bernstein and Koehler, "PBS Network Hit by Charges of Censorship."

15. Interview with Hilferty, November 6, 1991.

16. The other films included in *P.O.V.*'s "Short Notice" were "Who's Going to Care for These Children?" about foster parents of children with AIDS; "Mirror, Mirror," about how women view their bodies; and two shorts about people and their cars, "Auto Bond" and "Crutemobile." None of these films was deemed controversial.

17. Howard Rosenberg, "New 'P.O.V.' Flap Finds PBS at the Edge of Timidity," *Los Angeles Times*, August 14, 1991.

18. Quoted by Bernstein and Koehler, "PBS Network Hit by Charges of Censorship."

19. Robert Hilferty, "Why Is PBS Afraid of AIDS?" *New York Newsday*, September 4, 1991.

20. Quoted by Jay Sharbutt, "PBS Pulls Film about AIDS Protest" (Associated Press), *Bangor Daily News*, August 14, 1994.

21. Quoted in "PBS Pulls Film on AIDS Protest," *Boston Globe*, August 14, 1994. No reporter's name was given in this Associated Press story.

22. Julia Keller, "PBS Cancellation Knocks More Teeth from 'P.O.V.,'" *Columbus Dispatch* (Columbus, Ohio), August. 18, 1991.

23. Marvin Kitman, "P.O.V.: This Censorship Is Disturbing," *New York Newsday*, August 15, 1991.

24. The *Washington Times* editorial appeared on August 16, 1991.

25. The *Charleston Gazette* editorial appeared on August 16, 1991.

26. Catherine Saalfield, "Tongue Tied: Homophobia Hamstrings PBS," *Independent Film and Video Monthly*, October 1991.

27. Rosenberg, "New 'P.O.V.' Flap Finds PBS at the Edge of Timidity."

28. Bernstein and Koehler, "PBS Network Hit by Charges of Censorship"; Rosenberg, "New 'P.O.V.' Flap Finds PBS at the Edge of Timidity."

29. Telephone interview with Barbara Goen, January 22, 1992.

30. The strategy employed by KCET is described in *A Guide to Crisis Management*, a monograph distributed at the PBS annual meeting, June 1992. The next two paragraphs contain information from this document.

31. In our July 7, 1994, telephone interview, Hilferty said he was "a little apprehensive" about the ACT-UP/Los Angeles threat to jam the KCET phone lines during the pledge drive, feeling it would have been "too extreme," but he also said he encouraged his associates in Los Angeles to do "whatever you feel is right in L.A." He remembered telling them, "It's your Cardinal and public television station."

    The film maker told me ACT-UP kept the pressure on KCET to make sure the station would follow through on its decision to broadcast the show, and eventually the organization decided it should be broadcast "no matter what," meaning regardless of whether it was packaged with a wraparound.

32. Sharon Bernstein, "Gay-Rights Activists Plan National PBS Protests," *Los Angeles Times*, August 16, 1991.

    "Son of Sam and Delilah" was produced by Charles Atlas for a series called *New Television*. The program used a serial killer as a metaphor for AIDS. PBS rejected it because it contained "gratuitous violence."

33. Using "Stop the Church" as an example, the "Guide to Crisis Management" recommended several courses of action when dealing with "Third-Party Groups and the Public." (Section titled "Relations with Critics & the Community—'Preventing Smoke with Clear and Open Communications.'") Among them were notifying the local police to request increased security in the event of a demonstration, asking station staff to avoid discussing the controversy with any demonstrators, contacting the local telephone company to see if it could set up an alternative if threatened with the possibility of phone jamming, asking station supporters who have ties to the station's critics to help make the station's case, and presenting a consistent line that the station's decision was based on either "sound programming or funding policies." (KCET chose to stress "sound programming" policies in the "Stop the Church" case.) "Reach out to and maintain communication with any reasonable and serious critics, especially members of your local community," the "Guide" advised.

34. Quoted by Diana E. Lundin, "Gay Group Protesting PBS Plans," *Los Angeles Daily News*, August 21, 1991.

35. Quoted by Bernstein, "Gay-Rights Activists Plan National PBS Protests."

36. As recommended by the PBS *Guide*, the strategic team chose to invite the gay critics to the station, where access could be controlled and where the concerns could be discussed privately and without the media.

37. Bernstein, "Gay-Rights Activists Plan National PBS Protests."

38. Telephone interview with Goen, January 22, 1992.
39. Bernstein, "'Stop the Church' to Be Part of KCET Special."
40. "Chronology of Events Leading up to 'Stop the Church' Controversy, Excerpted from Memo Dated August 27, 1991," by Coiro. Coiro sent me this chronology in January 1992.
41. Ibid.
42. Telephone interview with the Reverend Gregory Coiro, January 22, 1992.
43. Ibid.
44. Ibid.
45. Ibid.
46. Telephone interviews with Coiro, January 22, 1992, and July 11, 1994. At his press conference that appeared in the KCET special, "Stop the Church: Issues and Outrage," Mahony said Kobin admitted to him in a telephone conversation that the station decided to show "Stop the Church" because of the pressure put on the station by gay groups, an allegation Kobin later strongly and adamantly denied when asked about this by the press.
47. Ibid.
48. Telephone interview with Coiro, January 22, 1992.
49. Telephone interview with Goen, January 22, 1992.
50. Sharon Bernstein, "KCET Unworthy of Public Support, Mahony Declares," Los Angeles Times, September 6, 1991.
51. "Statement on KCET-Channel 28 Program Decision," Catholic Twin Circle (weekly), September 29, 1991.
52. Sharon Bernstein, "KCET Pays Price in Flap with Church," Los Angeles Times, October 10, 1991.
53. Telephone interview with Goen, January 22, 1992.
54. Klosinski confirmed this in our telephone interview July 11, 1994.
55. Telephone interviews with Goen, January 22, 1992, and July 11, 1994. In her fax sent to me on July 12, 1994, Goen explained each Nielsen rating point equals 50,000 households in the KCET market area, and each household is estimated by Nielsen to represent 1.3 persons.
56. Telephone interview with Goen, July 11, 1994.
57. Fax from Goen to the author, July 12, 1994.
58. PBS, Guide to Crisis Management.
59. Telephone interview with Goen, January 22, 1992. The ratio is taken from PBS's Guide to Crisis Management.
60. Telephone interview with Goen, January 22, 1992.
61. Bernstein, "KCET Pays Price in Flap with Church." This figure was "as of Sept. 30."
62. Telephone interview with Goen, January 22, 1992.
63. KCET form letters to "Mr. John P. Sample," no date.
64. Telephone interview with Coiro, January 22, 1992.
65. Fax from Goen to the author, July 12, 1994.
66. Telephone interview with Goen, July 11, 1994.
67. Penelope McMillan, "Mahony Gets Mixed Feedback on Feud with KCET," Los Angeles Times, September 9, 1991.
68. Robert J. Hutchinson, "Cardinals Won't Let Bigots 'Stop the Church,'" Catholic Twin Circle (weekly), September 28, 1991.
69. Amy Kuebelbeck, "Under Fire?" Los Angeles Times, September 9, 1991. Cokie Roberts, the National Public Radio and ABC-TV correspondent, mentioned she is Catholic on This Week with David Brinkley.
70. "Air Time for Hate: KCET's Airing of an Anti-Catholic Video Was a Lowering

of Standards and a Lapse of Judgment," editorial, *Los Angeles Daily News*, September 10, 1991.

71. Howard Rosenberg, "'Stop the Church': All Parties Do Their Part," *Los Angeles Times*, September 9, 1991.

72. "Stop the Charges: No Double Standard in 'Church' Stance," *Los Angeles Times*, September 16, 1991.

73. Terry Ann Knopf, "Two PBS Outlets to Air 'Church,'" *Electronic Media* (weekly), August 26, 1991. "KQED Moves to Air Controversial Documentary," *Tribune* (Oakland, Calif.), August 22, 1991. The documentary also was scheduled to be shown at the Roxie Cinema at 11 a.m. the following Saturday and Sunday mornings. See "'Stop the Church' Will Screen at Roxie Cinema," *San Francisco Chronicle*, August 22, 1991.

74. Susan Bickelhaupt, "WGBH to Air Controversial Special," *Boston Globe*, August 31, 1991.

75. "Another Controversy Hits Public TV's P.O.V. Series," *Herald-Sun* (Durham, N.C.), August 30, 1991.

76. Steve Behrens, "Archbishop Blasts Airing of Documentary," *Current*, September 9, 1991.

77. Diana Lundin, "Decision to Air AIDS Show Angers Catholics," *Vancouver Sun*, September 7, 1991.

78. The "considerable number" of telephone calls was quoted by Jack Robertiello in "Some Stations to Air 'Stop the Church,' *Current*, August 26, 1991. The Chancey quote is from Verne Gay, "Station Might Air Controversial Film," *New York Newsday*, August 23, 1991.

79. Walter Goodman, "Prime Time vs. the Art of Ridicule," *New York Times*, September 1, 1991.

80. Ibid.

81. Telephone interview with Hilferty, July 7, 1994.

82. Peter Steinfels, "Channel 13 to Show Film on AIDS Protest," *New York Times*, September 13, 1991.

83. Transcripts of radio stories from *P.O.V.*'s monitoring service.

84. Steinfels, "Channel 13 to Show Film on AIDS Protest."

85. Telephone interview with Hilferty, July 7, 1994. Telephone interview with Joseph Zwilling, January 16, 1992.

86. Peter Steinfels, "Should a Movie about Disrupting a Mass Be Shown Simply Because It's Controversial?" *New York Times*, September 14, 1991.

87. Ibid.

88. "Why 'Stop the Church' Was Televised," Letters to the Editor, *New York Times*, September 21, 1991.

89. Telephone interview with Weiss, February 4, 1994.

90. Interview with Hilferty, November 6, 1991.

91. Telephone interview with Hilferty, July 7, 1994. The quotes by Hilferty in the following paragraphs are taken from this interview.

92. Telephone interview with Coiro, July 11, 1994.

93. Larry Stammer, "Mahony, KCET Make Peace, Disagree Anew," *Los Angeles Times*, December 2, 1992.

94. Telephone interview with Coiro, July 11, 1994.

### Chapter 7   *"Roger & Me" and "The Heartbeat of America"*

1. This worker was Ben Hamper, the author of *Rivethead: Tales from the Assembly Line* (New York: Warner Books, 1992).

2. Internet, to members of H-Film list, from Michael Moore, April 4, 1996.
3. Telephone interview with Michael Moore, August 10, 1996.
4. Henry Allen, "Have Grin, Will Film Despair," *Washington Post*, January 11, 1990.
5. Moore told the *Washington Post* his trouble with *Mother Jones* began when he interrupted a discussion about hiring more women and minorities and suggested that the magazine would be better off if a blue-collar factory worker were hired. He also did not want to publish an article that criticized the Sandinistas. (See Allen, "Have Grin, Will Film Despair.") The *Washington Times* quoted former *Mother Jones* publisher Don Hazen, who disagreed with Moore's account of events. He said Moore was fired because he ignored deadlines and was "impossible to work with." (See Rick Marin, "The Truth about Michael Moore and 'Roger & Me,'" *Washington Times*, February 14, 1990.)
6. Telephone interview with Moore, August 10, 1996.
7. Susan Stark, "Sparks from Flint," *Detroit News*, September 11, 1989.
8. David Sterritt, "A Documentary Grabs Attention," *Christian Science Monitor*, January 16, 1990.
9. Ibid. Some papers later wrote it cost $260,000.
10. Kathy Huffhines, "Movie Takes an Offbeat Swipe at GM," *Detroit Free Press*, September 11, 1989.
11. Roger Ebert, "'Roger and Me' Strikes Out at the Greed That Fuels General Motors," *Chicago Sun Times*, September 10, 1989.
12. Roger Ebert, "'Roger & Me' Is the Right Film at the Right Time," *Chicago Sun Times*, December 3, 1989.
13. Sheryl James, "Film Drives Home a Point about GM and the Fall of Flint, Michigan," *St. Petersburg Times* (St. Petersburg, Fla.), January 21, 1990.
14. Vincent Canby, "A Twainlike Twist for Flint, Mich.," *New York Times*, September, 27, 1989.
15. For an insider's description of the business side of "Roger & Me," see John Pierson, *Spike, Mike, Slackers & Dykes: A Guided Tour across a Decade of American Independent Cinema* (New York: Hyperion, 1995), pp.137–176.
16. Stephen Advokat, "'Roger & Me' Gets Big-Time Distributor," *Detroit Free Press*, October 31, 1989; Phil Primack, "'Roger & Me' Hits Home in Framingham," *Boston Herald*, December 11, 1989.
17. See Pierson, *Spike*, pp. 154–155.
18. Telephone interview with John Mueller, August 9, 1996.
19. Quoted by Nunzio Lupo, "Nightmare on Grand Blvd.," *Detroit Free Press*, September 24, 1989.
20. Quoted by John Foren, "'Roger & Me' Puts Flint in Spotlight—Good or Bad," *Flint Journal*, October 1, 1989.
21. Quoted by Patrick Lee, "Exasperated GM Chief Pans Satiric Film as 'Sick Humor,'" *Los Angeles Times*, January 4, 1990.
22. See Julie Hinds, "Roger & Them," *Detroit News*, October. 29, 1989.
23. Dennis Niemiec, "Flint Journalist Reportedly Fired," *Detroit Free Press*, September 27, 1989. The paper had planned to publish an editorial critical of Moore and his film, and accused Doug Sanders, a *Flint Journal* staff writer, of leaking the contents of the editorial prior to its publication. Sanders denied the charge and claimed his seventeen-year friendship with Moore led to his firing.
24. Telephone interview with John Foren, July 19, 1996.
25. Harlan Jacobson, "Michael and Me," *Film Comment*, November–December 1989.
26. Telephone interview with Harlan Jacobson, July 22, 1996.
27. Ibid.

28. Jon Pepper, "Fallout: GM-Flint Marriage Endures," *Detroit News and Free Press*, December 17, 1989.
29. Jacobson, "Michael & Me."
30. Pierson, *Spike*, p. 168.
31. Pauline Kael, "The Current Cinema," *New Yorker*, January 8, 1990.
32. Thomas Hazlett, "'Roger & Me'—Bad Economics and Phony Facts," *Newsweek*, February 4, 1990.
33. Richard Schickel, "Imposing on Reality," *Time*, January 8, 1990.
34. Marin, "The Truth about Michael Moore and 'Roger & Me.'"
35. Telephone interview with John Mueller, September 24, 1996.
36. John Mueller sent me one of the "truth packets." The "Talking Points about Michael Moore Film" was dated January 31, 1990, and included copies of Roger Smith's statement on the film, highlights of GM's activities in Flint, critical reviews from *Newsday*, Pauline Kael's review in the *New Yorker*, Harlon Jacobson's interview in *Film Comment*, and an editorial from the *Oakland Press* in Pontiac, Michigan.
37. Telephone interview with John Mueller, October 4, 1996.
38. Telephone interview with Moore, August 10, 1996. Moore also recounted this story in his article "'Roger' and I, Off to Hollywood and Home to Flint," *New York Times*, July 15, 1990.
39. Telephone interview with Moore, August 10, 1996.
40. Telephone interview with Mueller, September 9, 1996.
41. Joseph B. White, "GM Seeks to Keep Ads Off Talk Show about 'Roger & Me,'" *Wall Street Journal*, February 1, 1990.
42. Ibid.
43. No byline, "G.M.'s Response to 'Roger & Me,'" *New York Times*, January 31, 1990; White, "GM Seeks to Keep Ads Off Talk Show about 'Roger & Me.'"
44. Telephone interview with Mueller, September 24, 1996.
45. Telephone interview with Mueller, October 4, 1996.
46. Mitchell Block, a distributor of independent films and a faculty member of the University of Southern California, was on the Oscar documentary screening committee. Block confirmed that the sequencing issue and concerns about accuracy prevented "Roger & Me" from receiving a high enough score from members to be nominated. It was a "runner-up." He said some members of the committee were very enthusiastic about the film, and he spoke in favor of nominating it partly because he did not want the academy to relive the flak it had experienced for snubbing other commercially successful and popular documentaries in previous years. Others on the committee did not want to reward "Roger & Me," a film that was, in his words, "unethical and not respectful to others."
    In his twenty years on the nominating committee, Block recalled only one other film had lost a likely Oscar nomination due to a sequencing issue: "Vietnam Requiem." He said one committee member was familiar with the stock footage used in the film and argued that it was used out of context when post-Tet footage was used to represent scenes from the Tet Offensive. This was the only instance in his memory where a sequencing issue was ever discussed, and one committee member's outrage was enough to sink the nomination. (Telephone interview with Mitchell Block, July 19, 1996.)
47. Yardena Ara, "Documenting Their Outrage," *Los Angeles Daily News*, February 23, 1990.
48. Pierson, *Spike*, p. 174.
49. Ibid., pp. 173–174.

50. Telephone interview with attorney Steven Spender, March 25, 1997.
51. Telephone interview with Marc Weiss, February 4, 1994. This experience with "Roger and Me" prompted Weiss later to create a completion fund for especially promising documentaries. This account of events differs from Michael Moore's. Moore said he offered "Roger & Me" to Weiss for $10,000 about the same time he submitted it to the Telluride Film Festival in 1989 for possible inclusion in the festival. (Telephone interview with Moore, August 10, 1996.)
52. Telephone interview with Weiss, February 4, 1994.
53. Telephone interview with Jim Gaver, February 9, 1994.
54. Pierson, *Spike*, p. 175. I tried to confirm this account with Fred Ross, but I was unable to reach him.
55. Telephone interview with Glen Lenhoff, July 18, 1996.
56. Karen (Edgley) Martin's exact words were, "We don't hold any public offices. We're really nobody special, but he wanted our opinions and our views."
    News stations routinely use stock footage for visuals in their news stories, and it is not uncommon for independent film makers or commercial broadcasters to purchase tape from stations for use in their own productions.
57. Steve Behrens, "Woman Seen in 'Roger & Me' Sues PBS, Flint Station," *Current*, January 31, 1994, p. 4.
58. Moore's voice-over narration read, "Meanwhile, the more fortunate in Flint were holding their annual 'Great Gatsby' party at the home of one of GM's founding families. To show that they weren't totally insensitive to the plight of others, they hired local people to act as human statues at the party."
59. Telephone interview with Lenhoff. Lenhoff has been no friend to GM over the years and has represented numerous clients who have protested their termination by the company. Karen Martin, one of his plaintiffs in the "Roger & Me" lawsuit, was, however, the wife of a GM manager. Lenhoff said the employer of her husband was incidental to her lawyer's claim that Moore was damaging the reputation of private person.
60. Telephone interview with Foren, July 19, 1996. Michael Moore, "Michael Moore Says Comments by Journal Mayor Unfair," *Flint Journal*, August 11, 1996. See also Michael Moore, "How to Keep 'em Happy in Flint," *Columbia Journalism Review*, September–October 1985.
61. All quotes by Michael Moore in this section are taken from my telephone interview with the film maker on August 10, 1996. Moore went on to produce *TV Nation* for NBC, a six-episode, prime-time summer series that he described as a comedy version of *60 Minutes*. The series moved to Fox and then to Comedy Central.
    NBC premiered *TV Nation* on July 19, 1994. The one-hour program in its Tuesday night, 8 p.m. time-slot garnered an average 6.7 rating and was seen by an estimated 6.3 million households, according to NBC research. (Telephone interview with unnamed NBC researcher, September 7, 1994.) These figures are a dismal rating in commercial television, where programs with ratings around 16, like *Home Improvement* and *Frasier*, are considered a success. Yet even *TV Nation*'s relatively low rating was still more than three times PBS's 2.0 prime-time average fall season premiere and still exceeded, on average, the estimated 5.2 rating of Ken Burns's two-hour first episode of *Baseball: An American Epic*. (See de Moraes, "'Hope' Delivers; Burns Doubles.")
62. Telephone interview with John Foren, September 24, 1996.
63. Telephone interview with Mueller, September 9, 1996.
64. Telephone interview with Mueller, September 24, 1996.
65. In the other *Frontline* coproductions with the Center for Investigative Report-

ing, the center usually raised between 40 to 50 percent of the total budget and shared the copyright. In the case of "The Heartbeat of America," CIR was unable to raise its normal share, and *Frontline* agreed to cover most of the budget. (Note from Steve Talbot to the author dated October 12, 1994.)

66. Steve Talbot, the producer of "The Heartbeat of America," is an example of the independent producer I describe as a "pragmatist" in chapter 1. Talbot is one of a handful of independent producers who started their film-making careers by making political advocacy films during the anti–Vietnam war movement. Some of these independent documentarians later found work as staff producers at public television affiliates or in commercial network television. Many were also born, white and male, into the professional, upper-income class and attended private schools and colleges.

67. Donald W. Nauss, "U.S. to Drop Recall Probe of GM Trucks," *Los Angeles Times*, December 3, 1994.

68. Ibid. *The NBC Dateline* broadcast, however, was soon followed by an investigation by the National Highway Traffic Safety Administration. On December 1, 1994, the U.S. government agreed to drop a recall of five million GM pickups in exchange for a $51-million contribution from the company for safety programs.

69. The company has a reputation for playing hardball when media outlets for its commercial messages make editorial decisions unfavorable to GM. For example, GM pulled an eight-page insert from *Fortune*, which was owned by Time, Inc., after it published a cover story about Ross Perot, who had vehemently criticized the company. (See Raymond Serafin, "GM Yanks Ad Insert out of 'Fortune,'" *Advertising Age*, February 15, 1988.)

70. Telephone interview with William O'Neill, January 27, 1994.

71. Telephone interview with Ed Lechtzin, February 10, 1994.

72. Marc Gunther, "PBS Documentary Takes Aim at General Motors, Which Plays Hard to Get," *Detroit Free Press*, August 3, 1993. Also referred to by Eve Pell, "General Motors Clams Up," *Muckraker*, winter 1994, p. 4. (*Muckraker* is a publication of the Center for Investigative Reporting in San Francisco.)

73. Pell, "General Motors Clams Up," p. 4. Pell wrote that Hoglund made this statement at the *Automotive News* World Congress in Detroit on January 11, 1993.

74. Ibid.

75. Quoted in ibid. Talbot verified the accuracy of this quote on October 12, 1994.

76. Ibid.

77. The dominant style of *Frontline* documentaries resembles the old *CBS Reports*. *Frontline* documentaries appeal to viewers through a reasoned argument rather than more obvious manipulative means such as using dramatic music and images to reach into the viewer's heart and give it a twist.

78. The actual households numbered 2,826,000 according to ratings data provided me by *Frontline*.

79. Walter Goodman, "Diagnosing the Clank inside GM's Engine," *New York Times*, October 12, 1993.

80. Ben Kubasik, "Looking at Drivers Who Nearly Made GM Crash," *New York Newsday*, October 12, 1993.

81. Phil Kloer, "GM Gimmicks Fail to Mask Problems," *Atlanta Journal/Constitution*, October 12, 1993.

82. Warren Brown, "'Frontline' on GM: Faulty Steering" (TV Preview), *Washington Post*, October 12, 1993.

83. David Zurawik, "'Frontline' Relies on Wisecracks in Report on GM," *Baltimore Sun*, October 12, 1993.

84. Greg Gardner, "Carmaker on the 'Frontline': PBS Looks Back; GM Says It's Looking Ahead," *Detroit Free Press*, October 8, 1993.
85. Greg Gardner, "Stung by PBS' 'Frontline,' GM Reassesses Its Funding," *Detroit Free Press*, October, 14, 1993.
86. Quoted by Ben Kubasik, "TV Spots: Will GM Ever Learn?" *New York Newsday*, October, 18, 1993.
87. David Tobenkin, "PBS Docu May Drive Away GM's Funding," *Hollywood Reporter*, October 15, 1993.
88. Telephone interview with Lechtzin.
89. Gardner, "Stung by PBS' 'Frontline.'"
90. "PBS Statement on General Motors Funding of Public TV," no date.
91. Ed Lechtzin quoted the Ottenhoff letter to me *verbatim* on the phone but asked me to request the letter from Ottenhoff directly. I called Ottenhoff on February 10, 1994. He said he wanted to talk to Lechtzin and would get back to me that afternoon. He didn't. I called Ottenhoff's office the next day and left a message to follow up, but the call wasn't returned until I received a call from Karen Doyne, PBS's director of public relations, who said she would not give me the letter because PBS considered it "private correspondence." She suggested I get it from *Frontline*, but neither David Fanning nor Martin Smith knew about the letter until I told them about it. I have paraphrased the letter in the text because to quote from it directly would require written permission from the author.
92. *The Civil War* received the highest ratings of any program on public television and attracted an audience of forty million viewers.
93. GM spent nearly $4 million on a "Teamwork and Technology" insert for magazines alone, expecting to reach sixty million readers, according to *Advertising Age*, February 15, 1988.
94. GM isn't the sole funder, nor the majority funder, of Ken Burns's projects, but for *Baseball*, GM insisted on and got its logo and "Mark of Excellence" slogan prominently featured on air and in its educational and promotional print material associated with the series. For *The Civil War*, GM provided $1 million, the National Endowment for the Humanities contributed $1.3 million, the Arthur Vining Davis Foundation added $350,000, the MacArthur Foundation gave $200,000, and the Corporation for Public Broadcasting provided $200,000.

    With *Baseball*, CPB and PBS contributed about $2 million; General Motors gave $2.1 million toward production; the National Endowment for the Humanities came up with $2 million; the Pew Charitable Trusts gave $987,000, and the Arthur Vining Davis Foundation donated $550,000. (See de Moraes, "'Hope' Delivers; Burns Doubles.")
95. After interviewing several key sources who requested anonymity, I have been unable to confirm rumors that WTVS/Detroit lost a significant donation from GM in the wake of "The Heartbeat of America" broadcast.
96. Interview with David Fanning, Orlando, Fla., June 4, 1994.

### Conclusion

1. A few sources in public television also seem to have undermined Franklin-Trout's journalistic credibility informally through gossip and innuendo, but when I asked them to explain or to go on record about their concerns, they refused.
2. See Donald L. Barlett and James B. Steele, *America: What Went Wrong?* (Kansas City: Andrews and McMeel, 1992), p. 49.
3. While the typical Japanese or German chief executive makes less than twenty times as much as the average worker, the ratio for CEOs of major U.S. corpora-

tions climbed to 40:1 in 1980 and to 160:1 in 1991. (See Kevin Phillips, "A Capital Offense: Reagan's America," *New York Times Magazine*, June 17, 1990, and Karen W. Arenson, "The Boss: Underworked and Overpaid?" *New York Times Book Review*, November 17, 1991.)

4. Recent efforts to zero-out funding for the Corporation for Public Broadcasting and to privatize public television merely extend the process of balkanization begun by Richard Nixon in the early 1970s. Public television today is a semicommercial network of stations, no matter how hard employees try to pretend otherwise.

Some independent producers, such as Michael Moore, seem to have found not only larger audiences and more airtime but also more aesthetic freedom on commercial network television than on public television. Moore's program *TV Nation* has been shown on NBC, Fox, and Comedy Central. (Other independent producers have given up on national public television and now sell their work to cable networks.) Interestingly, Bill Moyers is diversifying his television presence, having signed a contract to give commentaries on *NBC Nightly News with Tom Brokaw*. (See "Quick Takes," *Current*, February 6, 1995, p. 4.)

5. From the perspective of independent producers, even more or regular government funding to PBS and public television stations through CPB would have at best an indirect effect on independent producers. Unless local stations expanded their relationship with the independent community (for example, through production and postproduction services), increased funding to stations would likely lead to more of the same programming that stations are known for, produced by station producers. On the other hand, increased, direct funding to the independent producers through government sources such as the NEA—and, through CPB, to the Independent Television Service—would be a more certain way to ensure that independent works continue to be made that reflect the aesthetic and cultural diversity of our society. (This would also depend on the courage of the NEA and other sources to fund provocative works.) Getting these works on the public television airwaves would be, as it is now, a second challenge.

## Epilogue

1. William Hoynes, *Public Television for Sale: Media, the Market, and the Public Sphere* (Boulder: Westview Press,1994), 105.
2. Quoted by John Day, *The Vanishing Vision: The Inside Story of Public Television* (Berkeley: University of California Press, 1995), p. 308.
3. In our telephone interview on March 24, 1997, Christensen confirmed that this was his view in 1994. He still believes that without government funding, public television will be commercial by the year 2000.
4. Interview with Ervin Duggan in *Broadcasting and Cable*, January 1994.
5. John Grant, June 5, 1994, roundtable meeting on "common carriage," Orlando, Florida.
6. The quote about the Sears series is from "Sears to Underwrite *The Puzzle Place*: A PBS Preschool Series Promoting Diversity," Sears Press Release, June 12, 1995.
7. *Wishbone* became the focus for an underwriting dispute when the *Washington Post* reported Frito-Lay was offering $1 million to underwrite the series, because the new, looser underwriting guidelines would allow the brand names of "junk food," such as Cheetos, to be attached to the program. Each half-hour episode of *Wishbone* costs approximately $500,000. See Karen Everhart Bedford, "When a Funder Arrives Bearing Cheese Puffs," *Current*, November 11, 1996, p. 1.
8. "Questions and Answers about the Public Broadcasting Trust," flier, May 1995,

prepared by America's Public Television Stations, National Public Radio, Public Broadcasting Service and Public Radio International.

9. Telephone interview with hotel security, Chicago Hilton, June 14, 1996.

10. My film "Circle of Plenty" was a coproduction with KCTS, and PBS scheduled it in prime time when it aired in 1987. "Earl Robinson: Ballad of an American" was also a KCTS coproduction that PBS rejected, but it was offered to other stations in the country over the Pacific Mountain Network.

11. Quoted by Karen Everhart Bedford, "Air Fare," *Current*, November 11, 1996, p. 8.

12. Telephone interview with Gail Christian, December 28, 1992.

# Selected Bibliography

## Documentaries

Videocassettes of "Dark Circle"(1989) are available for purchase from:
  The Video Project
  200 Estates Drive
  Ben Lomond, CA 95005
  (800) 475–2638 (4–planet)
  e-mail videoproject@videoproject.org
Film prints (16 mm) of "Dark Circle" are available for rental from:
  New Yorker Films
  16 West Sixty-first Street
  New York, NY 10023
  (212) 247–6110
"Days of Rage: The Young Palestinians" is available for purchase from:
  Pacific Productions
  22626 Pacific Coast Highway #4
  Malibu, CA 90265
  (310) 456-0403
"Earl Robinson: Ballad of an American" (1994) is available for purchase from:
  PBS Video
  1320 Braddock Place
  Alexandria, VA 22314
  (800) 344–3337
Although "The Heartbeat of America" (1993) is no longer in distribution, transcripts
  of the program, and of all other *Frontline* documentaries, are available from:
  Hyperscribe L. L. C.
  1535 Grant Street
  Denver, CO 80203
  (800) ALL-NEWS or (303) 831–9000
  fax (303) 831–8901
  e-mail timellis@800_allnews.com

"God and Money" (1986) is available for purchase from:
  California Newsreel
  149 Ninth Street
  San Francisco, CA 94103
  (415) 621–6196
"Pets or Meat: The Return to Flint"(1992) is no longer in distribution.
"Roger & Me" (1989) is available for rental at most video rental outlets.
"A Search for Solid Ground" (1990) is no longer in distribution.
"Stop the Church" (1991) and "Tongues Untied" (1989) are available for rental or
  purchase from:
  Frameline Distribution
  346 Ninth Street
  San Francisco, CA 94103
  (415) 703–8654/5
  fax (415) 861–1404

## Interviews

Chris Beaver, telephone, January 7, 1993; telephone, February 25, 1994.
Jeannie Bunton, telephone, March 4, 1995.
Barry Chase, New Orleans, June 21, 1993; telephone, March 3, 1994; telephone, September 27, 1994.
Gail Christian, telephone, December 28, 1992.
The Reverend Gregory Coiro, telephone, January 22, 1992; telephone, July 11, 1994.
Owen Comora, telephone, October 4, 1996.
Josh Dare, telephone, June 2, 1994.
Larry Daressa, telephone, May 10, 1989.
Glen Dixon, telephone, November 6, 1995.
Karen Doyne, telephone, February 22, 1994.
Ervin Duggan, Orlando (Fla.), June 6, 1994.
Steve Emerson, New York, September 21, 1995; telephone, July 9, 1996.
David Fanning, New Orleans, June 20, 1993; Orlando, June 4, 1994; telephone, October 7, 1994.
John Foren, telephone, July 19, 1996; telephone, September 24, 1996.
Jo Franklin-Trout, telephone, March 4, 1992; telephone, March 2, 1994; telephone, March 9, 1994; telephone, November 19, 1996.
Jim Gaver, telephone, February 9, 1994.
Barbara Goen, telephone, January 22, 1992; telephone, July 11, 1994; fax, July 12, 1994; fax, July 13, 1994.
Mable Haddock, telephone, November 4, 1994.
Lawrence Hall, telephone, September 1, 1989.
Sandy Heberer, Orlando, June 6, 1994.
Robert Hilferty, New York, November 6, 1991; telephone, July 7, 1994; telephone, September 27, 1994.
Judy Irving, San Francisco, June 23, 1992; telephone, December 15, 1992.
Harlon Jacobson, telephone, July 22, 1996.
Nathan Katzman, telephone, February 11, 1993.
Olivia Kim, Orlando, June 6, 1994.
Lee Klosinski, telephone, July 11, 1994.
Rabbi Anson Laytner, telephone, February 16, 1990.
Ed Lechtzin, telephone, February 10, 1994.
Glen Lenhoff, telephone, July 18, 1996.

Paul Lomartire, Orlando, June 4, 1994.
Glenn Marcus, Alexandria (Va.), April 14, 1993.
Mary Jane McKinven, Alexandria, April 14, 1993; telephone, November 22, 1994.
Michael Moore, telephone, August 10, 1996; Allentown (Pa.), September 11, 1996.
John Mueller, telephone, August 9, 1996; telephone, September 9, 1996; telephone, September 24, 1996; telephone, October 4, 1996.
William O'Neill, telephone, January 27, 1994.
Beverly Ornstein, telephone, February 21, 1994.
Robert Ottenhoff, telephone, February 10, 1994.
Richard Ottinger, Orlando, June 5, 1994.
Eve Pell, telephone, January 10, 1994.
Al Perlmutter, Orlando, June 6, 1994.
Marlon Riggs, telephone, May 12, 1989.
Hirsham Sharabi, telephone, February 1, 1992.
Martin Smith, telephone, January 31, 1994.
Steve Spender, telephone, March 25, 1997.
Steve Talbot, telephone, October 12, 1994.
Patricia Thomson, telephone, September 7, 1994.
Marc Weiss, telephone, November 5, 1991; telephone, February 4, 1994; Orlando, June 5, 1994; telephone, September 29, 1994.
Joseph Zwilling, telephone, January 16, 1992.
Many others were interviewed off the record.

## Published Sources

Accuracy in Media (AIM). *AIM Report*. Washington, D.C., 1975–1993.
American-Arab Anti-Discrimination Committee. *ADC Times: News and Opinions of the American-Arab Anti-Discrimination Committee*. Washington, D.C., 1979–1992.
Anderson, Benedict. *Imagined Communities: Reflections on the Origin and Spread of Nationalism*. New York: Verso Press, 1983.
Angus, Ian, and Sut Jhally, ed. *Cultural Politics in Contemporary America*. New York: Routledge, 1989.
Aufderheide, Patricia. "Controversy and the Newspaper's Public: The Case of 'Tongues Untied.'" *Journalism Quarterly* 71 (autumn 1994), 499–508.
———. "Controversy at Issue: The Press and 'Tongues Untied.'" Paper Presented at the International Communications Association Annual Convention, May 1992.
———. "Public Television and the Public Sphere." *Critical Studies in Mass Communications* 8 (spring 1991), 168–183.
Avery, Robert K., and Robert Pepper. "An Institutional History of Public Broadcasting." *Journal of Communications* (summer 1990), 126–138.
Bagdikian, Ben. *The Media Monopoly*. 2d ed. Boston: Beacon Press, 1987.
Baliles, Gerald L., and Ervin S. Duggan. *Taking Stock: A Report on "The Conversation" among PBS Member Stations*. Alexandria, Va., May 25, 1994.
Barnouw, Erik. *Documentary: A History of the Non-Fiction Film*. New York: Oxford University Press, 1983.
———. *The Sponsor: Notes on a Modern Potentate*. New York: Oxford University Press, 1978.
———. *Tube of Plenty: The Evolution of American Television*. New York: Oxford University Press, 1975.
Barthes, Roland. *Mythologies*. New York: Farrar, Straus and Giroux, 1989.
Bartimus, Tad, and Scott McCartney. *Trinity's Children: Living along America's Nuclear Highway*. New York: Harcourt Brace Jovanovich, 1991.

Becker, Carol, ed. *The Subversive Imagination: Artists, Society, and Social Responsibility.* New York: Routledge, 1994.

Becker, Howard S. *Art Worlds.* Berkeley: University of California Press, 1982.

———. *Writing for Social Scientists: How to Start and Finish Your Thesis, Book, or Article.* Chicago: University of Chicago Press, 1986.

Bennett, W. Lance. *Public Opinion in American Politics.* New York: Harcourt Brace Jovanovich, 1980.

Bullert, Bette Jean. "Art Is a Hammer! Independent Producers' Challenge to American Public Broadcasting." May 1990.

Cantor, Muriel. *The Hollywood Television Producer: His Work and His Audience.* New York: Basic Books, 1971.

Carey, James W. *Communication as Culture: Essays on Media and Society.* Boston: Unwin Hyman, 1989.

Carnegie Commission on Educational Television. *Public Television: A Program for Action.* New York: Bantam Books, 1967.

Carnegie Commission on the Future of Public Broadcasting. *A Public Trust.* New York: Bantam Books, 1979.

Center for the Study of Popular Culture. *Heterodoxy: Articles and Animadversions on Political Correctness and Other Follies.* Studio City, Calif.: Center for the Study of Popular Culture, 1991–1994.

Cohn, Carol. "Sex and Death in the Rational World of Defense Intellectuals." *Signs 2* (summer 1987), 687–718.

Committee on Media Integrity. *Comint: A Journal of the Committee on Media Integrity.* Studio City, Calif.: Center for the Study of Popular Culture, 1991–1995. (Publication later renamed *Comint: A Journal about Public Media.*)

Cook, Fay Lomax, Tom R. Tyler, Edward G. Goetz, Margaret T. Gordon, David Protess, Donna R. Leff, and Harvey L. Molotch. "Media and Agenda Setting: Effects on the Public, Interest Group Leaders, Policy Makers, and Policy." *Public Opinion Quarterly* 47 (1983), 16–35.

*Current* Publishing Committee. *Current: The Public Telecommunications Newspaper.* Washington, D.C., 1983–1995.

Daniel, Josh. "Uncivil Wars: The Conservative Assault on Public Broadcasting." *Independent Film and Video Monthly,* August–September 1992.

Day, John. *The Vanishing Vision: The Inside Story of Public Television.* Berkeley: University of California Press, 1995.

Duggan, Ervin S. "The Culture of Chaos: Remarks of Ervin S. Duggan, Commissioner, Federal Communications Commission to the Aspen Institute Lecture Series." Aspen, Colo., July 20, 1993.

Edelman, Murray. *Constructing the Political Spectacle.* Chicago: University of Chicago Press, 1988.

Edelstein, Alex. "Thinking about the Criterion Variable in Agenda-Setting Research." *Journal of Communications* 43 (spring 1993), pp. 85–99.

Emerson, Robert M. *Contemporary Field Research: A Collection of Readings.* Prospect Heights, Ill.: Waveland Press, 1983.

Emerson, Steven. *The American House of Saud: The Secret Petrodollar Connection.* New York: Franklin Watts, 1985.

———. "The System That Brought You 'Days of Rage.'" *Columbia Journalism Review,* November–December 1989, 25–30.

Engelman, Ralph, *Public Radio and Television in America: A Political History,* Thousand Oaks, Calif.: Sage Publications, 1996.

Fairness and Accuracy in Media (FAIR). *Extra!* (magazine). New York, 1987–1997.

———. *Extra! Update* (newsletter). New York, 1993–1997.

Film Arts Foundation. *Release Print: The Newsletter of the Film Arts Foundation, the Bay Area Organization of Independent Film and Videomakers*. San Francisco, 1978.

Fiske, John. *Television Culture*. London: Methuen, 1987.

Foundation for Independent Video and Film. *Independent Film and Video Monthly*. New York, 1978–1995.

Gans, Herbert J. *Deciding What's News: A Study of* CBS Evening News, NBC Nightly News, Newsweek, *and* Time. New York: Vintage Books, 1980.

Gibson, George. *Public Broadcasting: The Role of the Federal Government, 1912–1976*. New York: Praeger Press, 1977.

Gitlin, Todd. *Inside Prime-Time*. New York: Pantheon Books, 1985.

———. *The Whole World Is Watching*. Berkeley: University of California Press, 1980.

Goffman, Erving. *Frame Analysis: An Essay on the Organization of Experience*. New York: Harper and Row, 1974.

Greider, William. *Who Will Tell the People? The Betrayal of American Democracy*. New York: Simon and Schuster, 1992.

Habermas, Jürgen. *The Theory of Communicative Action*. Vol. 2, *Lifeworld and System: A Critique of Functionalist Reason*. Boston: Beacon Press, 1987.

———. *The Structural Transformation of the Public Sphere*. Cambridge: MIT Press, 1989.

Hall, Stuart. "Which Public, Whose Service?" In *All Our Futures: The Changing Role and Purpose of the BBC*, edited by Wilf Stevenson, pp. 23–38. London: British Film Institute, 1993.

Heins, Marjorie. *Sex, Sin, and Blasphemy: A Guide to America's Censorship Wars*. New York: New Press, 1993.

Herman, Edward S., and Noam Chomsky. *Manufacturing Consent: The Political Economy of the Mass Media*. New York: Pantheon Books, 1988.

Hertsgaard, Mark. *On Bended Knee: The Press and the Reagan Presidency*. New York: Farrar, Straus and Giroux, 1988.

Horowitz, David. *The Problem with Public TV: A Monograph from the Committee on Media Integrity*. Los Angeles: Center for the Study of Popular Culture, no date.

Hoynes, William. *Public Television for Sale: Media, the Market, and the Public Sphere*. Boulder: Westview Press, 1994.

International Documentary Association (IDA). *International Documentary: A Journal of the International Documentary Association*. Los Angeles, 1992.

Irvine, Reed. *Media Mischief and Misdeeds*. Chicago: Regnery Gateway, 1984.

Ivers, Susan C. "Congress, the Corporation for Public Broadcasting, and Independent Producers: Agenda Setting and Policy Making in Public Television." Paper presented at the Broadcasting Education Association Annual Convention, Las Vegas, Nev., April 1989.

Ivers, Susan C., and Charles E. Clift. "A Decade of Quiet: The Failure of Academic Research to Explore Public Broadcasting in the United States in the 1980s." Paper presented at the International Communications Association, San Francisco, Calif., 1989.

Kellner, Douglas. *Television and the Crisis of Democracy*. Boulder: Westview Press, 1990.

Latour, Bruno. *Science in Action: How to Follow Scientists and Engineers through Society*. Cambridge: Harvard University Press, 1987.

Lichter, S. Robert, Daniel Amundson, and Linda S. Lichter. *Balance and Diversity in PBS Documentaries*. Washington, D.C.: Center for Media and Public Affairs, 1992.

Lustig, R. Jeffrey. *Corporate Liberalism: The Origins of Modern American Political Theory, 1890–1920*. Berkeley: University of California Press, 1982.

McChesney, Robert W. "The Corporate Seizure of U.S. Broadcasting in Historical Perspective." March 1995.

McCombs, Maxwell E., and Donald L. Shaw. "The Evolution of Agenda-Setting

Research: Twenty-five Years in the Marketplace of Ideas." *Journal of Communications* 43 (spring 1993), 58–67.

Montgomery, Katheryn C. *Target: Prime Time: Advocacy Groups and the Struggle over Entertainment Television.* New York: Oxford University Press, 1989.

PBS National Programming and Promotion Services. *Program Producer's Handbook.* Alexandria, Va., 1991.

Pepper, Robert. "The Interconnection Connection: The Formation of PBS." *Public Telecommunications Review* 4 (January–February 1976), 6–26.

Public Broadcasting Service. *A Guide to Crisis Management.* Alexandria, Va., June 1992.

Rapping, Elayne. *The Looking Glass World of Nonfiction TV.* Boston: South End Press, 1987.

Said, Edward. *Covering Islam: How the Media and the Experts Determine How We See the Rest of the World.* New York: Pantheon Books, 1981.

———. *The Question of Palestine.* New York: Vintage Books, 1979.

Schiller, Herbert. *Culture, Inc.* New York: Oxford University Press, 1989.

Seidman, Steven, ed. *Jürgen Habermas on Society and Politics: A Reader.* Boston: Beacon Press, 1989.

Sheheen, Jack. *The TV Arab.* Bowling Green: Popular Press, 1984.

Special Committee on Program Policies and Procedures. *Report of the Special Committee on Program Policies and Procedures to the PBS Board of Directors.* Alexandria, Va., April 15, 1987.

Stone, David M. *Nixon and the Politics of Public Television.* New York: Garland, 1985.

Strauss, Anselm L. *Qualitative Analysis for Social Scientists.* New York: Cambridge University Press, 1987.

Tuchman, Gaye. *Making News.* New York: Free Press, 1978.

Twentieth Century Fund Task Force. *Quality Time? The Report of the Twentieth Century Fund Task Force on Public Television.* New York: Twentieth Century Fund Press, 1993.

Vaughan, Diane. *Uncoupling: How Relationships Come Apart.* New York: Vintage Books, 1987.

Warren Publishing. *The Public Broadcasting Report: The Authoritative News Service for Public Broadcasting and Allied Fields.* Washington, D.C., 1979–1995.

White, David Manning. "The 'Gate Keeper': A Case Study in the Selection of News." *Journalism Quarterly* 27 (fall 1950), 383–390.

Whitney, D. Charles, and Lee B. Becker. "'Keeping the Gates' for Gatekeepers: The Effects of Wire News." *Journalism Quarterly* 59 (spring 1982), 60–65.

Witherspoon, John, and Roselle Kovitz. *The History of Public Broadcasting.* Washington, D.C.: Corporation for Public Broadcasting, 1987. (Originally published in *Current.*)

# Index

WNEO-WEAO/Kent, 115
WNET/New York, xvii, 18, 20, 75–79, 83, 86, 89, 99, 100, 140–143
WNIT/South Bend, 115
WNYC/New York, 72–74, 77, 78, 86
Wood, William, 136
*World*, 26
Wortham-Brown, Mimi, 106
WPBT/Miami, 77, 104
wraparound: and "Days of Rage," 72, 73, 77–86; and framing of controversy, 187; and *Frontline*, 88; need for, 185; and "Stop the Church," 135–136, 140, 143–144
WTBS, 38, 59

WTCI/Chattanooga, 113
WTTW/Chicago, xvii, 195
WTVS/Detroit, 112
WXEL/West Palm Beach, 103, 104

Yandel, Gary, 105
Yates, Pam, xiii, 200n6
Yee, James, 197

Zionist Organization of America, 78
Zogby, James, 83
Zurawik, David, 113, 177
Zwilling, Joseph, 142

# About the Author

B. J. Bullert is an independent producer who has produced and directed several documentaries that have aired locally and nationally on public television. She holds a Ph.D. from the School of Communication at the University of Washington in Seattle, an M.Litt. in Politics from Oxford University, and a B.A. in philosophy from Boston University. She has taught at Muhlenberg College and Antioch University–Seattle and is currently an assistant professor of communication at American University in Washington, D.C.